ETTERS FROM THE
FRONT

ROM THE **FIRST WORLD WAR**
O THE **PRESENT DAY**

ANDREW ROBERTS

First published in Great Britain in 2012 by
Osprey Publishing,
PO Box 883, Oxford, OX1 9PL, UK
PO Box 3985, New York, NY 10185-3985,
USA
E-mail: info@ospreypublishing.com

Osprey Publishing is part of the Osprey
Group

First published in 2012 by Osprey Publishing
as *Love, Tommy: Letters Home, from the Great
War to the Present Day*.
This paperback edition was first published in
2014 by Osprey Publishing Ltd.

A CIP catalogue record for this book is
available from the British Library

ISBN: 978 1 4728 0334 4
e-book ISBN: 978 1 4728 0818 9
PDF ISBN: 978 1 4728 0817 2

Research by Emily Holmes and Kate Moore
Index by Sandra Shotter
Typeset in Adobe Garamond Pro & Akzidenz-
Grotesk
Originated by PDQ Digital Media Solutions
Printed in China through Worldprint

13 14 15 16 17 10 9 8 7 6 5 4 3 2 1

Front cover: A routine patrol in Afghanistan.
(Corporal Mike Jones © Crown Copyright
2011) © Imperial War Museum (CO 2533)

www.ospreypublishing.com

EDITOR'S NOTE:
**The letters in this collection were edited for
sense. Minor spelling and grammar changes
were made.**
**Material from the troubles in Northern
Ireland has not been included in this
volume as IWM could not allow access to
the archives they hold due to classification
and sensitivity surrounding the documents.**

CONTENTS

Introduction	**9**
The First World War	**21**
The Second World War	**113**
Modern Warfare	**227**
Glossary	**301**
Acknowledgements	**304**
Index	**307**

Also by Andrew Roberts

The Storm of War
Masters and Commanders
The Art of War: Great Commanders of the Modern
World (2 volumes)
A History of the English-Speaking Peoples Since 1900
Waterloo
Hitler and Churchill
Eminent Churchillians

To my step-mother Charmian, whose father, Lieutenant Colonel Robin Lindsay, won an MC fighting his way into Libya and a DSO fighting his way out.

INTRODUCTION

Soldiers' letters home to their loved ones have a raw power denied to almost all other epistolary writing. Written for the most part without thought to publication, or to live for the ages, they try to make that seemingly impossible connection: between the writer who has seen the terrible face of war and the reader who generally has not. The fact that the writer is facing the horrors of war precisely in order to protect his reader from those selfsame horrors adds another powerful dynamic to the correspondence. In publishing these superb letters home from British soldiers, sailors and airmen fighting in the wars of the 20th and 21st centuries, Osprey is performing a fine service to scholarship, as well as allowing us to glimpse into the lives of heroes on the front line.

The knowledge that each of these letters might be the last communication the serviceman ever had with his loved ones gives every page of this book a poignancy that is only otherwise found when hearing the voices of pilots of doomed aircraft from black-box flight recorders, or seeing a living-will videotape. The fact that all too often the writers of these letters did not survive gives them a profundity usually reserved only for deathbed confessions. And somehow the very fact that they are not over-written or self-consciously 'literary' merely adds to their haunting power. This is life and death in the raw, expressed by British serviceman across nearly 100 years.

The subjects the letters cover are the elemental ones that have not altered much since the dawn of war. Men writing home from the Peloponnesian and the Punic conflicts wanted to downplay their heroism but also their fears, to grouse about their rations, to discuss their love of country and city, to lament the deaths of comrades, to ponder the nature of the enemy, to ask for news and provisions, to comment on their leaders, to wish the war could end quickly but victoriously, to complain about their billets, and so on, but above all they wanted to express their love for their families and friends, whom they feared they would never see again. Human nature can't have changed much in the intervening two millennia, for those are also substantially the same subjects written about by the British Tommy in this fascinating and beautifully produced volume.

A man's immediate prospect of death, as Dr Johnson said in the inexact but related context of being hanged in a fortnight, 'concentrates his mind wonderfully'. Of course some housekeeping remarks do occasionally get written – 'Thanks so much for the hankies' – but overall it's remarkable how these letters are shorn of much of the minor paraphernalia that can otherwise fill day-to-day existence. They get to the point quickly, and in every area except one they tend to tell the truth, for what's the point of dissembling when on the brink of eternity? That is what makes soldiers' letters home such an important tool for historians. However, the one area where the soldiers routinely downplay the truth is in estimating their likelihood of death. This is not because they have not considered the odds themselves – of course they have – but because they desperately want to protect their parents, wives, lovers and children from the terrible thought that lies behind every letter written: that this could be the last.

When it comes to soldiers' testimonies about how to avoid the sniper's bullet, or what it's like to sleep in a lice-ridden blanket, or how to get by on three hours sleep a night, or what the 'weird shrieking noise' of shells sounds like compared to the high-pitched whistle of bullets, this book is a veritable treasure trove of invaluable first-hand information. These letters pulsate with immediacy: you are there with them, alternating between empathizing with the young man who has just returned from vicious, often hand-to-hand fighting in the trenches of the Great War and empathizing just as powerfully with his readers – 'My darling Mother and Father', 'My dear Vera', 'My own beloved wife' – who received the letter all those years ago. Trying to imagine their emotional response to getting a letter from the postman, rather than a constantly feared telegram from the War Office, makes this book an emotionally powerful experience. I defy you to read the haunting letter from Francis Herbert Gautier to his four-year-old daughter Marie, written for 'when she is able to understand', without experiencing a lump in your throat or a tear welling unbidden to your eye. I couldn't.

As well as being a fine tribute to the Tommy through the ages, this book is a very valuable social document. The Great War was fundamentally different from earlier conflicts in which Britain had taken part, in that ordinary Britons were conscripted for service. Besides the press-gang of the Napoleonic Wars, which generally only operated in coastal towns and largely on an *ad hoc* basis according to immediate manpower needs, Britain's wars had hitherto been fought by volunteers. The decision in January 1916 to allow the government to force citizens to serve was hugely controversial, and it radically changed the nature of the British Army. For the rest of the war, and into the Second World War when partial conscription was adopted even before it broke out, the services effectively became 'the nation in uniform', and a number of the letters in this volume reflect social concerns that were mirrored by the nation at large.

As well as relating the pulse-quickening, adrenaline-pumping rush of clashing arms, some of these letters reflect that other well-known side to soldiering: stultifying boredom. 'Nothing very exciting happens,' complains a soldier of the Great War here. Until, of course, it does. Also highlighted is the way in which the stress subtly affects social relationships among men living on the precipice, in ways one might not automatically have considered. 'We laugh much more readily these days,' writes a soldier, 'at things that normally we would consider merely amusing.' This book also underlines the importance of cups of tea to the Tommy, something that differentiates the British soldier from the Prussian grenadier or French *poilu*.

The enduring power of a soldier's letter home was reinforced as recently as October 2010 when the group *The Soldiers* released their album 'Letters Home', whose title song's lyrics featured words that were written in a real last letter of Tony Downes, a young soldier in the 1st Battalion, Grenadier Guards, who had died in Helmand Province, Afghanistan, in June 2007. It was the first time that a last letter had ever been set to music for commercial release, and it works on a musical, as well as emotional level. 'I'm sorry to put you through all this, I'm sorry there was no last kiss,' reads one stanza. 'I'm up here in heaven, you're free to start again. My love will never end. I'm sorry to my family and friends.' The group – composed of Lance Corporal Ryan Idzi, Staff Sergeant Richie Maddocks and Sergeant Major Gary Chilton – dedicated the title track to Downes, whose mother Sheryl said: 'It shows how much my son was a loving and caring person. I can just see him now, looking down on us all with his million-watt smile. He will be so proud.' If *The Soldiers* need any more last letter lyrics from earlier conflicts, they need look no further than this volume, several of which would not be out of place in an operatic libretto either, despite having been originally written for an audience confined to grieving parents or a widow.

The letters from this volume come from the Imperial War Museums (IWM), and form a tiny fraction of the vast collections that they expertly curate there. The IWM name has been put into the plural in order to reflect the fact that it now extends far beyond the magnificent central museum building in Lambeth, to the Churchill War Rooms in Whitehall, HMS *Belfast* moored on the Thames, the historic airfield at Duxford and IWM North in Manchester. The IWM is one of the truly great British institutions; its archive collection was inaugurated in 1917 and now comprises the largest collection of servicemen, servicewomen and civilian's wartime letters to be found in the British Commonwealth. Any reader of this book who would like to read the actual letters themselves, or continue investigating the life stories of individual soldiers mentioned in it, can do so easily at their superb research facilities in Lambeth, with iwm.org.uk as an invaluable first step.

So what do we learn from soldiers' letters home that can't be found in the multi-volume regimental histories that were published after the fighting was over, or the propaganda put out by the Ministry of Information while conflicts were still going on? The first thing is that, for all they might have tried to minimize the horror for their loved ones, war is hell. Not just the ever-present peril of death and mutilation, but also the flies, rats, exhaustion, exposure to the elements, the powerlessness – 'We are simply pawns in the great game' – and the catastrophic waste of time and effort and life that should have instead been dedicated to the progress of civilization.

The two world wars that were unleashed by Germany in the first half of the 20th century really were 'crimes against humanity', not simply because of what humanity had to suffer during them, but for what it was held back from achieving through having been sidetracked by war for a total of ten years. Reading these soldiers' letters reminds us of what might have been achieved if so many talented people had not been ground up into the charnel houses of the Marne, the Somme, Passchendaele, the Japanese death camps, El Alamein minefields, the massacre at Arnhem, and elsewhere. One is also reminded by this book just how young they were; the commanding officer of the 2nd Battalion of the 5th Lancashire Regiment, who lived to announce Armistice Day to the town he had liberated in November 1918, was only 27.

We learn how the British Tommy had – and indeed still has, because the last letter is from the ongoing war in Afghanistan – almost superhuman capacities for simply muddling through, and, grumbling and grousing all the time in best Army tradition, for making the best of what was happening. 'A good grumble eases our minds,' writes one soldier. Similarly, those other ancient army traditions of 'scrounging' (which is very often indistinguishable from petty pilfering) find their way into these pages, which is in no sense an unthinking hagiography. Overall, though, the picture of the British Army is hugely uplifting. 'Like good British troops,' writes one soldier from the Second World War, 'we always hope for the best.' Humour, modesty and *sangfroid* – 'We had a bit of a battle yesterday', or describing a trench as 'rather cosy', or calling a battle 'a picnic' – pervade this book. When a Great War second lieutenant writes 'I keep alive, and bucked my men up' his words obviously mask a very great deal more than that.

With death dealt on an entirely unpredictable basis, we are reminded how superstitious soldiers can quickly become. 'I have a strong feeling of Kismet,' writes one, 'but nevertheless do not go out trying to be hit.' This is a well-known phenomenon among soldiers, because there seems to be no rational explanation for why some men survive while others don't. The attitude towards the enemy ranges from genuine hatred to a more common healthy respect. 'The Germans in this part of the line are certainly sportsmen if they are nothing else,' writes one Tommy of the Christmas Day truce of 1914. Overall, Conscientious Objectors seem to be objected to more than the Germans, except of course the Nazis, who were cordially despised.

Censorship of these letters used to be undertaken by regimental officers in their (rare and much-prized) spare time during the Great War. So long as no operational details that could be of use to the enemy were included, the men's freedom of speech was widely indulged; it was one of the things for which Britain was fighting, after all. That explains why occasional remarks were let through in the Great War that would have been construed as demoralizing civilian morale by the professional, full-time censors of the Second World War. 'The idea of breaking the Germans is so much nonsense!' writes one squaddie from the trenches, for example. Yet, even if the soldier thought it he rarely wrote it, for the simple reason of not wanting to sound defeatist. There is also remarkably little about high politics, let alone individual politicians in these letters. The overwhelming sense is that they were doing the right thing in trying to stop German hegemony in Europe, but ultimately, in the words of the plaintive First World War song, 'We're here because we're here because we're here because we're here.' Local patriotism is present, of course – 'They did not disgrace the name of Ulster' – but not ultra-nationalism, let alone jingoism.

Censorship was thus not used as a means of controlling the men, let alone civilian morale. This book tends to support the theory prevalent among military historians today that the men glossed over the worst horrors and the most dangerous moments in order to avoid distressing their families, as the daily casualty lists were quite long enough to achieve that. Yet the fact that the soldiers tended not to dwell on the mutilation of friends by 'whiz-bangs' (German high explosive shells) does not mean that these letters are not invaluable to historians and the general reader for what can be gleaned about rations, billets, recreation, conditions, relations with officers and NCOs, training, leave, friendly-fire incidents, enemy abuse of the white flag and so on.

While some soldiers plainly enjoyed their Great War experiences, a point made forcibly in Professor Niall Ferguson's revisionist book *The Pity of War*, there were more who would have agreed with the soldier who writes, 'The Army is undeniably the most dismal experience I have had yet.' Osprey has done an excellent job in choosing testimonies from a broad cross-section of the theatres and campaigns, as well as witnesses from a wide array of the units that fought in them, providing therefore a really representative sample of opinions and viewpoints. A good summing up of the emotions felt by the troops, as well as an insightful commentary into the human condition, is provided by the soldier who writes, 'We are all fairly shouting with joy at going and I daresay we shall soon be cursing the day, and when we get back we shall say we had the time of our lives.'

One predictable and constant emotion that comes through strongly in this volume is the desire for news from home, any news, however trivial, that could take the soldiers' minds off their own circumstances. 'Write me any news – anything,' begs a soldier from the trenches. Of course there are some things they don't want to hear. 'Don't tell me you are lonely,' writes a soldier from the Second World War, 'or I'll probably desert.' Nazi black propaganda made a great play of the soldiers' sexual fears, trying to provoke suspicions that their girlfriends were being unfaithful while they were serving abroad, especially once over a million Americans were billeted across the United Kingdom in the build up to the Normandy landings. Today, the modern squaddie in Iraq or Afghanistan has a huge advantage over his First and Second World War counterpart through the use of satellite phones, which was technologically unthinkable in earlier conflicts when they had to make do with black-and-white photos of their loved ones. 'The most real and living thing in the life that I've had has been you, Phyl Kirby,' writes a romantic soldier from the Second World War, though he never posted the letter.

The role of rumour in the life of the Tommy is vividly demonstrated in these letters. The British Army has long been an active – some say wildly overactive – rumour-mill, where orders to camp, decamp, retreat and attack were vigorously posited by the men, often with nothing more than guesswork to go on. Here, too, modern technology has altered the dynamic somewhat, with websites like that of the British Army Rumour Service (ARRSE) taking the place of whispered speculation in the sergeant's mess. Endemic in the British Army too were swearing and obscenities, yet for obvious reasons these are not reflected in letters home to loved ones, although there are references to 'some other words I won't repeat'. Shell-shock, or something approaching it, is elliptically referred to as well, as in the admission: 'I am afraid I am a mere nervous wreck, in fact when we got back I sat down and had a jolly good cry.'

Britain was a far more religious country in the first half of the 20th century than in the first part of the 21st, so it is not surprising to see God mentioned regularly, not least because soldiers' closeness to death forced them to consider the concept of the hereafter much more than civilians. Lieutenant Eric Marchant of the 7th Battalion, London Regiment, recalled after the war how, when reading his men's letters, 'The percentage which showed a realization of religious truth and faith in God was tremendously bigger than I ever suspected, and such phrases as "We must go on trusting in God" were in dozens of letters I read.' The belief in heaven and a loving God was clearly a huge comfort for many Tommies as they contemplated the future. 'A firm belief in the Christian faith goes a long way,' writes one soldier in the Second World War, and when Lieutenant Leefe Robinson won the Victoria Cross for shooting down a Zeppelin in the Great War, he wrote to his parents to say, 'I thanked God with all my heart.' The cheering spread across London when the Zeppelin exploded into flames, which could be heard for miles into the suburbs and beyond. Robinson felt a powerful sense of 'the relief, the gratitude, the thanks of millions of people'.

If wild cheering and public celebration over what was, after all, the deaths of other human beings, is considered at all politically incorrect, it needs to be seen in the context of the death and destruction that the Zeppelins rained down upon London's civilians. Similarly the references to 'Huns', 'Chinks', 'Japs', 'gooks', 'Argies' and 'rag-heads' need to be seen in their proper historical context of total war. By contrast, those martial non-Britons who fought on Britain's side, such as the Sikhs and the Gurkhas, were held in high respect, and racial barriers started to break down during the world wars, just as shared experiences of trauma began the process of breaking down class barriers. 'In their letters I saw for the first time a new world,' wrote the Old Rugbeian Charles Douie of the platoon he commanded, 'with interests and standards of which I had previously no experience. Most of the letters were frank in a degree with surprised me. I found the world of the private soldier wholly natural and without reserve.' The future prime minister Harold Macmillan wrote in April 1915 of how 'some of the older men, with wives and families, who write every day, have in their style a wonderful simplicity which is almost great literature.'

The British Expeditionary Force (BEF) wrote a vast number of letters home during the conflict, with some estimates reaching up to 9 million letters and postcards sent per week during 1917. The officers who had to censor their men's mail quickly perfected the ability to, in the words of one of them, 'Glance over the page spotting censorable matter without reading line by line.' Another officer, who dismissed his troops' letters as 'mostly rot', nevertheless understood how important writing them was for morale, concluding, 'It certainly makes them happy, and that is the great thing.' In his excellent book *Six Weeks: The Short and Gallant Life of the British Officer in the First World War*, the historian John Lewis-Stempel points out how officers' censorship of the soldiers' letters 'gave a secret, God-like look into a man's soul; out of the resulting glimpse came a better understanding of the men.' He quotes Second Lieutenant Robert McConnell writing on a boat bound for Gallipoli: 'I have just censored the letters of my men. By Jove! If you could read some of those letters, they would do you good. The tenderness of those great, rough men is wonderful. I love them all for it.'

Certainly there is little in these letters of the fury against the officers, and especially the senior field commanders such as General Sir Douglas Haig, that was to be directed against them in the 1920s and 1930s, especially after Haig's Western Front strategy was criticized in print by both the former prime minister David Lloyd George and by Winston Churchill. Indeed, of one 1916 enemy offensive, a soldier is quoted writing about 'the Hun', saying, 'Haig seems to have found the way to deal with him.'

These pages also confirm something I've long suspected, which is that the Second World War army poets were just as good as those of the First World War. There are also some unsung philosophers here, too; look at the thoughts on life and death of Captain Charles McKerrow, for example, who writes of how 'death becomes a very unimportant incident'. I think you will feel, as I did, a keen hope that the author of each letter survived the war, and a pang when, as happens all too often, one learn that he did not.

'It is unbearable to describe our feelings', writes Lieutenant Woodroffe before the Great War had been going a month. 'I will give a full account later.' To write any such thing in 1914 was tempting Providence, and, sure enough, he never did give that full account, not living to see the year's end, let alone the war's. But with the compelling honesty of men who face death, he and his comrades have left us, in this volume, an inspiring set of living documents. Since history is nothing more than the collective experience of millions of ordinary people, these letters, written directly from the soul, help us to understand what made those ordinary people extraordinary.

Andrew Roberts
April 2012
www.andrew-roberts.net

THE FIRST WORLD WAR

The immediate *casus belli* for the First World War was Germany's aggressive support for Austria-Hungary, which wanted to punish Serbia for its alleged complicity in the assassination of the Emperor of Austria's nephew, the Archduke Franz Ferdinand, in Sarajevo on 28 June 1914. However, the long-term causes predate that, and can be found in Germany's lust for European hegemony. Fighting between Austria-Hungary and Serbia broke out on 29 July and Tsarist Russia's mobilization in support of Serbia on 30 July led to an ultimatum from Germany on the 31st and a declaration of war on 1 August. Fighting in the West broke out on the 4th when Imperial Germany invaded Belgium in accordance with its General Staff's Schlieffen Plan, under the terms of which France was to be invaded via its northern neighbour. On the same day, Great Britain declared war against Germany for violating Belgian neutrality, which she had guaranteed when Belgium was created in 1839, and also because she had a de facto alliance with France, known as the Entente Cordiale. After a general European peace lasting over four decades, the Great Powers were all at war within four days of Germany's intentionally provocative ultimatum to Russia.

Between 7 and 17 August 1914, a British Expeditionary Force (BEF) was despatched to the Continent, but it could not arrive in time to prevent the opening stages of the Schlieffen Plan from being put into operation, as German forces marched through Belgium and occupied Brussels on 20 August. France's subsequent attempt to invade Germany in 'the battle of the Frontiers' fizzled out by the

25th and over the following days the retreating BEF fought a delaying action at Le Cateau. Yet nothing could prevent the Germans crossing the River Marne to the east of Paris on 3 September. The original Schlieffen Plan, conceived in 1905, which called for a powerful right flanking movement through Belgium and northern France in order to capture Paris, now seemed on the verge of success. Crucially, however, subsequent German chiefs of staff had watered down the plan, weakening the right flank, and so between 15 September and 24 November the French and British armies managed to stabilize the situation in front of the French capital.

Due to the advances in firepower – with the advent of the machine gun and heavy artillery – the fairly evenly-matched size of the armies facing each other and logistical problems in moving the soldiers rapidly, the autumn and early winter of 1914 saw a relatively static line of trenches spread across north-west Europe from the North Sea through Belgium and France all the way to the Swiss border. These trenches were to form the front lines for the next three and a half years. On the Eastern Front, the German General Paul von Hindenburg defeated the Russian Army at the battle of Tannenberg in late August 1914, inflicting 125,000 casualties for the loss of 15,000, but there, too, the front later stabilized. On 28 October Turkey joined the Central Powers, bombarding Russia's Black Sea ports; the sides were drawn.

On 19 January 1915 the first Zeppelin raids were unleashed against Britain, first against East Anglian ports, and then from 1 June against London, culminating in the largest raid of the war on 13 October which caused over 200 casualties. Another sinister new invention of war, poison gas, was also introduced by the Germans in Poland in January 1915. On 4 February 1915 Germany declared Britain to be under blockade from its U-boat submarine fleet, a stranglehold the Royal Navy struggled to break throughout the war.

On 10 March 1915, British and Indian forces managed to break through the German lines and capture the northern French village of Neuve Chapelle, but as was to happen all too often over the coming years, they were unable to exploit their temporary victory. Such was the military technology, especially with regard to machine guns and heavy artillery, that the defensive proved superior to offensive, time after time. With poison gas being used by the Germans on the Western Front against the British-held Ypres salient after 22 May, the war entered a truly hellish new phase, from which it did not fully emerge until the summer of 1918.

In an attempt to turn the flank of the Axis powers, and hopefully knock the Ottoman Empire out of the war, thus relieving pressure on Russia's southern front and allow her to concentrate on Austria and Germany, the Allies attacked in the Dardanelles. British and French forces landed at Cape Helles and Australian and New Zealand (ANZAC) forces landed at Anzac Cove on the Turkish-held Gallipoli peninsula on 25 April 1915. Both the difficult terrain and stout Turkish resistance led by Mustafa Kemal (later Kemal Atatürk) denied the Allies the quick victory they needed, and instead led to a long and costly campaign, which only ended with evacuation in December 1915 and January 1916. (One of the letters in this volume refers to the 'Morning Hate'; the nickname given to the three-quarters of an hour of shelling that the Turks always began at 7.45am.)

On 7 May 1915 a U-boat torpedoed the British liner *Lusitania* off the southern coast of Ireland, drowning 1,198 passengers, 114 of whom were American. Widely considered a war crime, it turned American public opinion decisively against Germany and is widely considered to be a factor in America's entry into the war two years later.

On 25 September British forces used gas for the first time, at the battle of Loos, but, as so often on the Western Front, the small gains in territory were outweighed by the large loss of men. This was particularly seen in the battle of Verdun, which lasted from 21 February to 18 December 1916. There, the attritional tactics used between France and Germany led to the loss of 400,000 men on each side.

In late May 1916 the German High Seas Fleet left its harbours to contest maritime superiority with the Royal Navy's Grand Fleet in the North Sea. Although Admiral Sir John Jellicoe lost more ships than the Germans at the battle of Jutland on 1 June, he avoided defeat, which was all that was needed to ensure that the Germans remained in their harbours for the rest of the war. The Royal Navy was thereafter able to impose a gruelling blockade on Germany, many of whose citizens succumbed to malnourishment and starvation.

Britain and France were to undergo an even greater slaughter than they had experienced at Verdun during the battle of the Somme, fought between 1 July and 18 November 1916. The BEF suffered no fewer than 60,000 casualties (including 20,000 killed) on the first day of the Somme Offensive alone, as troops attacked across shell-pitted landscapes of death and destruction known as no-man's-land, against machine guns protected by barbed wire. The battle, which only succeeded in taking 5 miles of territory, resulted in 620,000 British and French and 450,000 German casualties.

An attempt to break the incredibly costly stalemate was made by Britain on 15 September 1916 with the introduction of the tank to the battlefield, which was a considerable advance in technology. However, the tank was not the breakthrough weapon that the Allies had hoped it might be. A genuine breakthrough was achieved on 6 April 1917, however, when, enraged by the sinking of American shipping and by the publication of the Zimmermann telegram,[*] the United States entered the war against Germany.

At the battle of Arras in April 1917, the British Third Army managed to advance a grand total of only 4 miles, yet on the Western Front this constituted a significant victory. That same month some of the French Army mutinied, destroying its ability to mount further offensives. Instead it was the BEF that mounted the Third Battle

---

[*] The Zimmermann telegram was a message from the German Foreign Minister Alfred Zimmermann to his ambassador in Mexico suggesting that if war should break out with the United States, Mexico should be encouraged to recapture the territory she had lost in 1848.

of Ypres (also known as Passchendaele) between 31 July and 6 November, another hugely costly operation in which only 8 miles were taken. During the latter stages of the battle, thousands of miles to the east, the Bolshevik Revolution broke out in Russia, ensuring that after the new Communist regime took over and made peace with the Germans at Brest-Litovsk in December 1917, the whole weight of the German Army would fall upon the Allies on the Western Front.

Sure enough, between 21 March and late May 1918, the Germans launched their massive Spring Offensives, winning the Second Battle of the Somme and advancing 40 miles, allowing them to shell Paris itself. Yet it turned out to be Germany's final 'big push' of the war, for on 18 July the Allies began their counter-offensive, which left the German Army reeling. Between 8 and 11 August the concentrated forces of the British Commonwealth, including Australian and Canadian divisions as well as 400 British tanks, broke the German lines in front of Amiens, advancing more than 12 miles and capturing 30,000 prisoners. General Ludendorff referred to 8 August as 'the black day of the German Army'.

With 1.2 million fresh American troops plunging into the battle of the Meuse-Argonne in September, Lille falling to the British in October and the Allies cutting the German supply lines in early November, it was only a matter of time before Kaiser Wilhelm II abdicated and an armistice was announced. This finally came about at 11am on 11 November 1918.

In the first year of the war much of the fighting was conducted by the 'Old Contemptibles' of the British Regular Army. This included Second Lieutenant Neville Leslie Woodroffe, an Anglo-Boer War veteran who joined the Irish Guards in 1913 and was sent to France with the 1st Battalion in 1914. He survived the retreat from Mons and the battle of Landrecies, details of which are described in the letters below.

3 September 1914

My dear mother,

I got your letter and father's the day before yesterday. They had obviously been round several places before they arrived where we were as I have had letters dated later than [them] which I received before…

Mons was an awful time and we had a terrible week of retirement as fast as we could go covering sometimes 30 miles per day, starting while it was dark and not stopping until it was again dark. Our men stuck it extremely well and we were complimented on our marching by the general. We had very little sleep as the time we ought to have slept was devoted to making trenches and barricades.

We have finished this continual trekking for a while and have up till now been in different engagements [and] we have lost considerably. In the first wood fight we had after Landrecies which I described to you in my last letter, but can with safety now mention the name, we lost nine officers. Landrecies was a terrible massacre! We lost few but the Germans many…

The day after Landrecies our brigade acted rearguard for the Division and our battalion was last of our brigade… We were however badly attacked and had to hold on till the main force had got away. We were all caught in the wood and bullets whizzed as close as anything to one through the trees. The Coldstreams and us were together but the wood was so thick that I fear many shot one's own men…

I can't explain to you every engagement as it is unbearable to describe our feelings and experiences which one has been through. Some are awful and when I return I shall have a great deal to tell you. We have been on the move incessantly and attacking and reforming and advancing for the whole time.

The 1st Brigade of Guards have lost heavily in regards officers, and besides that the very best of fellows many of whom ranked as one's very best friends... Lockwood was shot yesterday whilst he was standing up telling some wounded Germans to convey in their language to another party of Germans that if they held the white flag up they were to throw down their arms. John Mannen, who you know by name, shot himself, when he saw that the alternative was to surrender to superior numbers of Germans... The other day a large force of Germans showed the white flag and our men went out to take them prisoner, when they immediately fired on us and killed several.

The Germans are very fond of wood fighting and detail snipers to get up trees where they are not seen and pick off the officers, others lie on the ground and if caught pretend they are dead...

Love to all,
Neville

October 18th

My dear Vera,
Many thanks for your parcel and letter I received about ten days ago. The former was much appreciated by Borgin who was duly given all which he was entitled to, though it needed great self-control on my part! I expect you have heard of some of my doings, experiences and adventures from letters to mother. Really this war is terrible, quite a picnic South Africa is considered compared to this. I am afraid it will not be over by Christmas, as

once thought at the commencement of the campaign, though the actual German prisoner one meets, both officer, non-commissioned and private all seem really very much against the war and at the same time most heartily fed up with it. They say they get very little food and [fine] men five francs for a tin of bully and a franc for one cigarette! The day before yesterday we completed our five weeks of entrenchment along the line, the position which we held ever since the last fight we had in a wood which I described before and of which you have probably heard of. We have now, I am glad to say, left and have moved off to —— where I expect we will be engaged in a day or so. Our trenches were taken over by the French. When we handed them over a captain of ours took the French captain and showed him an advance post, which we had cut out at night in front of our trenches and not far from those of our German friends and told him to relieve us with some of his men, so he accordingly got some out from the trenches and our men came in, but before they had got back hardly, the French post was found in the trenches again, [whenever] our fellow told them that they had to remain out there 'oh no we don't' they said! They obviously thought better of it…

Love from Neville

His final letter home was brief and simply sent on the back of a postcard. He was killed in action during the First Battle of Ypres, on 6 November 1914, just three days after writing this note.

Nov 3rd 1914

I am afraid I have not time to write a letter though I have heaps to tell you. The last two days have been ghastly. The Germans broke through the line. We have lost ten officers in the last two days and yesterday the battalion was less than 200 though I expect some stragglers will turn up. All the officers in my company were lost except myself. All in No 3 Coy and all bar one in No 4. We have had no rest at all. Everyone is very shaken. I do hope we are put in reserve to reform for a few days. I will give a full account later. The whole Brigade has suffered heavily. Thanks for letter…

Love to all,
Neville

Many of the soldiers serving on the front lines on the Western Front were incredibly young, and a number were 'underage' when they joined up. One such soldier, George Danzig, volunteered as a private aged just 16 and served in the 2nd Battalion, Leicestershire Regiment, which formed part of the Indian Expeditionary Force in France.

19 August 1915
Private G. Danzig 11599
2nd Batt, B Coy
Indian Expeditionary Force
France

Dear Mum,
Just a few lines in answer to your two welcome letters which I received alright. I am pleased to hear that you and Dad and Auntie and Kit and Em and Jim are alright. I hope this will find you in the same health as it leaves me at present. You know in the last letter I wrote we had just come out of the trenches and we were expecting to come right back for a well earned rest, well we have got it (in the trenches for another 14 days or more) – the bloke who says a soldier don't earn his bob a day should come where I am writing this letter and then give his opinion. Well

Mum I suppose we mustn't grumble, but a good grumble eases our mind. It is about 11 o'clock now and the skies look about black enough to give us enough rain to last us the whole time we are in. So I expect we shall soon be up to our necks in mud.

It is August now but it's blooming cold of a night time so goodness knows how it will be round Christmas time. Well Mum I wouldn't give a tuppence for <u>sunny</u> France as some people call it.

… I must close now as the fleas are irritating me so I must look at my shirt, I find millions of them every day, goodness knows where they all come from.

With love to you from your <u>lousy</u>,

George
PS. This is the only green envelope I have got so I might not be able to write you another letter till we come out.* I hope Dad has plenty of work still.
Am killing millions (fleas)

Danzig lost his battle against both the fleas and the Germans. Wounded firstly in May 1915 he recovered but was subsequently reported missing in action presumed killed just a month after this letter was sent.

---

* This refers to the green envelope given to some soldiers as a privilege. The letters in these envelopes were sealed and exempt from the censors and the soldiers certified that the contents did not contain any military information.

Born 1890, Alfred Dougan Chater volunteered for service in the Artists Rifles, 28th Battalion, London Regiment, Territorial Army (TA) force, in 1909 and was soon promoted to corporal. With the outbreak of war he was called up for active service and sent the following letter on the eve of his departure.

Oct 25th 1914
Knowley House
Abbot Langley

I must write you one more line dearest to say goodbye before we go, as God knows when I shall see you again. I am so awfully glad we are going – it is what we have been waiting for [for] so long and it has come so much sooner than we expected or hoped. I heard about it yesterday afternoon when I was going home; I called at our headquarters at Euston where I found the 2nd Battalion being got together and was told that the 1st Btn [Battalion] were to leave for France on Monday.

Although there is not much doubt that we are really going: we were served with our new rifles this afternoon and we believe that we shall be at Southampton tomorrow night.

As to where we shall exactly sail we don't know but I daresay we may be at Southampton for 2 or 3 days and when we get over we may be at [Le] Havre for some time.

I wish I could have seen you today and I can't bear the thought of going without saying goodbye to you but feel also it is better as it is…

So now dear it is goodbye and may we meet again if God wills. You know that if I am allowed to come back I shall feel exactly the same to you as I do now and shall be ready for you…

It is a funny game this war! We are all fairly shouting with joy at going and I daresay we shall soon be cursing the day and then when we get back we shall say we have had the time of our lives.

Goodbye darling may God bless and keep you.

One of the legendary events in the first year of the war was the Christmas truce in 1914 when British and German servicemen brokered unofficial ceasefires. Chater recalled his reaction to the truce on his part of the front line in a letter to his mother back home in Britain.

Christmas Day

Dear Mother,

I am writing this in the trenches in my 'dug out' – with a wood fire going and plenty of straw it is rather cosy although it is freezing hard and real Christmas weather.

I think I have seen one of the most extraordinary sights today that anyone has ever seen. About 10 o'clock this morning I was peeping over the parapet when I saw a German waving his arms and presently two of them got out of their trenches and come towards ours – we were just going to fire on them when we saw they had no rifles so one of our men went out to meet them and in about two minutes the ground between the two lines of trenches was swarming with men and officers of both sides shaking hands and wishing each other a happy Christmas. This continued for about half an hour when most of the men were ordered back to the trenches.

For the rest of the day nobody has fired a shot and the men have been wandering about at will on the top of the parapet and carrying straw and fire wood about in the open. We have also had joint burial parties with a service for some dead – some German and some ours – who were lying out between the lines. Some of our officers were talking to groups of English and German soldiers.

This extraordinary truce has been quite important – there was no previous arrangement and of course it had been decided that there was not to [be] any cessation of hostilities. I went out myself and shook hands with several of their officers and men.

From what I could gather most of them would be as glad to get home again as we should. We have had our pipes playing all day and everyone has been wandering about in the open unmolested but not of course as far as the enemy's lines. The truce will probably go on until someone is foolish enough to let off his rifle – we nearly messed it up this afternoon by one of our fellows letting off his rifle skywards by mistake, but they did not seem to notice it so it did not matter.

I have been taking advantage of the truce to improve my 'dug-out' which I share with D.M. Bain, the Scotch rugger international, an excellent fellow… We leave the trenches tomorrow and I shall [not] be sorry as it is much too cold to be pleasant at night.

27th

I am writing this back in billets – the same business continued yesterday and we had another parley with the Germans in the middle. We exchanged cigarettes and autographs and some people took photos. I don't know how long it will go on for – I believe it was supposed to stop yesterday but we can hear no firing going on along the front today except a little distant shelling. We are, at any rate, having another truce on New Year's Day as the Germans want to see how the photos came out! Yesterday was lovely in the morning and I went for several quite long walks about the lines. It is difficult to realise what that means but of course in the ordinary way there is not a sign of life above ground and everyone who puts his head up gets shot at.

It is really very extraordinary that this sort of thing should happen in a war in which there is so much bitterness and ill feeling. The Germans in this part of the line are certainly sportsmen if they are nothing else. Of course I don't suppose it has happened everywhere along the line although I think that indiscriminate firing was more or less stopped in most places on Christmas Day…

I must stop now – I was up all last night on a false alarm. I suppose they thought we had had too slack a time of it the last 2 days.

With heaps of love and wishes to you and everyone for a happy new year.

Your loving son,
ADC

Hedley S. Payne originally enlisted as a private on 6 November 1914 and was attached to the 4th Battalion, Royal Fusiliers, and was subsequently posted to 2/4th Battalion, Royal Fusiliers. He had a busy war serving in both the Mediterranean and European theatres. Between 23 December 1914 and 19 August 1915 he was on active service in Malta. He served as part of the Mediterranean Force (Gallipoli) between 20 August 1915 and 16 April 1916 and was subsequently attached to the London Regiment in May 1916. From 17 April 1916 until 12 January 1917 he served in France.

29 August 1916, France

My dear Mother,
I received your letter of the 17th several days ago but 'tempus fugit' even in the Army and so we have only had time to sleep and eat for the last week. I have not written any letters. I find myself now with half a dozen letters to answer in about five minutes, seated on the straw with twenty people shouting and jumping all over me and my only light a candle – a candle at sufficient distance away to be well nigh useless.

At the same time someone is offering one salmon and fruit for supper and on the other side being told to get up and make my bed…

Try to picture the above scene (and the way I had to stop and have supper) and you will begin to realise the feelings of poor Tommy on entering the correspondence department.

I suppose I am allowed to tell you that the battalion is out of the trenches for a short time for a rest... I heard the astounding news today that I had been made a battalion scout – fancy me hiding behind a blade of grass and sniping a Hun that isn't there – what hopes.

Still, joking apart I quite like the idea.

Now I think I had better start answering your letter written amid the joys of summer by the sea. I am so glad to hear that you have been having a good time at Ryde with them all. I have just received your letter of the 25th as well and apparently the weather was fine too. It has been pouring with rain the last few days here so I am glad to be out of the trenches.

The village is very pretty and peaceful after those to which we had been used to and the scenery around reminds me very much of Devon. A stream like the Sid runs below our billet where we wash and swim.

I must close now and write later. Please give my love to all.

From your loving son,
Hedley

Payne was awarded the Distinguished Conduct Medal (DCM) following courageous actions in France as a scout and his official citation stated:

For conspicuous gallantry on several occasions when carrying messages under heavy machine gun and sniping fire. Twice on his own initiative he made dangerous reconnaissances, returning each time with valuable information and sketches.

(*London Gazette* No. 29824, 14 November 1916)

However, he was injured and was forced to spend a short time in hospital, sending the following letter to his mother after his release and return to the front line.

23 October 1916
Back with the Boys
France

My dear Mother,

I fear that I have been keeping you a long time for this letter but is has not been my fault entirely. After a few days down at the Base where there was always something to do I was sent along with a few others back to the battalion. As we were called out in the middle of the night I could not let you know very well.

Then the train journey took us two days. I found the battalion out on their well-earned rest but there are very few of the old boys left. The next day we had a nice little march of about twenty miles to the village where we are at present.

We are standing by to move again so no letters are being taken but as I received your letters and handkerchiefs last night I must write and send the letter off as soon as possible.

Thanks so much for the hankies. They arrived just in time as I have caught rather a nasty cold. I am so sorry to hear that Majorie is ill.* When will she be well enough to come home again? You must let me know because I might be getting [leave] soon and home would not be the same without Majorie to feed [and] greet me. I do also hope she will be better soon, is there anything that you can take her from me – fruit, flowers etc? I suppose Norman and Howard have returned to school by this time. They will have to plug away to make up for lost time.

Thank you so much for the messages. I thought they must have been stopped as I had not received any for so long.

* His sister Marjorie had spent some time in hospital due to illness.

It was like hearing Dad's voice again to read it. He is getting more of a poet than ever. By the way when you address my letters now you will have to put KCo. [K Company] instead of ACo. [A Company].

I must close now but before I do so you will all be glad to hear that I have been awarded the DCM [Distinguished Conduct Medal].

With the best of love to all.
From your loving son,
Hedley

British servicemen were joined by their Commonwealth compatriots in the army as well as the fledging Royal Flying Corps (later designated the Royal Air Force – RAF). To those on the home front, the pilots exuded a sense of glamour, unlike the troops bogged down in the mud of the trenches, despite the obvious dangers they too faced. The pilots' exploits frequently attracted both the attention of the media and the medal committees. Lieutenant William Leefe Robinson was flying with No. 39 Squadron of the Royal Flying Corps when he shot down a Zeppelin on 3 September 1916. His success against this new enemy earned him the Victoria Cross (VC), the British Empire's highest award for gallantry. He sent the following account to his parents, describing the momentous event.

October 22nd, 1916

My darling Mother and Father,
I do really feel ashamed for not writing to you darling old people before, but still, there it is – you know what I am.

Busy – !! Heavens, for the last 7 weeks I have done enough to last anyone a life time. It has been a wonderful time for me!

I won't say much about 'strafing' the zepp L21 for two reasons; to begin with most of it is strictly secret and secondly I'm really so tired of the subject and telling people about it, that I feel as if I never want to mention it again – so I will only say a very few words about it.

When the colossal thing actually burst into flames of course it was a <u>glorious</u> sight – wonderful! It literally lit up as in the fire light – and [I] sat still half dazed staring at the wonderful sight before me, not realizing to the least degree the wonderful thing that had happened!

My feelings? <u>Can</u> I describe my feelings. I hardly know how I felt. As I watched the huge mass gradually turn on end, and – as it seemed to me – slowly sink, one glowing, blazing mass – I gradually realized what I had done and grew wild with excitement. When I had cooled down a bit, I did what I don't think many people would think I would do, and that was I thanked God with all my heart. You know darling old mother and father I'm not what is popularly known as a religious person, but on an occasion such as that one must realize a little how one does trust in providence. I felt an overpowering feeling of thankfulness, so was it strange that I should pause and think for a moment after the first 'blast' of excitement, as it were, was over and thank from the bottom of my heart, that supreme power that rules and guides our destinies?

When I reached the ground once more, I was greeted with 'was it you Robin' etc. etc.: 'yes, I've strafed the beggar' this time I said, where upon the whole flight set up a yell and carried me out of my machine to the office – cheering like mad.

Talking of cheering, they say it was wonderful to hear all London cheering – people who have heard thousands of huge crowds cheering before say they have heard nothing like it. When Sowrey and Tempest brought down their zepps I had an opportunity of hearing something like it, although they say it wasn't so grand as mine, which could be heard twenty and even thirty miles outside London.

It swelled and sank, first one quarter of London, then another. Thousands, one might say <u>millions</u>, of throats giving vent to thousands of feelings. I would give anything for you dear people to have heard it. A moment before dead silence (for the guns had ceased to fire at it) then this outburst – the relief, the thanks, the gratitude of millions of people. All the sirens, hooters and whistles of all joined in and literally filled the air – and the cause of it all – little me sitting in my little aeroplane above 13,000 feet of darkness!! – It's wonderful!

… But the most glorious thing is that Sowrey, dear old boy, and Tempest, sweet soul, the two zepp strafers who have been awarded DSOs are both in my flight!! <u>Some</u> flight – five officers, of which there are two DSOs and a VC and <u>three</u> zepps to our credit – some <u>record</u>!!!

Well you darlings I'll close now or else I'll go on babbling on all night and I'm really tired. I'll just tell you I'm not at present in Hornchurch, I'm somewhere in England on a secret mission but I'm going back to dear old Sutton's farm again.

Well, <u>do</u> forgive me for not writing before.
Ever your loving son,
Billy

Many soldiers relied on both a strong sense of patriotism and their faith to see them through the darkest days of the war. One such was William John Lynas who enlisted on 5 September 1914 and served with the Royal Irish Rifles (North Belfast Volunteers). Lynas participated in the battle of the Somme in 1916 which he survived, but his involvement was not without its dangers as this letter describes.

15 July 1916

Dear Wife,

I received your very kind and welcome letters alright. I think altogether I am glad to know that you and all at home are well and in the best of health. I am pleased to say that I am in the pink and getting along first class.

Well Mina words cannot express how thankful I am to God for his guidance and goodness to me during the past nine months that I have been in France, especially Mina during our advance. Your prayers have been answered. I am sure you are wondering why I have not written [to] you before this. Well Mina we have been on the move most of the time since we came out of the trenches, we are away down country now to get made up to strength, it may be three or four weeks before we are back to the firing line.

I need hardly begin to tell you about the gallantry of our boys for I am sure you have read more in the papers than I am fit to tell you, there is one thing, Mina, they did not disgrace the name of Ulster or their Force – little did you think as you sat writing that letter on the first day of July that our boys had mounted the top and made a name for Ulster that will never die in the annals of history. No doubt Belfast today and the rest of Ulster are in mourning for the dear ones that gave their life. May the Lord comfort all of those who have lost a beloved husband or brother or son and lastly may the Lord watch over those dear orphans…

We had a miraculous escape, it was on the night of a big bombardment and a shell paid us a visit and buried us in our dug-out. As soon as I realised what had happened I dug out of the debris as best as I could and made for the door to feel if it was blocked as we were choking on the gas from the shell and suffocating us there after a few minutes.

I lit a candle to find Charlie just lying near by. We got him up and off he went to hospital. I was a little bit shaken at the time but I had a bit of work in front of me so I got stuck into it and forgot about my calamity. It was for work that night that I got recommended to my Colonel and Company Officer. For whatever little bit of good work I [did] I consider I only [did] my duty. The only thing I can say is that I hope I will be spared to do many a little thing for our boys in the trenches.

I was promoted to Lance Corporal just a few days before the big advance. I have been returned to the Company since we came out. I hope I will be able to hold it all together. I prefer being a plain Tommy…

Your loving Husband,
William

xxxxxxxxxxxxxxxxxxxxxxxxxxxxxxxxxx

William Lynas' luck held for a little longer. He survived a gas attack later in the war but his lungs were permanently damaged and he tragically succumbed to tuberculosis shortly after the Armistice and his return home.

Serving in the trenches in France presented a number of challenges for the British Tommy, from avoiding the sniper's bullet to the lack of sleep, as recalled by Harold Anderton who served with the 13th Battalion, London Regiment, in France.

No. 3008. 2nd Section.
5th Platoon. 13th London Regt.
British Expeditionary Force
France
Feb 26/15

Dear Mother and All,

I must first apologise for the filthy state of this paper but it rained and soaked my overcoat and its contents – hence the dirt apparent thereon. There is, so the newspaper correspondents put it 'nothing to report' as far as my doings are concerned. The usual rigmarole takes place each week when you're in the trenches, nothing very exciting happens. We're behind our parapets of sand bags and mud, and the Germans behind theirs. A veritable sea of mud separates the two havens of refuge, so attack at present would be hazardous and difficult to either side. Shells buzz about overhead and make weird shrieking noise whilst snipers bullets whistle about with monotonous regularity. You're middling safe if you keep down – if you don't – well the people who say Germans are poor at rifle fire [might] perhaps like to try their luck; personally I prefer the cover of the aforesaid parapet. The nights in the trenches are usually rotten. Either you're on sentry – one hour on and one hour off all night – or else on digging and patrol. If on the former you get cold and fed up – if on the latter you experience bodily weariness but a glorious warmth. Don't know which I prefer. The days are quite all right if fine – you cook your bacon and porridge in your mess tin, prepare stew for dinner and make tea when you're feeling down; its quite OK. The main difficulty in the trenches is to get sleep. About three hours per day and in the day time of course is all that is possible. Hence sentry go on the third night is the devil. The time in the billets is pretty good. You've got to scrape yourself free of mud and keep your rifle and ammunition clean – apart from this and [diverse] fatigue duties you're free to go to the Soldier's Club, a nice cosy retreat run by C. of E. or to the adjoining café and stuff.

I hope you've sent that money off, I'm almost stony. Also please send that chocolate fortnightly. It's grand stuff and I've regained my youthful love of sweets of any sorts…

Well, so long, no more news.

With best love to all,
Your loving son,
Harold

A sense of humour was crucial to many as shown in this ironic letter anonymously drafted while on the front lines, which is intended to mock a typical Field Service postcard as provided by the army.

In the Field
    /   /1917
My   dear
        dearest
        darling

I can't write much to-day as I am very   overworked
                                               busy
                                               tired
                                               lazy.

and the   Corps   is exhibiting intense activity.
                 G.O.C
                 G.S.O.I
                 A.A & Q.M.G
                 HUN

Things our way are going on   quite well

much as usual

pas mal.

We   put up a bit of a show   last night with   complete success.

The HUNS   yesterday   tolerable

-out any

Our   offensive   appears to be going well.

The Russian

The Italian

The Montenegrin

The Monagasque

The United States

The Brazilian

The Panama

The Bolivian

The French

The Belgian

The Serbian

The Roumanian

The Portugeese

The Japanese

The Cuban

The Chinese

The German offensive is   obviously   a complete failure.

apparently

we will hope

I really begin to think the war will end   this year

next year

some time

never.

The	flies	are	vile
	rations	is	execrable
	weather		much the same.

The [blank]	is	cheery
		weary
		languid
		sore distrest [sic]
		at rest.

We are now living in a	Chateau
	ruined farm
	Hovel
	dug-out.

I am	hoping soon to come on	leave, which is now	on
	about due for		off.
	overdue for		
	not yet in the running for		

| I am suffering from a | slight | wound.* |
| | severe | |

* Or state disease. If the whole of this sentence is struck out the writer may be presumed to be well or deceased.

| ....'s wife has just | sent him |
| | presented him with ..... |

What I should really like is......

Many thanks for your	letter
	parcel
	good intentions.

How are the   poultry (including cows)   getting on?
                    potatoes
                    child

I hope you are   well
                 better
                 bearing up
                 not spending too much money
                 getting on better with mother.

Insert here protestations of affection – NOT TO EXCEED TEN WORDS ....
Ever ....
xxxxxxxxxxxxxxxxxxxxxxxxxxxxxxxx (Delete or add as many be necessary.)

No war is more associated with poetry than the First World War, from Wilfred Owen's *Dulce et Decorum Est* to John McCrae's *In Flanders Fields* they have defined and coloured our perceptions of this war ever since. McCrae's poem is assumed to be the inspiration for the first ever poppy collection held in 1919. Less well known is the suggestion that it also inspired his fellow poet Isaac Rosenberg. Born into poverty in the East End of London, Rosenberg volunteered in 1915 chiefly to provide his mother with the 'separation allowance' and wrote a number of poems throughout his service until his death in April 1918. McCrae's poem was first published in *Punch* in 1915 and so may well have inspired Rosenberg's *In the Trenches* which first appeared in the letter to his friend Sonia Cohen (also known as Sonia Rodker) in autumn 1916.

Dear Sonia,

I have been anxious to hear from you about Rodker [the modernist poet John Rodker]. I wrote to Trevelyan [pacifist and poet Robert Calverley Trevelyan] … and asked him for news but I fancy my letter got lost. Write me any news – anything. I seem to have [been] in France ages. I wish Rodker were with me, the informal lingo is a tragedy with me, and he'd help me out. If I was taciturn in England I am ten times so here; our struggle to express ourselves is a fearful joke. However our wants are simple, our cash is scarce and our own time… Here is a little poem a bit commonplace I'm afraid.

In the trenches
I snatched two poppies
From the parapets edge
Two bright red poppies
That winked on the ledge.
Behind my ear
I stuck one through,
One blood red poppy
I gave to you.

The sandbags narrowed
and screwed out our jest
and tore the poppy
you had on your breast…

Dawn – a shell – O! Christ
I am choked … safe … dustblind, I
See trench floor poppies
Strewn. Smashed, you lie…

Spring 1915 brought a rapid return to hostilities with several major battles. This letter by Major Henry Granville Scott describes his involvement in the Ypres area while serving with the 1/4th Battalion, Alexandra, Princess of Wales' Own (Yorkshire) Regiment.

6.30am
Tuesday morning
27th April 1915

To Mrs Scott,

I will now try and give you a more detailed and connected account of what has happened since we left the little village 10½ miles from Ypres where we billeted for 3 days after journeying night and day from England.

On Thursday night at 11pm I was roused. Orders had come for the Brigade to stand by ready to move at a moments notice. By 12pm the Battalion was ready to march.

Orders then came cancelling former orders and we went back to billets. At 8am Friday orders again came to be ready to move followed by an order to assemble as quick as possible at a point 2 miles away on the road to Ypres. We did so by about 10am and found the No. 1 Batt. [Battalion] already there. We are No. 2 in seniority of the Brigade. At 11 a long string of motor buses moved us to a point 3½ miles east of Yp. and from there we marched to hutments just outside. The men were all carrying tremendous loads, all they had and extra ammunition – 200 per man.

The roads are bad for the feet where they are most pavé, they are very uneven with large loose stones which turn over when you stand on them – very heavy on [the] ankles when you are carrying a heavy load. The addition of a heavy bundle of maps, double rations etc made officers' lists heavier than ever. I know we all carry too much, but we do not know yet what to discard. Everything we have seems absolutely necessary.

Well the hutments were an agreeable surprise to us (we never know exactly where we are going until we get there, movements being made in a succession of bounds). We quickly started to make ourselves comfortable, a deafening cannonade was going on and we knew we were well within range of shell fire. We were to have no rest however, as orders came at 8.30pm to move.

My times after this are not to be relied upon as I am trusting to approximation. However they are real enough for a personal narrative. We moved at 2.45am (head of the column) and in the following order – 1, 3, 4, 2 (seniority of Batts in Brigade) in the direction of Yp canal and lay down in a field in readiness. We were moved back twice during the next few hours. At 6am I was sent back to hutments on a bicycle to arrange to bring hot tea for the men…

I was wishing I could shed some of my kit but couldn't risk it. Just as we were lighting fires four shells came right amongst us, fortunately doing only slight damage – six men slightly wounded including Lt Tugwell. De Legh was there with his stretchers and he quickly got to work. Our four stretchers were sent off to hutments so I lugged Tugwell on to a cook's cart … and De Legh dressed his wound (slight shell wound on lower leg)…

We reassembled in somewhat open order. The CO [commanding officer] came back with orders to move in the direction of the east of Ypres… We marched in a roundabout way to a point E of Yp., about 6 miles and squatted down again. We were intermingled with all sort of scattered troops, wounded men were continually passing, the deafening artillery fire never ceased for a moment… We received orders that the Bn. had to attack. Well I thought this was pretty sharp for troops that had only been a few days in the country…

Each Coy [company] formed its own method of formation, but they were mostly in diamond formation in column of platoons. While the CO was making his disposition, I took a careful compass bearing of the line. Off we started.

We were quickly observed and immediately the leading Companies extended into lines and pressed on in short rushes. Nos 3 and 4 acting as supports began to close up and thicken the lines. I have seen our men practise the attack drill and do it very well, but I never saw them do it so well as this. As a drill it would have been fault-less. As an actual action under frightful conditions of modern warfare it was superb...

Men began to drop quicker and quicker. Still we pressed on, taking advantage of every little undulation and there were not many. A man dropped just in front of me. Nevin and I could not see his wound. He said it was in his stomach. We lay on each side of him and tore his clothes apart. We found the wound (a bullet in the back behind his kidneys) put his first field dressing on and left him...

The CO in his anxiety was exposing himself too much, at least I think so, and some of the men told me afterwards that it later worried them. We were getting near to the enemy's position now and found other troops in front of us, who proved to be the Royal Irish. Suddenly the man lying next to me turned his head towards me and I saw his face from his eyes to his chin was literally blown away. He made a sort of moaning noise and looked at me in a questioning sort of way as if asking me what had happened to him. I rolled over to him, got his field dressing, turned him on his back and put the dressing on, but the pad would not nearly fill the hole. I injected 2 pellets of morphine into his arm and pressed on... I joined our second line about 30 yards ahead. Our front line was forming at 300 yards carefully and systematically...

The CO and I found the CO of the Royal Irish and he told us he had orders from the GOC [general officer commanding] to relieve at dusk as he could not hold the line we had advanced to. It seemed awfully hard to have to give up what we had apparently gained but we are simply pawns in the great game and know nothing more than is necessary and very often, we think, not even that...

That is all up to now. It is 10.45 and I have written this whilst my memory is fresh. I hope you will be able to decipher it. It is only a sketch, I could paint the picture but it would take me a week and I would not be able to see for tears.

Yours as ever

Some soldiers were not afraid of expressing their true feelings, from fear to despair, in letters home to loved ones. J.T. Keeping wrote the following letter on 20 May 1915 after surviving the Second Battle of Ypres in 1915. He served for the remainder of the war with the London Regiment, was subsequently promoted to captain and won the Military Cross (MC).

Miss E. Keeping
44 Digby Road
Finsbury Park
London
20.5.1915

Dear Elsie,
I am very sorry not to have written before but I dare say by this time you have got some idea of where we <u>have</u> been in fact in your first letter you had it right although I cannot think how you got it. We had about a fortnight of <u>Hell</u> and are now back resting again some 150 strong out of a total of 1,600 in all and I can tell you the ones who have got back are lucky. You could never believe what it has been like and you can guess I did not feel much like writing. It was all so sudden, one day we were back resting and the next we were in the thick of it being shelled to pieces. But there is one thing about the regiment, the regulars retired and passed us along the [road] but we stuck it till dark

and then of course were reinforced. I am afraid I am a mere nervous wreck, in fact when we got back I sat down and had a jolly good cry. I am absolutely alone now, the only one of my section left.

There is some talk of leave so will write further tomorrow as soon as I get any news.

Cheer up and tell them all I will drop them a line in a day or so.

J

Death was an ever present feature of the battlefield, regardless of rank. The following letter of condolence was sent to the brother of Lieutenant Gerry M. Renny who was killed while serving with the Royal Field Artillery.

7th May 1917
C/92 RFA
BEF

My dear Renny,
I have just got your letter and will send you all the particulars I can about poor old Gerry. First now I can only scribble a note. I can well understand how hard you must find the blow and how it must hurt. I know it all the more for having been so fond of him myself and for the blank that his death leaves in the Battery. He was such a cheerful lad and quite irresistible as a pal. It is hard that he had to go, when so many rotters still live. I have always hated the Boche, but now I shall have a very deep personal [sense] to pay back and by God he shall get it every time I sit down to measure our [angle]! I am sending you his revolver and belt... His belt has the bullet hole in each side

– the bullet that robbed you of a brother and me of a very dear pal…

With very deep sympathy to you and all the family.

Sincerely yours,
J.H. O'Kelly

For servicemen knowing what active duty on the front line would bring there was often little sympathy towards conscientious objectors, as shown by this letter from Norman Thomas, who served with the London Regiment.

Seaford
Sussex
Wednesday 25 April 1917

My Dear 'Weenie',

… I have some rather interesting news today – our battalion have moved to Aldershot. I do not know the exact place. We are supposed to be in some barracks. What luck isn't it 'Weenie', [I] shall be able to see old 'Reggie' again, will seem like the old days.

I cannot get leave from here as I expect I shall be going away next week. So I may be able to get the week-end when I rejoin my new battalion. I am writing to Reggie today, hope he will be able to obtain leave, if he does succeed he will be extremely lucky.

There are a great number of 'Conscientious Objectors' near Seaford. They have been employed for the past 4 months constructing one of the roads leading the Newhaven, the road is just the same as it was before the operations of the 'C.O.s'. They all were allowed leave at Easter and Xmas and get real good food. Don't you think it's rather unfair to us fellows? We often march past them and pass a good deal of comments etc; some-times there is a 'rough-house' ending in a few C.O.s being badly 'mauled' and a few of us chaps escorted back to the guard-room and then punished 'C.B' [confined to barracks] etc. This is an every-day occurrence. I can see some fun shortly if they continue to keep them here.

Well 'Weenie' dear, I hope you are not 'bored', this must seem very uninteresting?!!!

Have no more news. Give my kindest regards to the Girls.

Write soon – dear

Concluding,

With love and kisses
Yours,
Norman
xxxxxxxx
xxxxxxxxx

PS. Please excuse writing and mistakes as I am in a hurry to catch the post.
Love,
Norman

The following are a series of extracts from the letters sent by Second Lieutenant Robert Peyton Hamilton describing the trials and tribulations of constant service in the front-line trenches while serving with the 20th (County of London) Battalion (Blackheath and Woolwich), London Regiment.

24 May

I have just come out of the trenches. As luck would have it, our crowd were doing a spell of fire drops, of which they had done three when we reported at 9 o/c at night. We went straight in and stopped until 8 o/c last night. The trenches are a manual of clean, mechanical workmanship. These particular trenches were built by the guards, and one cannot too highly praise the splendid way they are built; much better than our previous ones, and they were built at leisure, and these under fire... The men are all very cheerful. I've had shells drop very near me, and have been near guns going off, but do not think the noise will do me much havoc, though of course I am yet but an infant in such things. For the moment our feelings are interested very; want letters from England very; and a game of cricket very; and that's just all.

27 May

I have seen it, and am a little older, I can't write a collected letter. I am supposed to be sleeping now; I have two hours on and two hours off. Our Battalion has been getting used to things, and when I arrived they were being pushed up a bit.

I started at 4am Tuesday for a reconnaissance, which went well and took till 8.30. Had breakfast, censored letters and had a sudden call to go with 100 men and take ammunition from the rear to a reserve depot in the back trenches held by another Brigade who were attacking that night. Did this, got back at 5.30; had no lunch. Had to parade with Battalion at 6 o/c and stand in reserve in case we were wanted for the attack. At 12 o/c midnight I was told to take my platoon up to the trenches and take ammunition to the firing line. In the communication trenches we [were] stuck, with dead and wounded and reliefs etc, and we couldn't move either way, and all the time we were under constant shell fire. Men were dropping all round, and some were horrible sights. Oh, Govenor, it was awful to see those poor boys... My platoon was most fortunate and got off practically free. The Brigadier thanked me nicely for helping...

It was the worst show my battalion has been in, they tell me, so I had a pretty good introduction. I keep alive, and bucked my men up, which helped me considerably... At 5 o/c we took over the trenches which were the scene of shelling and attack. We had to clear up; it was awful. We went out in front when it was dark, and got some poor wounded devils in, and dragged the dead to the back and buried them. I mustn't give you the figures of the casualties, but it is a high price to pay for an advance of any description, and it's due simply to our not having enough shells to cope with their artillery.

I don't know when we come out, and can't get an envelope till we do. I am writing this in my message-book, and will put your address on in case.

June 5

I hope you won't think from my letters that I'm wailing. Of course things shocked me, and I was very much checked into bully beef, no sleep, and the usual hardships of a picnic of this sort; but now I have got over that, and can cheerfully eat every course and every meal from the same plate... I really do feel that I'm lucky to be here, and that after all it's something beside beastly slaughter. It's sort of taking a part in the biggest game [that] ever happened, and the whole place has no room for any petty or artificial feelings. One is on rock-bottom all the time...

June 13

I've had two new men from home who came up on Friday and it was their first time in the trenches. I was talking to one, who was on look-out, about 12 o/c when a whizz-bang came over. We both ducked and I got up when the thing had finished, but the poor fellow didn't; a bullet from the shell had gone through the peak of his cap into his temple, and he died in ten minutes. Later on – about an hour – his friend, the other new man, came up from further down the sap with his nose blown about, he'll get better. Rotten luck, though; isn't it?…

July 1

I will talk anon of my men and their ways and my overlords. This I do know. I had 50 of my platoon up working the other night. They did fairly well; but all the time they're much too well educated and intelligent to dig with ease. My platoon are all products of Goldsmith's School, nearly all half and fully fledged schoolmasters, not so badly brought up. They quote poetry, and can't see that digging trenches is 'fighting'. You know that cursed education that leaves them half stranded on decency's shore. They do well when they forget and their true selves come out. If they think of their job or of their superior education, they're very boring. My general attitude to them, except in the trenches, is one of great scorn, and I jump on them severely for not 'washing behind their ears'… I'm trying to get them to realise they're stupid babies – know nothing and must do what they're told. In the trenches they do it, because they know there's death knocking very near, and a prompt obedience might save 'em. Out of the trenches they begin slacking, and turn up with dirty equipment, and other odd things and I just give them all the punishment they've got time to do. It ain't popular but the CO told Hooper, my OC, that my platoon was decidedly smarter.

Peyton Hamilton would see active service for just short of a full year. He died on 25 September 1915 as a result of wounds received in action.

For some servicemen life in the armed forces was simply abhorrent and they struggled to see the point of the war. One such soldier was

Lance Corporal J.H. Leather who served with the Royal Fusiliers. In a series of letters he described his loathing of army life and his lack of enthusiasm for the conflict.

Monday
No 8, Barrackroom
B Company
20th S. Battn: Royal F usilluiers
No 7 Lines: Clipstone Camp
Nottinghamshire

Dear People,
Thank you all so very much for the letters that I have had from you at Woodeste, and the one I got the other day. I should really have answered them a great deal better but, as a matter of fact, one always feels either too tired or too bored, or something, to write any letters at all. What usually happens with all the people I know is that they write to me, don't get an answer; write to remind me and still don't get an answer; write a postcard asking if I am dead or something, still don't get an answer; then give me up with a final angry note. Four months after that I write and make the best excuse I can…

The Army is undeniably the most dismal experience I have had yet… I haven't got the faintest enthusiasm about this war; and I feel pretty sure now that the question is not whether we shall win or lose, but whether we shall lose or just manage to save our bacon. The idea of breaking the Germans is so much nonsense, and you have only to be in this Army to see the mess and muddle of everything; the lack of training in the men and the thick-headedness of the officers – nine out of every ten of whom I wouldn't touch with a yardstick in civilian life – to realise that this nonsense about beating the Germans is so much water on the brain. I compare everything I see around me with what I saw for the last eight years or so in Germany, every year, and I compare the foolish, ill-educated, stupid officers here with the German officers, many of them my own friends, one or two of them very dear friends indeed: and the only thing I think is that Germany is as strange and unknown a country to most English people as the Sudan...

Shall write again quite soon.

Yours,
JH

Lance Corporal Leather was subsequently killed fighting at High Wood during the battle for the Somme in 1916. Ironically, the letter of condolence sent to his father expressed the usual platitudes about commitment to the cause.

August 20th 1916

Dear Mr Leather,

In answer to your enquiry about Lance Corporal Leather, which I received today, I can only say that your son met his end in the Wood on July 20th almost in the forefront of the battle.

He was first wounded in the legs, and more than one of his comrades was killed in trying to bring him in, and a little while later he was killed outright by a shell. This is all that I have been able to gather, but everyone tells me that your son bore himself, as always, like a man and a soldier.

We were all of us exceedingly sorry to hear of his death, as we appreciated his good fighting qualities, whilst his thorough knowledge of German made him a more than ordinarily useful man to have in the company.

Please accept our sincerest sympathy with you in your great loss. It has not yet, so far as I know, been possible to recover his body, as the spot where he fell is still disputed territory, but he may have been given burial by another Division; but be that as it may, may it be of some comfort to you to know that your son met his end as a soldier should, in that great cause for which we are fighting.

Faithfully yours,
E. Mannering

Even Army chaplains were not immune from the depravations of the front lines. Reverend Canon Cyril Lomax served as a Church of England Army chaplain in France between July 1916 and April 1917, attached to the 8th Battalion, Durham Light Infantry. An accomplished amateur artist, many of his surviving letters are illustrated including this surviving extract entitled 'The First Tanks' sent on 7 September 1916.*

… Everybody hates shells – the man who is naturally fearless is almost a wash out in this war – but in spite of hating them so everybody goes on solidly doing whatever his job happens to be with a really fine dry humour and stoicism.

Everybody too hates mud, but we bathe in it, wade in it, sleep in it and clods of it adorn the most secret recesses of one's clothes, books and papers.

To see the poor brutes of horses straining through ankle deep mud with food for the hungry guns goes to my heart. Even more than seeing the unfortunate men coming out of the front line. The poor beasts have such a pathetic droop, look so patient, and miserable, and respond so bravely to some tremendous effort to suck a timber out of mud…

But of course, one thing that has put the wind up the Boche more than anything else is our perpetual artillery fire. Ever so

* See the image insert for the sketch of the tanks in action at Cambrai, drawn by Reverend Lomax.

many have gone mad under the strain. So the horses must be overworked to keep the rain of shells up. It is a rain of shells.

I was humping stretchers all one night through mud nearly as bad. The stretcher-bearers had been at it for 36 hours and I was a bit tired with just one night, especially as I ran into a Boche barrage and had to take cover in a trench where I cried my eyes out for an hour in response to his tear shells.

The tanks were a great success. I did not see them in action but our men were full of them. They certainly put the wind up the Boche. His favourite strong places were as nothing, and they crossed trenches with ease. An RAMC [Royal Army Medical Corps] man said to an upstanding wounded German who knew the vernacular, 'Well, we've got you properly beat this time.' The reply was, 'What can you expect when you come over in bl—dy taxis.'

I saw a quaint sight myself in which one of them figured. They had been heavily shelling the scrag end of a wood just behind a ridge where I was in a Collecting Post for the wounded.

Great gouts of flame, black smoke, stones and balks of timber had been flying thirty feet in the air at least. We all felt rather glad we were well out of it and that it was well behind our line. When it was all over, out from what had been the thickest of it, waddled a tank painted green and yellow, as it might be rubbing its eyes and saying 'Dear me, I believe somebody woke me! I think I must find a quieter spot.' Thus it proceeded to do waddling over trenches into shell holes, out of shell holes, until it came to rest…

In April 1915 the Gallipoli campaign was launched on the Dardanelles. A joint British-French operation, using a large quantity of ANZAC troops, an attempt was made to seize the Gallipoli peninsula from the Ottoman Empire and thus secure a sea route to Russia. It was one of the major Allied failings of the war and became renowned for the terrible fighting conditions experienced by the troops.

Lieutenant Patrick Duff served with the 460th Battery, 147th Brigade, Royal Field Artillery (29th Division) on Cape Helles, Gallipoli, and wrote a series of letters home describing the general conditions and the determination of his Turkish adversaries with a resolute cheerfulness.

May 18th

Dear Ma,

I got your letter of April 27 yesterday. I was so sorry to hear of Grannie's death and am afraid you'll miss her a lot. Hope you're not tired with the long journeys – but I forget that when this reaches you it will be a month or so after the event.

I suppose you'll be hearing news of this expedition in the papers by now: we don't hear much either of what goes on here or anywhere else except in a small leaflet circulated daily from Headquarters and entitled 'Peninsular Press'. This contains extracts from what Lord Crewe says in the House of Lords about ten days old; and even when fresh from the mint I have never felt much thrilled by the utterances of the noble peer.

Am having a slightly more peaceful time than when last I wrote: the 'Morning Hate', as we call the shooting the Turks do from 7.45am till 8.30, didn't come near me this morning, and there has been no Lunchtime Hate at all… Life here is any amount nicer than when I was on Hounslow Heath last August with the HAC [Honourable Artillery Company]; mayn't [sic] be quite so safe, but it's more interesting…

Am going to send this off now, as I've been writing it for three days. Picture me walking about in the sun all day long, and the Turks missing me by rods, poles and perches.

Best love to all.

May 27th

Dear Ma,

Many thanks for your letters. I suppose you'll be getting mine by now tho' [sic] you always say you haven't heard in your letters. I am again with the Battery and living in the Eagle's Nest, as we call it: incidentally, it's not a bad name, as I saw a Sikh a bit further up the ravine feeding a young eagle about the size of Uff which he must have found here.* The Sikhs are good to see in the mornings combing their long black hair: in this setting it puts one in mind of the Spartans before Thermopylae. The Gurkhas are ripping too: I never saw such fine little men…

We had a water-spout here two days ago: in 20 minutes the ravine was a rushing stream, in the gullies the harness and even the men's clothes were nearly washed away. My dug out, cut in the side of the cliff and heavily protected with a tarpaulin, kept out the rain wonderfully. It doesn't matter how wet one gets here as the next day it is baking hot. We are now getting up at the loathly hour of 3.45am and exercising the horses in the semi-darkness so that Gallipoli Bill won't see us.

By the way, parcels and papers etc reach us perfectly easily: in fact we send in an Indian with a little cart and two mules to fetch the mail when there is one. Had rather fun the other day: I had gone down to the beach and saw that the ship I came from Alexandria in was here. I managed to get on board and [get] a bottle of fizz and a bottle of whisky. Seemed so funny to have it out here. I had tea with some officers at their mess yesterday and had butter, which I hadn't tasted for a month: one poured a spoonful of it onto the bread.

I want to see the papers awfully, because for one thing it makes writing so much easier when you know what you can say. Wish I could send my films home to be developed, as I'm so

---

* Uff was the name of Patrick's cat back at home.

afraid of them getting spoiled or lost. When we came down this morning we found that the battery had been augmented by one foal – which is a very jolly little beast – I had lost one on the way from Alexandria...

We have had news in the 'Peninsular Press' that Italy has joined in and the *Lusitania* has been sunk. Wish one could have weekends here to learn all the news... Hope all goes well with you and that you're all going strong; and that people don't talk war all the time.

Best of love to all,
P.

June 6th

Dear Ma,
Got your last letter in the midst of a huge bombardment – I had been shouting orders to the guns from 8.30am till 4.30pm almost continuously and found your letter when I came away for a bit of food. That was June 3rd or 4th; expect there will be something in the papers about our advance on that day, as things had been very quiet just before and probably will be quiet again for a bit. It is an extraordinary sight to look out of our observation trench, which one mostly does with great caution through a periscope; one sees simply a maze of trenches, and it is awfully hard to tell which are ours and which are the Turks'. In one trench there were English and Turks throwing hand bombs at each other like mad. Seen a fair number of Turkish prisoners lately – they stick them for [the] time being in compounds closed in by barbed wire and guarded by sentries. Rather aquiline evil-looking men, but devilishly strong and hardy looking...

Have some long days now and again, getting up at 4am and going to bed about 1am occasionally: but sleeping practically out of doors makes what sleep one has go further, and after all, war is war. The time one feels it most is about 2pm when there is no shade of any kind; in the trenches the sun simply beats down on one, and one's clothes get full of sand… The great comfort is having the sea so handy: by means of a communication trench we can go from the guns to the edge of a cliff and so down to the great and wide sea also without showing ourselves on the skyline…

We are indenting for respirators, but I don't expect we shall have much asphyxiating gas, as the wind is generally from us to the Turks. The latter set fire to the heather the other day, as a matter of fact, thus hindering the infantry from advancing and burning our wounded; when the Turk sees a wounded man in front of his trench he calls to others and they solemnly shoot at him and throw bombs. Guy saw them doing it. They also blazed away like mad with guns at a trawler flying the Red Cross, which was engaged in taking our wounded from the beach; but happily just missed it.

Hope you're managing to get on the river: one feels in a foreign climate here, and doesn't realise that possibly you're having fine weather at home as well. One feels at times a great yearning to get back; but most times one's too busy to think of anything but work; as a matter of fact, it's not quite as deadly as that. They days pass very quickly: I shall soon be sending along a fresh instalment of [the] diary…

Must now go and see horses fed. 'God bless you till I come back' as the men say in their letters – implying that on their return, He can stop: be sure that my fortune or your prayers have preserved me so far and should continue to do so with luck.

Best of love to all.
Your very affectionate,
P.

June 21st

We have been blazing off ammunition in great style since above was written: you'll probably see in the papers that an advance was made today. The part of the peninsula which we and other batteries were shelling this morning was simply a mass of dust which spread down Gallipoli and out to sea. We have been 'standing by' all subsequent parts of the morning… By the way, I believe we can send cables quite cheaply from here, so don't be alarmed if you get one, because it will only contain a request for two boot-laces by return of post and not a notice that I'm pushing up the daisies of the Thracian Chersonese*…

Had better finish up this letter now, or a bombardment will begin again and I shan't have a chance to send it off for another day or so.

Best of love to everyone: I hope you are keeping in good spirits and defying the evil Germ-Ottomans' attempts to create despondency.

Yours very affectionate,
P.

June 28th

Dear Ma,
… I write this in the midst of a terrific battle: it is now 5.30pm and since 7 this morning we have been hard at it. From what I hear on [the] telephone we are doing very well – I know we meant to make a real business of it today. I am pretty deaf and fearfully hot: everyone else is all right.

War is so full of chances: three signallers today who really took considerable risks in lying wires out in the open and along

---

*   This is the ancient name for the Gallipoli peninsular.

the fire trenches, return unscathed to our camp here where they promptly get hit drawing their rations and filling their water bottles at the water carts!

We went for the Turk in proper style today, with mine and maxim and rifle and gun and aeroplane and destroyer (at sea) and howitzer and heavy gun and balloon. Expect after today we shall have a quiet time for a bit…

I write with my last stump of indelible pencil by one of the guns and with the ground strewn with empty cartridge-cases. The gunners are sitting about on the trails of the guns … and drinking tea… (More action) Am now standing by all loaded up in case of counter-attacks, so that if evil Turk shows his nose round the counter it may be blasted off him by one word.

8pm Have had more firing and am again standing by. I believe we have made a biggish advance; anyhow they sent up the right troops last night. It was the most impressive sight seeing them simply crowding up, all proper men, and with all the same expression on their faces. Hope they are all comfortable in the Turkish trenches.

I shall be dashing about most of tonight getting ammunition: am inclined to think that one earns one's money occasionally. It will be rather a stirring night, as each side will be so nervous of the other that will be constantly shooting up flares which momentarily light up all the ground between the trenches and tho' [sic] one is miles away, one feels most 'conspicuous'…

Must go and eat. Best love to all. Will write a better letter soon.

Your very affectionate,
P.

July 2nd

Dear Ma,
… We did a big advance on June 28 and I have been walking about [the] last day or so looking to find where the new positions are.

You know the things at exhibitions called 'mazes', where you walk into a room full of passages and try and find your way out? It is no exaggeration to say that the trenches are worse than that. They run in and out, never straight for more than 10 yards (so that if a shell comes in it won't kill more than three or four) and there are duplicate firing trenches, supports, reserves, communication-trenches and so on; it is awfully difficult to find one's way about, or to find where the enemy's trenches actually begin. Generally the infantry put up a flag or biscuit-box to show how far they have got...

Had rather fun the other day: we were looking down a big ravine where we could see the Turks scuttling about at the further end, and we had machine guns popping off like mad at them. I did a bit of observing for one gun – a machine gun, you know, just presses a button like our dining-room bell and off go the bullets as long as you press.

It's pretty hot here, and the glare off the whitish earth in the trenches is trying at times: but we go about without coats on generally. We are going to have khaki drill shortly, like the Gurkhas wear – little short bags like one wears for football...

I expect you can see from my letters that the war doesn't worry me much, or what I run up against leave an impression on me that I can't get rid of. One gets perfectly dispassionate – not, that is, being devoid of pity, but quite incapable of horror. These things are infinitely more ghastly in the reading than in the seeing. The great comfort is that we nearly always get back from the trenches at night, and where we are everything is quite sweet and clean. So you needn't imagine me in a state of mental despair: but rather as very brown and getting much fatter, and thinking exclusively of what we shall get to eat...

Best love to all,
P.

The Highland Division also served alongside the ANZAC contingent in the Dardanelles. Eric Townsend served as a captain in 1/5th (City of Glasgow) Battalion, Highland Infantry Division (157th Brigade, 52nd Division). His letters home offer an interesting insight into the general movements up and down the line.

The Dardanelles
3rd July, 1915

Dearest Mother,

We are at last somewhere in the Dardanelles and living the luxurious life in the trenches, though I couldn't quite exactly tell you where we are even if I wanted to. There are not many square miles on the peninsula where I could be, so you know fairly exactly where I am…

These trenches are old ones and not in the form of a continuous trench, but consist of individual dug outs in a double line a few yards apart. There is plenty of room to lie down in them, but they provide no shelter from the sun which beats into them. I have rigged up a waterproof shelter which affords a little shade, but it is very hot, tho' [sic] we had some rain last night and this morning, and last night the lightning played continually and was very bright… Our company is in the front line of the Battalion trenches and the next line is about 400 yards to the rear. Exactly how many lines we have at present I don't yet know… We have had no shells on our trenches yet, but we were told that the Turks had this exact range and until we got one or two and have a few casualties I don't think we shall be able to keep the men properly down in their dug outs. There has been a fairly steady but very slight gun fire all day, and no rifle fire that we could hear. Our sole fare today is bully beef and dry bread and very little water. I expect water and supplies will come up during the night.

Sunday, 4th July (Not a day of rest). Still alive in the same trenches with the shrapnel buzzing overhead, but none on us yet…

Last evening the remainder of the Battalion straggled past our lines after nine days in the firing line on their way back for a rest. You will have heard how badly the Scottish Rifles were cut up – terribly sad…

Tuesday, 6th July. The scene changes again. The Battalion is in fairly advanced reserve trenches to which we came up last night. It was a long and weary job, and took from 8.30pm till about 1.30am today, at which point officers and men fell down together and slept. We are safer here than before for the trench is very deep and never gets shelled. The only dangerous thing in the front line is a charge. The heavy firing of [yesterday] morning I spoke of was a Turkish attack, repulsed with great loss. There is no rifle fire by day, but there are other sharp bursts at dawn and sunset when attacks are made and the Turks fire all night at random, just to show us they are still here. It lulls us to sleep! – At present we are very crowded – too short a trench. No casualties. Quite well.

Hope you are all the same.
Eric

4 Nov 1917

Dear Mother
The war has started again here, but we are entirely out of it in the meantime – in fact enjoying baths in the sea! More later.

Love to all,
Eric

Despite the cheerful optimism of this short note it was in fact his final letter home and Eric was killed in action shortly afterwards.

For most soldiers on the front line regular contact with the home front was crucial for maintaining morale. The British Forces Post Office (BFPO) could trace its history back to 1799 when the office of the Army Postmaster was initially established, but during the First World War its service expanded greatly with millions of letters exchanging hands.

Rifleman Bernard Britland sent a series of letters home to his mother during his time on the Ypres Salient in 1915 describing the general conditions in the rear echelons, his first sighting of a dogfight and even the occasional gas attack.

Ypres, Thursday June 17, 1915

Dear Mother,

I received your letter and parcel quite safe and in good condition. Thank you very much for the parcel it was a treat. Thank Aunt Pollie and our Bertha for the butter, milk and sweets. The bread and butter tasted a treat. The bread we get out here is nothing near so good as English bread and it is not so often that we can get butter. I would like a few teacakes if you could send them, either white or brown. I have never seen one since I left England.

We have done some moving about since we came over here and all marching too. From what I can hear we are a kind of flying column, ready to go where we are needed at a minute's notice. We are seeing the country through it, so that is one consolation. At the present time we are in reserve trenches. The only thing we have to be afraid of here is when they start shelling us and that is not so often.

When we are marching through the country place, only a mile or two behind the firing line, you would never think there was a war on except now and then you come across a village which has been shelled and then you realise what it must have been like to the Belgians. It is mostly farming round here and we see the farmers going on with their work as unconcerned as if nothing was going on and yet all the time there will be the roar of the big guns and the rattle of rifle fire all around. It does seem a contrast to me...

I am getting as hard as nails and keeping in very good health. Many a time we have to sleep out in the open and up to now I feel no worse for it...

I think I will close now with best love to everybody at home and my best respects to all enquiring friends from your affectionate son,

Bernard.

Field Post Office
Saturday July 3, 1915

Dear Mother,

I received your very welcome letter and the [parcel] from G. Howard. I also received a letter from Pollie in the same post. They were delivered to me in the trenches and at the time of writing we are still in the trenches. We are still at the same place I told you about in my last letter, we are in the support trenches here and we have to carry rations up to the troops in the firing lines. We do this at night but in the daytime we are not allowed to leave the dug outs, for if we do the enemy are almost certain to start shelling us and we have a lively time for about an hour. The Germans have sent gas bombs over our trench several times but the only effect it had on us was to make our eyes smart. You would have laughed if you had seen us sitting in the dug out with tears streaming down our faces. As soon as we smell it we put our smoke helmets on, and if we get these on in time it does not affect our eyes. The smoke helmets we use seem to be very good ones. They are made like a bag and fit right over our heads and we fasten them inside our tunics. In the front is a transparent piece of tale or mica, so that we can see what we are doing. There has been a lot of shelling here this week but I am still one of the fortunate ones. I am still keeping in good health and hope you are all the same at home…

I think that is all just now so I will close with best love to everybody from your loving son,

Bernard.

Field Post Office
Monday July 26, 1915

Dear Mother,
We have left the rest camp and we are at present living in dug outs outside the town which I mentioned before. We are a few miles from the firing line but expect to go there any day now…

Yesterday we had an open-air service and after the service the chaplain held a communion service in a loft over a barn. We had to climb a ladder to get to the loft. It was a very interesting service and was a strange contrast to the communion service I attended at Easter at Mossley. The chaplain is trying to make arrangements for a confirmation service for those who have not been confirmed. I should think it should be a very interesting service.

We had a very interesting experience here last night just after tea. We were outside our dug outs when we saw a German aeroplane flying about. Our anti-aircraft guns started firing at it and then three or four of our own aeroplanes appeared. All at once we saw the German machine burst into flames, tipple over a few times and then dive straight down to the earth. Whether it was the guns or one of the aeroplanes which hit him I do not know, but whichever it was, both the men in it were killed and the machine wrecked. It fell from a terrible height. It is the first I have seen fetched down and I must have been terrible for the two men…

Give my kindest regards to all enquiring relatives and friends. I am your affectionate son,

Bernard.

Rifleman Britland's letters are quite different in tone to Charles Tame who served with the transport section of the 1st Battalion, Honourable Artillery Company, also in Ypres. Tame did not hesitate to tell his sister about some of the bloody and brutal fighting he witnessed on the front line, including the execution of prisoners.

Transport Section
1t Battn HAC
British Expeditionary Force

My darling Hilly,
How can I thank you for your kindness to me on so many occasions, my wants you have so quickly supplied in such extremes as these. The medicine which has just arrived is appreciated more than words can say, and in fact you have done for me as much as mother could do. I shall always be very grateful to you and when I return I shall worship the ground upon which you walk…

Now this is my private letter home, I therefore intend to tell you everything concerning this Great War and myself. We have just been through a very rough fight at Ypres, capturing three German trenches under very heavy shell fire, we were in the charge with the Royal Scots, First Rifles and Worcesters. I am sorry to tell you two officers have been killed (Stone and Dathow), two officers wounded, including the colonel, the doctor, Capt Lancaster, Capt Osmond and Capt Boyle, 250 men killed, wounded and missing. I do not know who they are yet, but no doubt you will see the list in the daily papers before I shall. Please send it out here.

Thanks to you for your good prayers. I am unhurt, the chap next to me had the back of his head blown off, and the fellow next but one on my left was shot through the right lung. Seven of our transport horses were killed, three were blown to atoms. 'Owen' is quite well but did not like it I am sure, as he pushed me over on my back twice in his excitement.* We were under shell fire for eight hours, it was more like a dream to me, we must have been absolutely mad at the time. Some of the chaps looked quite insane after the charge was over, as we entered the German trench hundreds of Germans were found cut up by our artillery fire. A great number came over and offered themselves as prisoners, some went on their knees and asked for mercy, needless to say they were shot right off which was the best mercy we could give to them.

The Royal Scots took about 300 prisoners, their officers told them to share their rations with the prisoners and to consider the officers not with them, the Scots immediately shot the whole lot, and shouted 'Death and Hell to everyone of ye s—' and in five minutes the ground was ankle deep with German blood and this is the life we had for two days. All that I saw were men and horses all mixed up in death, it was as I have said just like a dream, I could not believe my own eyesight, and could not realize what I saw to be reality, only a dream, or, I might say a nightmare. War makes every man turn to his God, and asks Him for help. He is the only protection he has, it also helps him to understand death more clearly, his life out here is not worth a blade of grass, unless God says otherwise. It does seem indeed very strange to me to be in such a position as to see dead men and horses, and to smell them all day and night, everywhere, and at all times, it is really an awful life and unnatural one…

They are badly in want of officers out here, I do not want promotion, I want the war to finish and to go home. The weather

* Owen was Charles' horse.

now is getting very hot indeed, most of our chaps sit about in the fields naked, the poor horses feel it very much also. We are having a trouble with the water supply which is very short. I believe someone is trying to have it pumped inland from the coast, the man who succeeds should receive the VC. The water we are now drinking is absolutely thick and muddy, but yet it seems to do us no harm so it must be good. I drink as little as possible. I have found a new invention which suits me very well and quenches my thirst better than anything else, it is to chew a small quantity of long grass and then put the old pipe on.

Ypres is absolutely in ruins, churches, mansions, convents, monasteries and streets of homes are no more, all are in piles of bricks and the once beautiful town, the capital of the region, has been destroyed by German artillery fire. It is this place we are now helping to hold where the Kaiser is trying to break through the British lines so as to march on and capture Calais, of course this he will never do. The British are losing 2,000 a day on an average in deaths, wounded and missing, the Germans are losing three or four times that number…

Well now my darling old girl, I think I must draw to a close, after writing a good long letter which I know will interest you very much. I wish you and the children the best of health, and good luck, keep smiling as I am doing, and I hope we shall meet again shortly…

Your affectionate old brother,
Charley

Ypres witnessed some of the bitterest fighting of the entire war. Situated directly in the path of Germany's planned sweep into France, the Allies managed to recapture the city after the First Battle of Ypres (19 October–22 November 1914). Between 22 April and

25 May 1915 a second battle was fought which saw poison gas used for the first time on the Western Front, and as a result mustard gas was originally called 'Yperite'. A third and final battle, also known as the battle of Passchendaele, was fought between 31 July and 10 November 1917.

In total millions of British soldiers would fight over just a few miles of Belgian ground and Charles Tame was not alone in feeling bitter towards the enemy as well as those who had yet to volunteer for active service. Captain Edward Simeons served with the 8th (Service) Battalion, Bedfordshire Regiment (16th Brigade, 6th Division) in the front line north-west of Wieltje on the Ypres Salient. Captain Simeons died of wounds sustained on 17 February 1916 and is buried at Lijssenthoek Military Cemetery, Belgium.

Belgium
Monday November 1, 1915

Dear Mr Clemmans,
Just a line to thank you for your kind thoughts, I was delighted to hear from you again.

We have been having a really thick time lately, as you will see by that I am going to tell you.

We took over these trenches last Thursday after having a few days rest. The rain has been coming down on and off since the day before. Everything is simply soaked through including ourselves and [we] simply long for tomorrow evening when we are relieved. Can you imagine being soaked through for 6 days…

The trenches we are in are falling in part, although we work hard day and night riveting and in parts the water is well over the ankles, although the pumps are kept hard at it.

We have been shelled very heavily by our friends the Huns and am sorry to say lost numbers. It is a sight one can hardly bear to see when a shell burnt amongst the men, killing some, wounding others and others losing their minds.

Yesterday I had a near shave, three shrapnel shells burning within 10 feet of me, but by falling flat on my face immediately got through without a scratch…

You can never imagine how simply awful and what the poor Tommy has to put up with until you have tried it – but with all of it we are a very cheery lot. All we want is to hear that the cads who have been trying to shirk it [are] made to come out and put their nose well into the thick of it which is simply unimaginable…

My very kindest regards to your wife, self and all inquirers.

Your affectionate,
Eddie

Service in the trenches inspired even the inexperienced poet to try to describe life on the front line. The following poem was sent home in August 1915 by Captain Charles K. McKerrow, a regimental medical officer of the 10th Battalion, Northumberland Fusiliers.

By hedge and dyke the leaves
Flame to the clay
Fanned by the wing
Of Death. Yet Life achieves
From such decay
The buds of spring.
By air and sea and earth
To glorious death
Our loves we gave
Certain that Death is Birth
Love blossometh
Beyond the grave.

— Flanders, October 1915

But most of McKerrow's correspondence took the form of traditional letters, sent largely from the Armentières section of the Western Front between August 1915 and February 1916 and also from his service during the battle of the Somme. He was a prolific correspondent and the following are extracts from the dozens of letters which detail his service as a medical officer on the front line.

January 28th, 1916

We have had such a pleasant first night in the trenches. The 15th Royal Scots are attached to us for a few days and we all came happily into our front line thinking what a nice fellow the Hun was to keep Wilhelm's birthday in so quiet and religious a manner. There had been very little shelling and rifle fire all day. We had dinner in our mess dug out and went to bed. At 10.30 I woke to the most appalling uproar I have ever heard. The Hun had turned all his guns – big and little – into our support and reserve trenches and, incidentally, our headquarters. The noise was simply indescribable. Shrieks and whistles of the arriving shells, and burst and crashes of the arrived ones, all blended together in one wild nightmare. I thought that most certainly we were going to have a proper smash up of everything – including ourselves. The shells poured on without a stop for half an hour. Our guns joined in the din, and then there was quiet. When we counted the bag, came the bathos. There had been two dug outs knocked in, the Adjutant's dug out badly mauled, and yet there was not a man even scratched. They had all, including myself, taken to [the] earth in time to escape annihilation. Of course, a bombproof [shelter] will give way before a big shell, but it has to hit it direct, and, fortunately, this did not happen. We then went off to bed again and thought the Kaiser's birthday had been sufficiently celebrated.

Would you believe it? They started off at 4 again in the morning, fortunately this time, not paying quite such direct attention to us. When we did get to sleep it was 5, and, as I had to get up at 6, I cannot say that I shall remember the Kaiser or his birthday with any enthusiasm or pleasure. When I walked across the field this morning towards the Medical Aid Post I found nice big holes, big enough to hide a decent-sized man, every few yards. I was pleased to see that the majority had been aimed too high to hit us, and not high enough for the reserve trenches. If they had all come down on us, it would have been very unpleasant indeed.

January 29th, 1916

The neighbourhood has been particularly unhealthy lately. As I told you we had two séances the night before last, one at 11pm and the next at 4am. We thought that this must about finish Fritz's birthday present, but not a bit of it. He re-commenced at 9.30 yesterday morning and shelled us till 12. He then had an hour's interval till 1, and started off once more. This shelling was not very heavy but at 3 the floods were let loose again.

I have never imagined such a noise and commotion could be attained by artificial means. The shrieks and bursts of the shells were absolutely continuous for an hour. I was in my Aid Post and it rocked and swayed like a ship in a storm. Fortunately it was not hit, but some shells were by no means far distant. Altogether, we had about 20 casualties, which was not much considering the heaviness of the bombardment. I don't know whether we are going to have any more or not, but I should think that it is probable that a few souvenirs will arrive. Last night we were all ready for the Hun to attack, but everything was quiet – hardly a rifle shot. It is rather as if he were bombarding us out of sheer frightfulness. We go out of this the day after tomorrow, and shall have a week to regain our presumably upset nervous tone. I have not noticed much upset myself, but, if it were continued for a week or so, one would certainly begin to feel some ennui. There has been nothing like this on any part of the line for some time.

January 30th, 1916

It is Sunday, and very damp and misty with a slight morning frost. We are being allowed a rest for the present but the Bosch may arouse himself and speak at any moment.

He has given tongue pretty regularly since we came in. We had 18 casualties on Friday, 5 on Saturday, and 3 already today and it is only 3 o'clock. We had one officer badly wounded. He will probably lose his right arm. This morning we had one Company Sergeant Major killed and one wounded, but only slightly. In fact, none of us will be sorry to get safely out of this tomorrow night. Of course, our casualties are not heavy considering the number of shells, bombs and aerial torpedoes which have showered on us for three days. Certainly, shells are not efficient as man-slayers, but they are most unpleasant. It is a queer thing that, as soon as one gets some work to do amongst the wounded, one ceases even to notice the shelling. It is a blessing because otherwise the doctor's life in the trenches would be undoubtedly trying. I am glad that I have a fairly healthy nervous system.

I daresay, though, that by June I shall be quite willing to take on some less exciting job. We are getting along with the winter, and it will soon be spring. What a relief to have dry ground again.

January 31st, 1916

I expect that everyone will be glad to have a rest. Some of our men have only had an hour or two's sleep in three days. They have been most awfully good, and their endurance and pluck are beyond all praise. The 15th Royal Scots, who were in with us, were also very good, and stuck it out well. It must have been an eye-opener to them. I do not think that any of us imagined that the Hun had such a lot of fun in him still. I do not believe that even a big 'Straf' could produce heavier shelling, though it might, of course, last longer. We feel quite 'blooded' now. We are all more confident. I hear that we go back in about three weeks now. They say that it means very hard work for the men, so I expect I shall be kept hard at work preventing them from skrimshanking…

I am looking forward to a bath tomorrow, and I shall need it. The mud of four days will take some removing. I wish you could see me.

February 1st, 1916

I have been strafed [reprimanded] by the ADMS [Assistant Director Medical Services] today over a silly little red-tape thing – a return I sent to the wrong place. The regular RAMC are great believers in this power of ink. Well, I left him in bitter pain, and went down to see some of the chaps who had been wounded … on the Kaiser's birthday and whom we had got out of the trenches under heavy shelling and safely into the ambulance. They were all doing famously, though their wounds had been most severe, and, when they smiled and shook my hand, I realised that it is in action and not in ink and paper that life and happiness lies. I never realised before what a magnificent lot of work there is for the young chaps out here, and how the old birds like the ADMS must sit in offices and bite their thumbs.

I forgave him at once for all his strafing. No wonder he has a strange perspective. I have quite decided that, if I am still going strong in June and our Colonel is away (perhaps, even if he is with us) I shall try and find some job a little bit back, away for a while. I shall have been 10 months in the trenches, and if the war is going on for some time longer, as seems possible, then I should like to keep a spurt for the finish. I know that my decision will please you. If you were not there nor George, I should stay where I am, not that I am doing any extra good work, but because there is no doubt that work with a regiment rather appeals to me. I suppose for the same reason that scorching a motor bike does. I expect that though a VC, MC or DSO would please you, yet you would prefer me than it.

However, Captain McKerrow stayed in the front line and saw service throughout the battle of the Somme (1 July to 18 November 1916).

July 10th, 1916

I am so penitent for I have only sent you a field post card during many days. We have been right in the midst of things and I am safe. I would add 'so far' but, as we are at present safely in the country, that would seem merely a Scotch superstition. As a matter of fact if I could come through my experiences of the last week unscathed, I think you may consider me pretty tough. The Division has done well and scuppered many Huns, but has been rather knocked about. We were about the most fortunate, losing only 2 officers and 180 men or thereabouts. This was due to our being by chance less opposed. The 11th had less luck. Their MO was wounded and several officers wounded and killed. Poor Tullock was killed. You may tell Mrs Carrick that his death was quite sudden and painless as the bullet went right through his heart. This may be some consolation to his people.

I had one stretcher-bearer killed and five wounded. I am glad to say that Kirtly and Coulson were untouched. They were both lucky as they worked unsparingly. We had about 1,000 men through our Dressing Post in 3 days. They came from all sorts of regiments: Welshmen, Englishmen and a few Scots. The fighting, so far, has been very Northumbrian. I believe we are doing fairly well. I had a Red Cross sergeant major (a prisoner) working with me for a day. He had been caught in the Aid Post. He came from

Karlsruhe. Was that not a strange coincidence? He wept with joy when I spoke to him in German. There were about 15 wounded Huns in the Aid Post also. They were very thin and smelly. I got them away as soon as possible.

Coulson is a great stand by. As you may imagine, I had no sleep for 3 days or nights while the rush was on. Well, he made coffee and soup for me and chased me round till I took them. He made me change my socks, and rubbed my legs for me. He is really quite priceless. His language is sometimes hard to decipher, but what of that.

July 11th, 1916

I made my Aid Post a great success for the four days I held it, and I can say that we have saved many lives. I daresay others could have done as well if not better than I did, but no one could possibly have equalled my stretcher-bearers. As one hard-bitten chap said to me: 'They are doing what Christ would do.' It really is very fine to see these chaps passing through storms of shell to help their comrades. I am very proud of them and hope they will get some rewards, apart from the inward ones of their conscience. After all, there are no holocausts here as there were at Loos. The percentage of these wounded, only about one-third are serious at all. You are far more likely to have me home with a broken arm or a nice flesh wound than to have me not come back at all, while the vast probability is that I shall not even be scratched.

Poor Rix was killed by a chance shell the other day, some way behind the front line. I am very sorry as he was a good chap. He was killed out-right. Such accidents will occur, but, perhaps one such sacrifice will satisfy Moloch for a time.* Otherwise our RMOs are safe, though two are slightly wounded.

---

* Moloch, the name of an ancient Semetic god, is often used to describe an entity, either a person or thing, demanding a very costly sacrifice.

July 19th, 1916

We have now been under shell-fire (not, fortunately, continuous) for a fortnight and are becoming hardened. As a battalion we have had amazing luck. Two or three officers wounded, and, so far, none killed. We have not yet, however, had to make an unsuccessful attack, which is where the losses occur. The other Battalions in our Brigade have lost much more heavily. Twice we were to have stormed strong points, and both times the battalion ahead of us was cut up, and we had to dig in and wait. No doubt, our turn will come.

This will not affect me except that I shall lose some friends, and be very busy. Where I am, and where we are likely to be, the cover is not at all bad, and I do not neglect it. I have a strong feeling of Kismet, but nevertheless, do not go out trying to be hit. The weather is perfect, and all our aeroplanes are up, nosing round to see what they can discover. Between you and me, the Hun is having a rotten time. We fairly smother him with shells. In spite of that, he puts up a plucky fight though his methods are abominable. Of them I shall talk later. Never ask me to know or to write to or think of anyone who is a German, in the future. They are – one and all – the most vile, loathsome, crawling reptiles that kultur could produce. As a matter of fact, they are all brains and little soul. They talk much of the latter and of their various virtues. They have only one virtue and that is courage. After all, the stoat and the rat are about the bravest of animals.

I have an idea that we are going into rest very soon now. The oracles suggest it. How long a rest, no one knows. The last rest was 3 days, and we were shelled constantly. The Hun resistance is undoubtedly nothing to what it was, and in this one sees a happy omen. Many consider the War nearly won. Certainly, this offensive of ours, though slow, is very complete, and must be worrying the Hun quite a lot. Haig seems to have found the way to deal with him.

Poor wee Jake. I am very sorry for John. I shall write to him. Death is a very dreadful thing to those who are not flung into slaughter. It will take months for me to gain a truer perspective. When the dead lie all around you, and the man next to you, or oneself, may puff out, death becomes a very unimportant incident. It is not callousness, but just too much knowledge. Like other things, man has ignored death and treated it as something to talk of with pale cheek and bated breath. When one gets death on every side the re-action is sudden. Two chaps go out for water and one returns. Says a pal to him: 'Well, where's Bill?' 'A bl——whizz-bang took his bl—— head off' may not appear sympathetic, but it is the only way of looking at the thing and remaining sane. You may be certain, however, that the same man would carry Bill ten miles if there was any chance of fixing his head on again. They are great men, but rough outwardly. I expect that they have their reward.

July 20th, 1916

It is the third week of our offensive and I am still going strong… There are those who say that our next move will be into some quiet trenches up north, and that they will send new men to carry on here. I can scarcely believe it, but there may be some germ of truth in it. Anyway, I do not think that the offensive can go on for many more weeks, as at present. I know very little about what is happening except for a square mile of country. In the front is [a] slight rise, surmounted by a much ruined village in a much tattered wood. There have been four attacks made up this slope, all cut short by machine gun fire. The dead lie like sheaves in the harvest field. Day and night our shells rain down on the ruins, and the sign of their passage is like the beating of a heavy sea upon a sandy beach. At times, the roar is terrible and continuous, and then it fades away, but only for a few minutes. The shells are not all what we call 'outers', for the Hun has rushed up many batteries, and they are not idle. Every few minutes there is a threatening shriek and the rapidly following crash of an explosion. Pieces of iron and steel beat on the hillside, and everyone who can find a little head cover crouches for a moment till the storm is past. Those who are in the open whisper, 'Kismet,' and pass on their way outwardly indifferent.

Every now and then, down the hillside, comes a stretcher with its uncomplaining burden. However vicious the shelling, the wounded will never be neglected. A stretcher-bearer may fall, but another fills the gap. The practice, as opposed to the theory of Christianity, is here for men to wonder at. As the twilight darkens, our shells fly overhead ever more importunately. The bursts of exploding shrapnel merge into a streak of brilliant yellow flame above the enemies' trenches. The crimson flare of the heavy shells as they scatter trees and houses and men in horrible confusion, lights up the hillside with baleful gleams.

More and more intense becomes the bombardment, then, suddenly, as though a curtain fell, silence reigns. Only for a moment. From the trenches before us two red rockets soar into the night and all is once more a riot of noise. This time the shrapnel curtain drapes our trenches, and, high and sharp above the din, stammer the staccato voices of the Hun's machine guns. Rapid rifle fire breaks out along the line. For a few minutes the stray bullets fly like bees down the hill, and then all is again silence. From the trenches, bright magnesium lights soar into the air. Soon, down the road come wounded men limping in twos and threes; then come stretchers and more stretchers. Lucky indeed are those who fell near our line, or could crawl back in the dark. Many must lie out between the lines till death releases them.

We have attacked and been beaten back. Such is the daily happening in the great offensive. Often, however, we are not beaten back. Then the machine gun and rifle fire dies spasmodically. No magnesium lights go up to show that the Bosch line is still held. In the silence and the dark our men work remorselessly. We have advanced. Some German prisoners may come down the hillside under a guard with fixed bayonets, but more probably the bayonets will have done their work up there already.

In October 1916 Captain Charles McKerrow was transferred with his battalion to the Ypres Salient. Two months later he was wounded in action and died – just over a month before he was due for leave. This was his last letter.

December 19th, 1916

It freezes, but not with conviction. The shell holes are covered with the thinnest coating of ice and the ground is quite dry in places. Last night I went fishing. The results were not vast. We cast our 'nets' on the other side of the ship, but got no more than we deserved. It is an exciting sport under such circumstances. The question is whether we shall catch the fish or be straffed by Fritz. So far we have won. It was mighty cold on our private lake but hard rowing with shovels restored the circulation. I am going to try putting some tasty morsels in a spot known to myself, and then try a cast there. My leave will be any time between 25th and 27th Jan. At present the arrangement is ten days at home. The boat reaches Folkestone in the forenoon, and I should be in town for lunch. It is fun talking about it, but I shall go raving mad if it does not come off. It would be most distressing. You say this is our longest separation so far… It has only just struck me that I am coming home. I shall tick off each day carefully in my diary when it arrives. I dearly wish to see George.

His wife received the sad news of his death by official telegram.

London, Dec. 21st
Regret to inform you that Capt. C. K. M'Kerrow, R.A.M.C., attached 10th Northumberland Fusiliers, was dangerously

wounded by shell in abdomen. Particulars will be sent when received. It is regretted permission to visit cannot be granted.
Secretary, War Office

London, Dec. 22nd
Deeply regret to inform you Capt. C. K. M'Kerrow died of wounds, December 20th. The Army Council express their sympathy.
Secretary, War Office

Some of those who were wounded in action on the front line had the opportunity to write a farewell letter to their loved ones, knowing it was their last letter, and therefore a chance to say goodbye properly.

One such was Sergeant Francis Herbert Gautier who had served with the 11th Battalion, Cheshire Regiment, and who wrote the following letter to his young daughter Marie while he lay dying in the Voluntary Aid Detachment (VAD) Hospital in Earls Colne, Essex.

For my daughter Marie when she is able to understand.
F.H.G.
V.A.D. Hospital
Earls Colne
Essex
2 April 1916
To my darling daughter Marie,

Dearly loved daughter,
This, my letter to you, is written in grief. I had hoped to spend many happy years with you after the War was over and to see you grow up into a good and happy woman. I am writing because I want you in after years to know how dearly I loved you, I know that you are too young now to keep me in your memory. I know

your dear Mother will grieve. Be a comfort to her, remember when you are old enough that she lost her dear son, your brother, and me, your father, within a short time. Your brother was a dear boy, honour his memory for he loved you [and] your brothers dearly and he died like a brave soldier in defence of his home and Country.

May God guide and keep you safe and that at last we may all meet together in his eternal rest.

I am your loving and affectionate father.

F.H. Gautier

xxxxxxxxxxxxxxxxxxxxxxxxxxxxxxxxxxxxxxxxxxxxxxxxxxxxxxxxxxxx
xxxxxxxxxxxxxxxxxxxxxxxxxxxx

Gautier died just over two months later on 11 June 1916. His son, Albert, who is referenced in the letter, was also killed at Ypres, while Wilfred, another of Marie's brothers, volunteered for the army while underage and died later in the war.

Like the Gautiers, many families had more than one member on active service. The following is a letter from Acting Sergeant David Fenton to his brother Second Lieutenant William Fenton.

Both brothers served in the 1/4th Battalion, Duke of Wellington's (West Riding) Regiment, which was the local Territorial Force Battalion near their home in Cleckheaton, Yorkshire. William was commissioned in September 1914 but was injured and invalided home at the time of this letter. David was selected for service as a bomber probably due to his reputation as a good bowler in the local cricket team and was sadly killed behind the lines when a bomb with a faulty fuse exploded. William returned to front-line service for the duration of the war, winning the Military Cross and bar and was later promoted to Major.

The Grenade Company
1/4 West Riding Regiment
147th Infantry Brigade
B.E.F.

July 18th, 1915

Dear Willie,

Many thanks for the splendid parcels and the letter.

Your knee seems to be improving splendidly, and so long as it doesn't improve so nicely as to bring you out here again before the war is over, I hope the improvement will be maintained.

Bill, you did your whack and were absolutely worshipped by your men. You know what warfare is. Yet it hasn't been your lot to know the worst of war, dead comrades and dead men of the Regiment, if not friends more than mere acquaintances. I saw one newly promoted junior Captain, Captain Lee, a brawny virile man in life, carried out on a man's shoulder, an inert lifeless mass dripping from head to toe with blood. Poor fellow! He got shot through the head – faulty sandbag.

I don't ask you to skulk I know it would be useless. God forbid that I should be mean enough! Yet if you do come out again, don't come out as an ailing man as perhaps you would be tempted to do so…

We are mudlarking into the first line tonight where we shall remain at least 5 days. You have the situation exactly. Looking South East half as far again is the place you mention. The trenches are somewhat different to those to which you have been accustomed.

The first line is similar only not quite as good as at — and is of course always manned. 25 yards behind another line much lower than the first, unmanned. Then 25 yards further behind unmanned. 25 yards behind that [is] what I call the second line, manned. This we hold for 5 days and then we retire 300 yards to the canal into strong dugouts. The canal is continually shelled and the dugouts need to be strong. Since coming up here we have seen two bombardments, one on our left owing to a German attack and capture of one of our Brigade trenches which was successfully countered. Here I may mention that we Brigade bombers were called up for action but, on arriving at our post, the job had already been accomplished and we were dismissed without a chance, as the Brigadier puts it, of honour; as the men put it, of going under.

The second was whilst in our present position when we were the aggressors. It was a terrible bombardment and we were in the thick of it. They used poison shells at times. These flash much more than ordinaries on exploding and after a few seconds our eyes began to water and finally to gush. Then a rotten headache comes. Of course we wasted no time in putting on smoke helmets which are thoroughly efficient. Though this is reckoned the most dangerous line we have not yet lost a single man.

Old 'Colours' Parkin got his arm taken off by a shell last week when in the second line. 30 seconds before he was with me looking at some bombs. A shell whizzed over our heads and dropped about 30 yards behind. Colours said 'I'll bet that's in our lines' and he ran back to the Company. I, of course, went on preparing my bombs. A few seconds after another shell came. It can't have missed my nut by much because I did an uncommonly sharp duck and it dropped 20 yards behind. Then I went back and saw old Parkin getting bandaged. His left arm was, except for the jugular, severed at the bicep. He never flinched and <u>walked</u> out of the trenches. As he passed I said: 'Stick at it, old chap.' He smiled faintly and said, 'I'll try David'. He is a hero and I have written to his wife telling her so.

There is nothing more to tell you and as I am on fatigue now I shall have to chuck it up.

Thanking you for the fine parcels.

Your affectionate brother,
David

Lieutenant Rowland H. Owen served as a platoon commander in the 2nd Battalion, Duke of Wellington's (West Riding) Regiment from August 1914 until he was killed in April 1915. He exchanged a number of letters with his brother John who served in the Royal Navy for the duration of the war.

22/9/1914

Dear John,

Yes, I am sorry for you not getting an actual hand-to-hand brush with the Allemander, but you are helping to do the most important work of all. The strain must be awful for you – I am keeping you company through most of the nights.

Do you have any news? We have none, except very roughly a month afterwards. The naval attack must have been very wonderful, but I know nothing whatever about it.* M[other] and F[ather] seemed to know more than I did of whatever I had even done myself! I was quite mystified by references in their letters to our show: 'These two great battles' etc.

I should give over wishing you were here – you have nothing to grouse about. One goes thro' [sic] a fortnight of alternately sitting down under hellfire and hobbling away, without

---

* The naval battle referred to here is likely to be the battle of Heligoland Bight (28 August 1914), the first naval battle of the war.

necessarily seeing a single enemy, and then one's parents write and say 'it was glorious!' and refer to all sorts of names of battles. No part whatever of one's conception of fighting gained during peace training has been realized; an encounter with some infantry would be a real treat, whenever an encounter is necessary...

24th

We are about 60 yards away from some of the enemy and 300 from the remainder. We have been here sometime now – we get about 4 hours artillery fire a day, and some of our own shells drop very short. That is the battle we are fighting. When their guns open we get in the bottom of the houses or in two shelter trenches we have made. Yesterday a shell came into the house where I was, and into another house of the outpost position and three into headqrs [sic]. Also there were about five shot holes in the ground within 50 yds of us. I slept in one of them – it was a terrific luxury. So we were well bombarded yesterday, nobody was hurt, not even the sentries in the lofts which were hit by the lyddite.

The chief offender is Long Maria – there are four of her; about ten miles away I suppose. She was brought to settle Paris with. They say some Marines have arrived with 13.5[mm] guns to deal with her. I don't think they are in position yet.

In addition there are snipers on the edge of the wood and up trees. They make very merry when they see an officer: but, if I may say so without seeming rude, they are not good shots. One can continue what one is doing as a rule without paying much heed. It is rather funny taking field glasses and a rifle when I have been on the go. A lot of them came down yesterday to within 40 yards of us in the open gathering beans! The sentry was so excited that instead of doing them in, or kicking the arses, he sent a message that the enemy was advancing!

I am daily awaiting the news that the defeat of a certain German Army is assured and that the war will then end. However the news takes the Hell of a time to come. I hope you get a show, but at the same time that you won't go under. I am very anxious that both of us should get home again. I am afraid that hope has ranked all the way thro' [sic] in my mind second only to the success of the venture and prosperity of the Empire. It seems rather selfish, but damn it.

Well, good luck,

Your loving brother,
Rowland.

For many soldiers, service with the British Army meant their first trip outside the United Kingdom. For the vast majority this meant France and Flanders but British service personnel also served in Gallipoli, Egypt, Salonika, Mesopotamia and Palestine. Jack Beer, of the London Regiment, served in Palestine, and his hospitalisation following injury in battle brought a welcome reminder of home.

British Red Cross and Order of St. John
4th November 1917

My dear Father and Mother,
You will be surprised to know I am in hospital, wounded in the left upper arm during the scrap in front of Beersheba [in Palestine]. I am glad to say I am going on quite well. The same shell that caught me, killed the corporal of my Lewis Gun team and another gunner, also wounded another gunman and myself, and two other men of our platoon, so there were 6 of us altogether.

The shell burst right over us, and a piece of shrapnel went in my shoulder, through the equipment strap and came out of my upper arm, leaving an open wound, also a piece just scratched my upper right arm, but very slight. My pith helmet stopped 2 small pieces of shrapnel from going into my head and my second finger of my right hand, which I grazed two days previous, has gone septic.

Our company were waiting in a gully to go over, and old jacko found out we were there and shelled us like blazers. I was in the first batch to catch it, so I do not know how Chimney [his colleague] got on. We had done a long march over night, and as soon as we arrived, we had shoals of Rifle and Machine Gun bullets whizzing around. I have been four days getting here, being in different CC stations, and having walked, ridden on camels, motor ambulance and train. I was inoculated at one of the dressing stations, and it is wonderful how God has looked after me, as some of the poor chaps were awful sights. Now, it is the first time I have been in a bed between sheets for 16 months so you can guess how fine it feels, and not having heard an English woman speak for so long a time, it sounds very funny with their little voices. To get some decent food again is quite a treat, and I do look comical in my big baggy blue trousers and carpet slippers.

We have all kinds of chaps in out our ward, Welsh, Scotch and English.

I think it would be better if you send letters to the same address. I hope things are going on alright at Watford and you are not being worried by air raids.

Well I must close now with fondest love and kisses to all at home.

I remain,
Your affectionate son
xx Jack xx
xxxxxxxxxx

For many soldiers, the earlier patriotism and enthusiasm for the 'great endeavour' had given way to exhaustion, cynicism and a desperate desire for the war to simply end. D.L. 'Laurie' Rowlands expressed this in a letter to his future wife while serving as an NCO in France with the 15th Battalion, Durham Light Infantry.

5/2/18
France
Evening

Sweetheart Mine,

Now barring accidents, you will get to know all about it. I know you'll have a big surprise when you get <u>this</u> letter – I hope it lands without mishap. If anybody in authority was to see it – !

Well girlie, perhaps I'd better let you know where I am first of all. At the time these words are being <u>written</u> I am in a cellar. All that remains of what had evidently been a fair sized house, and which is now serving as a kitchen for the Mess in the ruined village of Learmonts (near Peronne). When you <u>read</u> this however I shall in all probability be in the front line on the left of Epehy. We do a week in and then come a short distance back for a fortnight. I believe the BEF is under the process of re-organisation. Instead of four, there are now to be <u>three</u> Battalions to a Brigade. To ours has been amalgamated – what do you think? The Tenth, Billy Allen's old lot – of all Bats…

The front is very quiet just now. It is the part Fritz broke through a few weeks ago you remember. We should have been in <u>Italy</u> now if it hadn't been for that. You remember when I came back from that Course, this Battalion was at Bray then being fitted out for the climate of the land of ice cream. Then we were suddenly ordered to pack up one afternoon and were marched off in the evening, had a train ride, got to Tincurt in the morning and marched up to the line a few hours later. Oh, it was <u>great</u>! We were all dead beat when we relieved the Bengal Lancers on the railway. We had a lovely four days digging trenches etc. etc. We are still on the same front. In the part of the line allotted to us, Fritz is several hundred yards away and, bar a few machine gun bullets now and then, a tour in the line is very quiet indeed.

Of course you have guessed by now where I had my first experience of the line. Yes it was on the Ypres Salient. Our Division (the 21st) was on Divisional rest when our draft landed up to then. We didn't go in till October the 2nd. Our Bat. [Battalion] was to have gone over the top and taken the final objective. Oh, it was a lovely 'baptism of fire' that night. We had to dig ourselves in, and early in the morning Fritz started straffing. Oh Lord, if ever a fellow was afraid, absolutely frightened to death, it was this child. Then one of my Section took shell shock when a big 'un dropped a couple of yards off the parapet and then the instinct of the leader, or one whose place it is to lead, came to the top and I became as cool and steady as a rock. I had twelve men when we went, I came out with three... Oh it was ghastly.

We did three tours of 'Wipers',* and the Division left the front when I was on the Course. But that October the fourth 'Do' [battle of Broodseinde] I shall never forget. Our Bat. lost so heavily during the third from shell fire whilst lying in reserve preparatory to going over the following morning that we could not attempt our job and consequently we remained in support till the attack was over.

Perhaps you would like to know something of the spirit of the men out here now. Well, the truth is (and as I said before I'd be shot if anyone of importance collared this missive) every man Jack is fed up almost past bearing, and not a single one has an ounce of what we call patriotism left in him. No one cares a rap whether Germany has Alsace, Belgium or France too for that matter. All that every man desires now is to get done with it and go home. Now that's the honest truth, and any man who has been out within the last few months will tell you the same. In fact, and this is no exaggeration, the greatest hope of a great

---

* Tommy slang for Ypres.

majority of the men is that rioting and revolt <u>at</u> <u>home</u> will force the government to pack in on <u>any</u> terms. Now you've got the <u>real</u> state of affairs 'right from the horse's mouth' as it were.

I may add that I too have lost pretty nearly all the patriotism I had left, it's just the thought of you all over there, you who love and trust me to do <u>my</u> share in the job that is necessary for your safety and freedom. It's just <u>that</u> that keeps me going and enables me to 'stick it'. As for religion, God forgive us all, it hasn't a place in one out of a million of the thoughts that hourly occupy men's minds. The Padres, and it's anything but pleasant to say so, they absolutely fail to keep up a shred of their Church's reputation. Nay, behind the line every man, and it's almost without exception, relies solely on <u>drink</u> for his relaxation, amusement, pleasure – everything.

Aye girlie, it's ghastly, but thank God for those dear ones at home who love true and trust absolutely in the strength, the courage and the fidelity of those who are far away midst danger and death. These are my mainstays, and thoughts of them always come to stay me and buck me up when I feel like chucking it all up and letting things slide. God bless <u>you</u> darling, and <u>all</u> those I love and who love me, for without their love and trust I would faint and fall. But don't worry dear heart o' mine, for I shall carry on to the end be it bitter or sweet, with my loved ones ever my first thought and care, my guide, inspiration and spur.

Au revoir my own sweetheart and God will keep you safe till the storm's over, with all my heart's deepest love.

Your own loving

Laurie

In spring 1918, the German forces on the Western Front launched a series of offensives widely known as the Spring Offensives, utilising troops suddenly available as a result of the peace on the Eastern Front. Fully aware that their only chance of victory was a major onslaught before the arrival of US troops in large numbers, the sheer force of the offensive resulted in many hasty Allied retreats. These proved to be a strategic failure when the Germans failed to follow up the gains they initially made. However, as recalled in a letter to his wife, Major Thomas Horatio Westmacott of the 1st Cavalry Division witnessed the chaos of the 5th Army's retreat on 21 March 1918.

The Queens made a heroic stand at Le Verguier only falling back in perfect order when their flanks were left in the air owing to other units giving way. German officers told me long after that the losses inflicted on them by the Queens were enormous.

I told Rudge to move back to Vendelles if the shelling got very bad, and then I rode back to my third post at Vermand. When I reached the village I saw a lot of shells falling in it and a stream of wounded men coming up hill in some confusion. I left Golden Rod outside the village and went down to the bridge, where I learned that the enemy had got right on top of the 1st North Staffords in the fog and wiped them out. There was also an ugly story of two companies of the 3rd Rifle Brigade having put up their hands.

Anyhow, the enemy had broken through as far as Maissemy (one of my traffic control men was wounded here) and was pouring on Villecholles, a mile from the bridge. Col Green of the Middlesex with a few men was digging in south of the bridge. I stood in the middle of the bridge and held up the fugitives (mainly Gunners) with my revolver and lined the bank north of the bridge and made them dig in, but the moment I went back to the bridge they bolted…

At 4am, on the 23rd March, GSO1 sent for me and said that the position was most critical and that I must get all the wheels across St Christ bridge. The fact that I had spent over 6 months in this part of the country with the 4th Cavalry Division in 1917 was of great help to me in controlling traffic…

I now began to realise how utterly inadequate the 5th Army's preparations had been to provide for a possible retreat. Not one tree was felled across the road; not a single crossroad was blown up. St Christ bridge itself was not destroyed though there was ample time to do it, and it was eventually by this bridge that the enemy crossed the Somme. Our huts, ammunition dumps, canteens and railways were all left for the enemy to take over as they stood. What trenches had been dug were 6 inch scratches (as if dog-tired men could be expected to deepen them!). The whole thing was a great contrast to the thoroughness of the German preparations for their retreat in the spring of 1917…

Hedley Payne who had written to his parents to inform them proudly of his DCM award in 1916 was wounded in action and taken prisoner in the fighting against the Germans during the 1918 Spring Offensives. A compatriot in his unit sent the following letter to Payne's mother while he himself was recuperating in hospital. For many parents, wives and sweethearts, letters such as this were the only way they received any additional information about how their loved one had been killed or taken prisoner.

Brook Hospital
Shooters Hill
Woolwich
London
26 April 1918

Dear Mrs Payne,
I was more than pleased to have a letter from you and to learn

that Hedley is still alive although it was very unfortunate that he has fallen into the hands of our enemy but I trust that he will soon get over his wound which I hope will not disable him in any way.

You must excuse me for not writing to you before this as I wanted to find out for certain what had really happened to Hedley, I met a Mr Irving in hospital but he did not know so as soon as I was able to write I dropped a line to the Battalion and am now waiting for an answer.

What Really Happened on the 24th of March was, Hedley went out with a few men to get in touch with the Battalion on our Right, looking in that direction some 5 to 10 minutes later I saw Hedley on the ground waving his left arm so I ran over to see what had happened and was sorry to learn that he had been hit by a 'sniper', the bullet leaving his body just behind the right arm and so it was impossible to get him away. I bandaged up the wound, my stay with him was very short as we moved forward so I knew that Hedley was pretty safe and hoped that some Stretcher Bearers would pick him up but before long I was hit in three places – arm, hand and leg and was unfortunate enough to lose the arm but I managed to get back – how is a miracle to me.

Hedley was loved by all officers and men in the Battalion and I am sure that one and all Regret to hear that he is a prisoner and wish him a speedy and safe return to his home.

His last words to me were 'Please write and tell my Mother that I have done my Best' and I hope you will excuse me for not doing so before as I wanted to find out for certain what had Really Happened to him.

If there is anything more I can do for you I am only too pleased to try my best.

I remain
Yours Sincerely,
Roland Brown

Another brother-in-arms also wrote to Payne's mother to give further detail of what had happened in the action which saw him taken prisoner.

Torquay
S. Devon
29 April 1918

Dear Mrs Payne,

I was waiting to write as I hoped to get some definite news of your son. It is no use offering you false hopes, and I am very much afraid the he must have been among the missing on March 24th. I have already written to the battalion, but am doing so again, and if I can hear anything I will let you know at once. But I am afraid there is very little hope. I wrote to Pickering who was in the same company and was hit that day, and is now at the 2nd Western General Hospital, Manchester, but he could give me no news of him. I believe you would certainly have heard if he had been in hospital anywhere.

On March 23rd the Germans attacked our line very heavily, but never got past our unit. Your son's platoon was there in the front line, and he was slightly wounded in the chest. He refused to go away, saying that he could quite well carry on. That night I saw him, and insisted on his going to the doctor and having the wound dressed, which he did. The last time I saw him was the next afternoon, about 5pm when the Germans had got through our right and we were forced to retire about 200 yards. He was then with his platoon and I gave him an order to take some men out to one flank. I was hit myself at that moment, and when I had to leave [he] was busy in a flank, and I never saw him again.

I can only say that he behaved very gallantly, as I knew he would, and showed exceptional courage and devotion in not leaving the line the day before. I commanded 'A' Company while we were in Italy, and so knew your son very well. He was an exceedingly good officer, and looked after his men very well, and a very faithful friend, and as I have already said he behaved in an exceptionally gallant manner on March 23rd and 24th.

May I offer my very deep sympathy in your anxiety and grief, and my earnest hopes that you may soon hear some definite news.

I will let you know as soon as I can hear anything.

Yours sincerely,
A. Chichester

Although Hedley Payne was subsequently released from his POW camp he died of his wounds in February 1919.

Many soldiers had to face up to the fears of their own mortality throughout the duration of the war. The following is a touching farewell letter written by Colour Sergeant Major James 'Jim' Milne (1/5th Seaforth Highlanders, 51st Division) immediately prior to the Second Battle of the Marne, July 1918.

BEF
Sat 20th July

My own Beloved Wife,
I do not know how to start this letter or note. The circumstances are different from any under which I ever wrote before. I am not to post it but will leave it in my pocket and if anything happens to me someone will perhaps post it. We are going over the top this forenoon and only God in Heaven know who will come out of it alive. I am going into it now Dearest sure that I am in His

hands and that whatever happens I look to Him, in this world and the world to come. If I am called my regret is that I leave you and my Bairns but I leave you all to His great mercy and goodness, knowing that He will look over you all and watch you. I trust in Him to bring me through but should He decree otherwise then though we do not know His reasons we know that it must be best. I go to Him with your dear face the last vision on earth I shall see and your name upon my lips, You, the best of women. You will look after my Darling Bairns for me and tell them how their Daddy died.

Oh! How I love you all and as I sit here waiting I wonder what you are doing at home. I must not do that. It is hard enough sitting and waiting. We may move at any minute. When this reaches you for me there will be no more war, only eternal peace and waiting for you. You must be brave my darling for my sake for I leave you the Bairns. It is a legacy of struggle for you but God will look after you and we shall meet again when there will be no-more parting. I am to write no-more Sweetheart, I know you will read my old letters and keep them for my sake and that you will love me or my memory till we meet again.

Kiss the Bairns for me once more. I dare not think of them, my Darlings.

Good Bye, you best of women and best of wives my beloved Sweetheart.

May God in his mercy look over you and bless you all till that day we shall meet again in His own good time.

May He in that same mercy preserve me today.

Good Bye Meg.
Eternal love from Yours for Ever & Ever
Jim

Jim Milne survived the Second Battle of the Marne and the rest of the war.

Lieutenant P.R. Hampton served with No. 62 Squadron RAF flying a Bristol F2B. By the latter stages of the war aerial superiority had become increasingly important but fraught with dangers for the pilots. During an offensive patrol over Armentières in spring 1918 he was brought down by German anti-aircraft fire and taken prisoner. He sent the following letter to his mother back home in Canada from his hospital bed and was realistic about the fact that he was probably safer as a prisoner than patrolling the skies above the Western Front.

19 May 1918

My dearest Mother,

I am still in hospital in fact I expect to be here for a week or so yet. I am getting better but a little slower than I first expected. I have now recovered from the shock but the burns are not healed yet. My nose, which was knocked almost flat between my eyes and a little to one side, is now back in its normal position. It is very painful but that is the only pain I have. The doctor is fixing it well, probably it will be better looking than before. I had a very narrow escape with my right eye, I have a nasty cut between the eyeball and eyebrow but that is nearly alright. My burns are not serious, the big toe of the right and ankle of the left are slightly burnt and also my right thumb and arm, but nothing to worry about.

I think Lane, my observer, will be better before me. I am not in the same ward but I hear he is getting on well. It has now been ascertained that I was brought down by Archie fire, a thing I never expected or even contemplated. I don't know how it set me on fire; of course the front petrol tank was burst but I don't know what lighted the petrol. I believe my machine was burnt to nothing after I hit the ground, so I am lucky to have undone my belt.

I don't yet know my address in Germany, I will have to wait till I get there… I have no idea where I will be sent to from here as there are a lot of camps in Germany. Being a prisoner, I don't think I am entitled to a wound gratuity. I lose about £50 but will make sure of it. This happened at an unfortunate time as I was looking forward to some letters and the parcel you said you were sending me for my birthday. I am wondering have you moved yet, and if so, where. I will have to wait a long time until I hear. It is now summer, but I can hardly believe it. I don't think you can send newspapers to a Prisoner of War but you can find out from the Red Cross. I am wondering how many days it was from the time you heard I was missing, until you heard that I was a prisoner. This must have been an anxious time for you. In case you don't know, I was shot down on 3rd May. I suppose Harry knows by now. He used to write me every week. I hope that there is no limit as to the number of letters I can receive. I suppose I am lucky in one way to be a prisoner, because I am reasonably sure of seeing you all when the war is over, and I wasn't before. Life as a prisoner will not be so bad once my letters and parcels start coming but that will take some time yet.

I must close now as I have no more news,

P.S. I have some books to read so I am alright in that respect. A German officer very kindly gave me cigarettes, but I long for sweets. I have just been moved to the officers' quarters and Lane and myself have a nice room. We are very comfortable here.

Ultimately, however, the German Spring Offensives failed, partly because they failed to take advantage of the gains they had made, and also as a result of a successful Allied counter-offensive. The war dragged on into the autumn but the end was clearly in sight. On

11 November an armistice with Germany came into effect. Many could scarcely believe it, including the 27-year-old commanding officer of the 2/5th Battalion, Lancashire Fusiliers, Colonel George Stanley Brighten DSO, although it is clear that hard fighting continued in some areas right up until the ceasefire.

BEF
13 November 1918

My dearest Father and Mother,
Well, isn't it wonderful? I can't realise it yet. We have not yet had the complete terms of the Armistice, but more or less know some of them. It is of course more or less unconditional surrender, an absolute abject defeat. Of course they have had their internal troubles, but it is the military defeat which has forced and won the situation.

Have been living during some wonderful days. After I last wrote, we remained some days in [the] same village and then commenced advancing again on our special job which was a flying column specially formed of all arms to chase the Hun, and we got three days of it before the Armistice. It was really most interesting. Very hard marching as we were the only infantry, and in addition to marching in the day and keeping up with cavalry, had to find out-posts ... as well. The men were simply splendid, and not one fell out. Needless to say we were in action the last moments of the war, we should be, and had a rather hot time of it afternoon and night of the 10th. Early 11th: we entered a fairly large town amidst an enormous reception, cheering the whole way, and passed through to the XXXXXXXXXXX further side, and then heard armistice. It was a wonderful moment; I was able to announce it to the people of the town.

Later same day we billeted in this nice quiet little village (near the same town) where we are now. The same night, Brigade, who have a beautiful place in the town, gave a dance to the local inhabitants to which I went, a great show, almost historic.

We are expecting to be part of the forces to go forward and occupy but do not know yet when we go; probably not the first. During the advance we used to get the most wonderful receptions in the towns, the moment the Germans had gone, and we arrived, flags everywhere. The Batt [Battalion] looked like an army of flags. Received officially by the Mayors etc. We had the funeral of some of our men who were killed the last day, and the people here gave a wonderful show, they made the coffins, and all turned out with a band, heaps of flowers. The Bergomaster read a very nice little eulogy, chiefly about what England had done.

As time goes on I hope censorship regulations will be relaxed and that we shall be allowed to name places. It is too early to imagine how things are going to settle down, and when and at what moment: one wants a few days to collect and re-arrange one's thoughts and ideas.

I have seen armistice terms since writing the commencement of this. They are simply wonderful. What more complete victory could have been desired?!

xxxxxxxxxx
Stanley

Major Westmacott who less than a year earlier had been part of the Allied retreat during the German Spring Offensives, was with the victorious Allied armies as they crossed into Germany. He later recalled his thoughts on marching into the homeland of his former enemy in a letter to his wife on 13 December 1918.

I have seen a sight today which I shall never forget. There are three bridges over the Rhine at Cologne, known as the Mulhelm bridge, the Hohen-Zollern bridge, and the suspension bridge. Our infantry began to cross the Rhine at 9.15am, the 9th Div. by the Mulhelm bridge, the 29th Div. by the Hohen-Zollern bridge and the Canadians by the suspension bridge. Until 1.15pm they poured across in three dense columns. So as to do things really well, the German police were told to see that no wheeled German traffic was allowed on the streets, and they obeyed their orders to the letter. There were big crowds of Germans looking on in spite of the rain, but they seemed more curious than anything else. I saw one women in tears, poor soul, but bar that it might have been almost an English crowd. General Jacob, my Corps Commander, stood under the Union Jack by a big statue of the Kaiser, at the west end of the Hohen-Zollern bridge, and took the salute of the 29th Division, one of the finest fighting divisions in the British Army, being the division which earned undying glory in Gallipoli.

The men marched with fixed bayonets, wearing their steel helmets, and carrying their packs. I wish you could have seem them – each man making the most of himself, and full of pride and élan. Then came the guns, turned out as our gunners always turn themselves out. Mind you, the Division was fighting hard all through the last battle, and they have been marching steadily through Belgium and Germany for the last 30 days, but the horses were all fit and hard as nails, and the buckles of the harness were all burnished like silver. The mules were as fit as the horses, and went by wagging their old ears as if they crossed the Rhine every day of the week. A German looking on said that the Division must have just come fresh from England. It is difficult to remember what we were like last March and April, during the retreat of the 5th Army, and to find ourselves here as conquerors in one of the proudest cities of Germany.

THE
SECOND
WORLD
WAR

The Second World War began shortly after dawn on Friday 1 September 1939 when two German Army Groups thrust deep into Poland. Supported by Junkers Ju 87 dive bombers ('Stukas'), and employing the tactic of *Blitzkrieg* or 'Lightning war', the Wehrmacht raced forward, enveloping and capturing entire Polish armies which were soon overwhelmed, especially when on 17 September the Red Army of Soviet Russia also attacked Poland from the east.

Two days after Hitler's assault on Poland, the British and French governments – which had guaranteed Poland's sovereignty that March – declared war on Germany. That same day, Sunday 3 September, Prime Minister Neville Chamberlain brought Winston Churchill into his cabinet as First Lord of the Admiralty, the minister responsible for the Royal Navy.

To the public eye, the next thing that happened was … very little. The 'Phoney War' lasted seven months while the Nazis ingested Poland and moved their forces westwards, but there was no fighting on the Western Front. Both the war in Finland and the war at sea were fought aggressively, however, with many sinkings on both sides, including the British aircraft carrier *Courageous* and the German battleship *Graf Spee*.

The months of uneasy waiting suddenly ended on 9 April 1940, when Hitler covered his northern flank by successfully invading Denmark and Norway, and forcing the Royal Navy to evacuate British and French forces from the latter country. This humiliation brought down Chamberlain's government after a tumultuous debate over Norway in the House of Commons, and on 10 May 1940 Winston Churchill became prime minister. In his first appearance in the Commons in this role, on 13 May, he told the British people that they could expect nothing but 'blood, toil, tears and sweat', in the first of many sublime morale-boosting speeches of his wartime premiership.

On the very day that Churchill became prime minister, Hitler unleashed his *Blitzkrieg* on the Low Countries. Neutral Holland and Belgium were invaded, as well as France, and by 20 May General Heinz Guderian's leading Panzer tank formations had reached the English lines at Abbeville, cutting the Allied line in half. Hopes of an effective counter-attack soon faded, and on the evening of 25 May, the British commander Lord Gort took the decision to retreat to the Channel port of Dunkirk and re-embark as much as he could of his hard-pressed British Expeditionary Force. There started a desperate race to the sea. Through a brilliant naval operation, supported by brave RAF sorties against the Luftwaffe, no fewer than 338,226 soldiers, including 120,000 French troops, were saved by 3 June, from what had at one point looked like inevitable capture. As the writer of one of these letters observes: 'Imagine carrying 56 pounds of potatoes on your back for five hours and you can imagine how I felt.'

Yet as Churchill told the House of Commons, 'Wars are not won by evacuations,' and by 11 June the Germans had crossed the River Marne. The French premier Paul Reynaud resigned soon afterwards, and the Great War hero of Verdun, Marshal Philippe Pétain, filled the gap, becoming leader of the French state. He immediately appealed to Hitler for an armistice, and a peace treaty was signed on 22 June.

Contrary to the cliché, Britain did not 'stand alone' against Nazism after the fall of France: the British Empire remained utterly loyal to the motherland, with declarations of war against Germany and the sending of troops from Canada, Australia, South Africa, New Zealand and the West Indies. India provided the largest all-volunteer army in the history of mankind, and in East Africa the native populations enthusiastically joined up and took part in the attacks on the Italian empire there.

Now the undisputed master of the continent, Hitler began to draw up plans to invade and subjugate Great Britain, codenamed Operation *Sealion*. In order for them to be put into effect he needed command of the skies, so he allowed Hermann Goering to undertake the great aerial struggle that became known as 'the Battle of Britain'. In July, throughout August and for the first half of September 1940, the Luftwaffe – with 875 bombers, 316 bombers and 929 fighters – contested the air against the RAF, which had around 650 fighters (having already lost nearly 500 in the battle of France).

Through the careful husbanding of resources by Air Chief Marshal Dowding, increased fighter construction under the new Minister of Aircraft Production, Lord Beaverbrook, invaluable early warning information from recently installed radar and observation posts, the slight performance edge of the Hurricane and Spitfire over the Messerschmitt, but above all the superb aggressive spirit of the young pilots of Fighter Command, the RAF won the Battle of Britain, in which Germany lost 1,733 planes by the end of October 1940, to Britain's 915. On 7 September 1940, after taking heavy losses, Goering decided to switch the main target from the aerodromes and radar stations to the metropolis of London itself, a tacit acknowledgement that Britain had won. The 'Nazi doctrines' which one of the authors of these letters, a RAF pilot, refers to, were not about to pollute Britain after all.

The bombing of London and many other British cities – including Coventry, Glasgow, Portsmouth, Bristol and Southampton – in what was called 'the Blitz', was to cost the lives of nearly 43,000 British civilians. It brought the war home to ordinary Britons in a way that the Zeppelins had not really achieved during the Great War. In order to protect urban children, millions were evacuated to safety, often to rural parts of the country. If a little more brutal honesty about the horrors of war can be detected in the Second World War letters than the first set in this volume, it might be because the soldiers at the front knew that the Blitz had brought the ghastly realities of death and destruction home to civilians in 1940 in a way that hadn't really happened before.

Although the RAF's Bomber Command responded by attacking German cities, and the Royal Navy blockaded Germany and attempted to sink raider battleships and U-boats, for a while after the Battle of Britain there was nowhere for the Allies and the Wehrmacht to clash on land, since the Axis powers controlled the European continent and an attempted invasion there was judged suicidal. In Libya, Egypt, the Sudan, Ethiopia and along the North African coast, however, the British Army under General Wavell was able to score several significant victories over Marshal Graziani's Italian troops, despite being heavily outnumbered.

This was not to last, however, as in February 1941 Churchill ordered forces to be diverted to protect Greece, just as the brilliant German commander General Erwin Rommel arrived in Tripoli to take command of the German Afrika Korps. On 6 April, Germany, having suborned Romania and Hungary onto its side, invaded Yugoslavia, which fell after only 11 days' fighting. Soon afterwards, British forces had to be evacuated from Greece to Crete, where they were followed by a daring German airborne landing of over 17,500 troops under General Kurt Student. After eight days' fighting the British were forced to evacuate Crete.

The war was going badly for the British Commonwealth, but in 1941 Adolf Hitler made two disastrous blunders which truly globalized the war and allowed the British their first genuine glimpses of possible future victory. The first mistake was Operation *Barbarossa*, Hitler's invasion of the USSR on 22 June 1941, which inaugurated a life-or-death four-year struggle between him and the Soviet dictator Josef Stalin.

The other mistake came after the surprise attack that Imperial Japan launched against the American Pacific Fleet as it lay at anchor at Pearl Harbor in Hawaii on Sunday 7 December 1941, which succeeded in sinking four battleships, damaging a further five, destroying 164 aircraft and killing 2,403 US servicemen and civilians. What President Franklin D. Roosevelt called 'a day that would live in infamy' brought the world's greatest industrial power into the conflict. Hitler's near-lunatic decision to declare war against America four days later effectively spelt his doom.

Between 22 and 28 December 1941, Churchill visited Washington and Ottawa with his service chiefs and hammered out with the Americans and Canadians the key stages by which victory was to be achieved. To their great credit, Roosevelt and the US Army chief of staff, General George Marshall, eschewed the obvious response to Pearl Harbor – a massive retaliation against the immediate aggressor, Japan – to concentrate instead on a 'Germany First' policy that would destroy the most powerful of the Axis dictatorships first, before then moving on to crush Japan.

'Germany First', while making good political and strategic sense, did, however, mean that the Japanese were permitted to make enormous advances throughout the Far East in the early stages of the campaign, advances that were characterised by dreadful cruelty to the peoples they conquered and to the prisoners-of-war they captured. Catastrophe for the Allies followed, along with humiliation at Japanese hands. On 10 December 1941 Japanese aircraft sank HMS *Prince of Wales* and HMS *Repulse*, on Christmas Day Hong Kong surrendered and in January 1942 the Japanese invaded the Dutch East Indies and Burma and captured Kuala Lumpur. On 15 February Britain suffered her greatest defeat since the American War of Independence when the great naval base of Singapore surrendered to a much smaller Japanese force. The Americans were also forced out of the Philippines.

Meanwhile, the struggle in North Africa surged back and forth between Tripoli and Tobruk. Wavell was replaced by General Claude

Auchinleck, who was himself replaced by Lieutenant General Bernard Montgomery. It was Montgomery who convincingly defeated Rommel in a well-planned battle at El Alamein, Egypt, between 28 October and 4 November 1942. On 8 November, Allied forces under the American commander Lieutenant Colonel Dwight D. Eisenhower landed in French North Africa, and it was not long before the Germans were in full retreat. Tobruk, which had been taken by Rommel in June, was recaptured by the British Army on 13 November 1942.

Between January 1943 and June 1944 the Axis powers were forced to pull back in Russia and the Mediterranean, which they did in a hard-fought rearguard action, contesting every important nodal point, defensive line and communications centre. On occasion, such as at the monastery of Monte Cassino in Italy, their dogged resistance held up the Allied advance for weeks.

At the Casablanca Conference in January 1943, Churchill and Roosevelt agreed that once the Germans were expelled from Africa, the Allies would invade Sicily. After that was undertaken successfully on 10 July, Mussolini fell from power, and the new Italian government began secret negotiations to switch sides. In early September Montgomery crossed the Straits of Messina onto mainland Italy, and the American Lieutenant General Mark Clark landed an amphibious Anglo-American army at Salerno. The fighting up the Italian peninsula, which was relatively easy for the Germans to defend, proved long, hard and costly, yet too early a cross-Channel attack would most likely have been disastrous. Rome did not fall until 4 June 1944.

The very next day the eyes of the world turned to the beaches of Normandy, where – after two night-time airborne landings inland – 4,000 10-ton landing craft took six infantry divisions to five beachheads, codenamed (from west to east) Utah, Omaha, Gold, Juno and Sword. In all, Operation *Overlord* on 6 June involved 6,800 vessels, 11,500 aircraft and 176,000 men. 'I hope to God I know what I'm doing,' Eisenhower said on the eve of the attack. With total air superiority, German confusion, ingenious inventions such as the PLUTO oil pipeline* and artificial 'Mulberry' harbours, and the courage of the English-speaking peoples, victory was assured. 'To us is given the honour of striking a blow for freedom which will live in history,' Montgomery told his troops, 'and in the better days that lie ahead men will speak with pride of our doings. We have a great and righteous cause.' The casualty figures from D-Day are estimated to be around 10,000 servicemen killed and wounded, including men from the USA, UK, Canada, Australia and New Zealand.

Yet the town of Caen held out for a month, the battle of the Falaise Gap was not won until 21 August and Paris was not liberated until 26 August. The ever-present capacity for Nazi punishment of Allied tactical over-extension was proven on 17 September, when a huge Anglo-American airborne operation of glider landings and parachute drops codenamed Operation *Market Garden* attempted to secure the bridges over the key Dutch rivers and canals ahead of their armies. The Allies took Eindhoven, Grave and Nijmegen, thereby securing access over the Meuse and the Waal rivers, but the British First Airborne Division was dropped to the west of the town of Arnhem, capturing the bridge over the lower Rhine. It proved to be a bridge too far, since by 25 September it was impossible to relieve them and they were ordered to withdraw, with just over 2,000, one-fifth of the total, managing to escape death, wounding or capture.

On 16 December the Germans then launched a major counter-attack, coming once again through the wooded mountains of the Ardennes. Twenty divisions – seven of them armoured – assaulted the American First Army, while to the north SS-Oberstgruppenfuhrer Dietrich's Sixth Panzer Army struck for the Meuse and General Hasso von Manteuffel Fifth Panzer Army tried to make for Brussels. Seeing the American front effectively being sliced in half, Eisenhower

---

* PLUTO stands for Pipeline Under the Ocean, and was designed to supply petrol from depots in the south of England to the advancing troops in Europe.

Lieutenant William Leefe Robinson VC, famed for shooting down a Zeppelin over London during the First World War. © IWM (Documents 200)

Company Sergeant Major Milne, 1/5th Battalion, Seaforth Highlanders, who fought in the Second Battle of the Marne in July 1918. © IWM (Documents 1635)

Corporal Laurie Rowlands, 15th Battalion, Durham Light Infantry, experienced his 'baptism of fire' on the Ypres Salient. © IWM (Documents 2329)

Sergeant Francis Herbert Gautier, who wrote a heart-rendering letter to his daughter, Marie, after he'd been wounded. He sent similar letters to other family members. Courtesy of the family of F. Gautier.

Reverend Canon Cyril Lomax, a Church of England Army chaplain, served with the Durham Light Infantry in France from July 1916 to April 1917. He illustrated his letters from the front line, providing his family with an insight into the first tank attack (top) and the arrival of post in a billet (bottom). © IWM (Documents 1289)

Men and horses from the Cavalry Division, British Expeditionary Force, retreat from Mons, August 1918. © IWM (Q 60695)

Front line trenches during the First World War. © IWM (Q 4649)

TOP
A Company, 11th Battalion, Cheshire Regiment, occupy a captured German trench at Ovillers-la-Boisselle on the Somme in July 1916. One soldier is on sentry duty, using an improvised fire step cut into the slope of the trench. The more established fire step facing the other way was used by the Germans before the trench was turned. © IWM (Q 3990)

BOTTOM
The trench system was often very confusing due to the sheer number of trench lines and the ziz-zagged pattern they followed. As a result, the different trenches often gained their own names, as seen here. © IWM (Q 4180)

OPPOSITE
This letter, written in the shape of a kiss, was sent by George Hayman, a private in the Lancashire Fusiliers, to his wife in June 1916 before he was sent to France. He died two months later. © IWM (Documents 1647)

me   our baby   you

By the way, my dear Marie, I am in the class but now instead of the six, soldiers forget when you write to me. Some of our fellows went home on well end pass last Saturday and you can bet I was wishing it was me again so that I could see and kiss that dear old face of yours. We are drilling as hard as ever, in fact harder if anything if we do not do it right the first time. They make us run all the time we are drilling instead of walking, and with a heavy pack on at that. So then we were first fixed us were all puffing like fish out of water. The bugle is just going for soup, and I am going to have some to warm me up. That I am absolutely frozen. so will start again after. My own Darling. At last I have got a nice letter, for which I thank you very much you dear girl too. I feel very happy because your letter is very nice and cheerful, just what you and I'd

... lots about going a nice trip kiss. So I promise you a jolly good time. that I do sometime I thanked your written effort so as to catch the post. only I had been pushed but will do as I see of apt to go so it was late when I — back so you will get it a little later. last Saturday I went to Stafford to see all the nice girls and I was wished whilst there & do you believe it I have gained one stone heavier so you may not be as fat as a little pig will feel it too. Well my dearer it will remove these. I hope so if you more news so will show you I can't think of any because it is good a hope it will be better very soon. give my love to Maude a little Charlie, and a very great big kiss for my dear little fat boy — a heap of love & kisses for my dear boy little fist naughty. Waits to see as soon as you can. for I shall be looking out for a letter every post. as usual. Well I hope you are all right quite well and happy and be a good girl till I get home. take just some nice rosy red cheeks for me to kiss. I wonder if you will be able to read and understand this scribble as it a long letter. and it has taken a long time to write. Good bye for a little while from your loving boy George

Bob Connolly, an NCO with 8th Battalion, Rifle Brigade, on his wedding day. Connolly landed on Juno Beach on 13 June 1944 and took part in a number of battles around Caen. © IWM (Documents 13168)

Captain Samuel Gordon served with the British Army as a doctor during D-Day on an American Landing Ship Tank (LST) which was later used to evacuate casualties. © IWM (Documents 774)

Lance Corporal John A. Wyatt, 2nd Battalion, East Surrey Regiment. He fought to contain the Japanese invasion of Malaya in 1941. © IWM (Documents 8531)

Lieutenant Brin L. Francis, 8th (Belfast) Heavy Anti Aircraft Regiment, Royal Artillery, served in the Far East, while his brother, David, was involved in fighting around Caen in 1944. © IWM (Documents 8240)

TOP
'The Withdrawal from Dunkirk, June 1940' by Charles Ernest Cundall. The troop-filled beaches, evacuation attempts by the Royal Navy and bombing by the Luftwaffe are all clear to see. © IWM (ART LD 305)

MIDDLE
In a posed propaganda photograph British pilots are seen 'scrambling' to their aircraft during the height of the Battle of Britain. © IWM (HU 49253)

BOTTOM
The Blitz: a Heinkel He 111 bomber flies over London on 7 September 1940. © IWM (C 5422)

Captain Christopher Cross of 2nd Battalion, Oxfordshire and Buckinghamshire Light Infantry, is shown here relaxing and writing. He took part in the glider landings across Normandy in June 1944. © IWM (Documents 771)

The 5th Cameron Highlanders prepare Christmas puddings in the Western Desert, December 1942, illustrating the fact that there were sometimes periods of light relief. © IWM (E 20598)

gave Montgomery command of the whole northern sector on 20 December. Montgomery managed to fight 'the Battle of the Bulge' successfully until the Germans ran out of petrol by Boxing Day 1944.

In January 1945, Eisenhower and Montgomery adopted a two-pronged strategy for the invasion of Germany, with the British and Canadians pushing through the Reichswald into the Rhineland from the north, while the Americans came up through the south. The land battle was supported by the heroic bombing missions of the RAF and the United States Army Air Force (USAAF), over such cities as Dresden, Hamburg and Berlin, as well as other cities and industrial and military targets. The diaries and memoirs of senior Nazis such as propaganda minister Joseph Goebbels and armaments minister Albert Speer suggest that these were highly effective in breaking German morale and dislocating industry. They came at a terribly high cost though: no fewer than 58,000 men died in Bomber Command during the war.

By mid-March most of the territory west of the Rhine had been cleared, with the German Army suffering 60,000 casualties and 300,000 taken prisoner. On 11 April the American Ninth Army reached the River Elbe at Magdeburg, only 80 miles from Berlin, and joined up with the Red Army. Two weeks later the Russians completed the encirclement of the German capital.

Adolf Hitler committed suicide in his bunker in the Reichschancellery on 30 April 1945, two days after the Italian dictator Benito Mussolini had been shot by partisans in northern Italy. Berlin surrendered on 2 May, and on the 7th, at Eisenhower's headquarters at Rheims, General Alfred Jodl and Admiral Hans-Georg von Friedeburg signed the document of total unconditional surrender on behalf of Germany, before representatives of the United States, Great Britain, France and Russia. The next day – 8 May – was declared Victory in Europe Day (VE Day).

In the Far East, since their startling victories of late 1941 and early 1942, Japan had become bogged down. It had been fought to a standstill by General Sir William Slim's Fourteenth Army in Burma, by General Douglas MacArthur in the Philippines and Admiral Paul Nimitz in the Pacific. There were a number of notable Allied victories, including the battles of Midway, Monywa and Iwo Jima and the fall of Mandalay, Kyushu and Okinawa. But they were all at a cost and despite these successes it was estimated by the US chiefs of staff that the invasion of mainland Japan might cost the lives of up to a quarter of a million Allied servicemen. The fanatical, often suicidal, resistance that the Japanese had offered during the island hopping campaign – and as kamikaze pilots against American ships – has convinced scholars and historians that this prediction was probably not exaggerated when extrapolated onto the Japanese home islands.

To some degree then, it was fortunate that by early August 1945 scientific developments were had been and what had been codenamed the 'Tube Alloys' and 'Manhattan' projects brought forth two different bombs, both of which were capable of using nuclear fission to create explosions of hitherto unimaginable force, and hopefully bring about peace. One was dropped on the Japanese city of Hiroshima on 6 August, killing around 140,000 people. Japan refused to admit defeat, so a second bomb was dropped on Nagasaki three days later, killing a further 73,884 people. Japan finally surrendered on 14 August 1945, bringing to an end a conflict that in total, over six years, is estimated to have cost the lives of over fifty million people.

With the outbreak of the Second World War the professional element of the British Army, including reservists, was once again posted to France. However, following the swift fall of Poland a period of calm descended. Ernest Probst, serving with the Royal Artillery, was able to write several letters to his wife back home in England during this quiet period as he adjusted to life in the military and active service.

Somewhere in France
November 13th, Monday

My dearest Winifred,
I received a letter from you yesterday posted on the 8th so you see I am getting your post quicker than you are getting mine. That, of course, is unavoidable as the officers censor our letters in their spare time – when they get any.

Rumours about leave abound and I do not trouble to believe them. I shall expect to get leave when I open the front door with my latch-key and not before. None the less for that I'm hoping hard and trusting in Cyril's lucky star because I've decided I was not fortunate enough to have been from under so continually a beneficent orb.

Don't tell me you are lonely, darling, or I'll probably desert. I certainly cannot get used to being without you and still expect to wake up and find myself working at [P…]. Even that would be heaven or at least a taste thereof.

It is very interesting to note that since I joined up migraines have been conspicuously absent. It's the open air. Do you fancy the open road and a caravan? Shall we become tramps when I return? Failing that an open air job… I fancy you will have to resign yourself to that because apparently the open air is the cure for it – and having written that I shall probably be attacked tomorrow…

That firing camp I mentioned has been cancelled for some reason unknown to me so digging is once more in full swing. I today am not digging as I have a battery duty but I shall be out again tomorrow. I have just written to mother and told her I am beginning to enjoy it in suitable weather. It's certainly bringing my muscles up…

We went to the pictures last Friday, I saw *Merrily we Live*. What a riot, I nearly fell of my bench laughing and it is by far the best film I've seen for many months. It is a peculiar thing, though, whilst on the subject of humour, that we are finding that we laugh much more readily these days at things that normally we would consider merely amusing. Maybe our sense of appreciation is becoming less critical…

Do you know that a French private receives but ½f pour jour? Ain't that bloody awful. We must appear like millionaires to them, although I am personally broke…

Well my dearest, there is no more for now. Hurry up peace! And don't you, wife, forget you owe me a photograph of yourself.

With all the love in the world,
Forever yours,
Ernie

The lull in the war continued throughout the winter of 1939–40 and Probst was indeed able to enjoy some leave with his wife in mid February before re-joining his unit.

20 February 1940

My darling Winifred,
I don't know quite what to say but I must leave you a little note.

We have had a wonderful reunion but like all things it has had its ending.

Remember, darling, how much I love you in my perhaps rather undemonstrative way.

I'll soon be home again so don't cry about me.

I shall think of you reading this at about 7 tonight (if I have not been already attacked by sea-sickness!).

Darling, I love you,
Ernie
xxxxxxxxxx

Unbeknownst to Ernie Probst he would be making the short journey back across the Channel sooner than he would have expected. In May 1940 Hitler unleashed his *Blitzkrieg* on the West. Storming through Belgium and the Netherlands in short order, the British Army and their French allies were pushed back to the sea to make a final stand at a small fishing port, Dunkirk. At first it seemed unlikely that the British Army could be saved in the face of the German juggernaut. But then something miraculous occurred and from the ports and estuaries of southern England a flotilla of Royal Navy ships and civilian crafts gathered. Brilliantly coordinated by the Royal Navy, with the aerial support of the RAF, nearly 340,000 Allied servicemen were rescued from the beaches of Dunkirk. Lance Sergeant Ernie Probst was amongst those who survived the crossing despite the best efforts of the Luftwaffe.

4 June 1940

My most darling Winifred,
It doesn't seem as though I shall get leave as quickly as I, at first, thought.

Apparently we stay here until our divisional reforming area is decided upon after which we are transferred there to refit and then it is not until we have refitted that we can hope for leave.

Anyway, darling, I am in England and absolutely safe in mind and limb with every prospect of seeing you within a fortnight.

This is a delightful place, which would be appreciated more under different circumstances. We are all getting very tired of doing nothing as we are confined to camp owing to the possibility of transfer orders arriving at any moment.

There are thirty 92nd men here including Howard Walls. I am afraid that we left Cyril somewhere in Belgium, during a retirement and I really don't know where he is. I can only hope he is safe with some other unit.

John did not return to the unit from leave as by the time his leave was up we were moving about all over the place and so I don't know what has happened to him either.

I am very glad that Howard is here with me as we are now pretty nearly inseparable.

We had a very narrow squeak at Dunkirk as just as we reached the boats moored to the ¼ mile long jetty five German bombers came over. Howard and I jumped on board and crossed to the outside boat of three which were moored together. The Germans dropped some bombs but we were not hit and our boat, a torpedo boat, left first and dashed hell for leather across the channel.

Howard and I solemnly shook hands when England hove in sight.

Well, sweet, looksee after yourself, more news when I see you and may it be soon.

All my love,
Yours everlasting,
Ernie
xxxxxxxxxxxxxxx
Drop a line to M & Dad saying I'm safe. E

Some soldiers were not as fortunate as Ernie Probst and the evacuation was fraught with danger. A French liaison officer, Lieutenant Le Maitre, serving alongside 3 Corps of the Royal Signals, vividly described his experiences in a letter to his fellow officer J.W. Thraves, an extract of which is below. Thraves himself was on the beach at the time and witnessed the burning of the boat as well as the death of many fellow Royal Signallers.

On Wednesday, May 29th (1940), after escaping heavy bombing in the harbour and along the pier of Dunkerque, I sailed aboard the Crested Eagle at about 5.30pm with my liaison agent, Bassett. Two miles beyond the pier our boat was attacked by German diving bombers who dropped some big incendiary bombs. I was then standing in the inside deck on the left of the staircase; a bomb fell on the right of the staircase and I fainted for a few minutes. When I recovered myself I expected the sinking of the boat and I saw that my hands and my face were terribly burned by the fire of the bomb. All around, some wounded soldiers were shouting and roaring: I saw a small window through which I dropped myself head first and I fell on a small outside deck two yards below; there I recovered better with fresh air and was happy to find again Bassett, who was suffering from the shock but was uninjured.

In the meantime the steamer was set on fire and was beached at about 700 yards off the sand, towards which it was possible to swim quickly, but we were afraid to be made prisoners the next morning. So we decided to reach farther a British destroyer. Bassett took off my field-boots and we jumped into the sea. I saw then that it would be impossible to swim quickly enough with my uniform breeches; unhappily my hands were so badly burned that the skin was going off with the nails, like gloves... Nevertheless, I succeeded to undo all the breeches buttons, including the leg buttons, and keeping only my short pants. I swam half-an-hour before being picked up near the destroyer. Then I fainted again and when I recovered I was in a small room inside the destroyer, rolled up in a blanket: a sailor was putting some oil and bandages on my hands.

The next morning we reached Great Britain and I was carried to a First Casualty Station and afterwards to hospital. There the surgeons anaesthetised me to clean my hands and my face, and sprayed tannic acid on my hands. After further sprayings of this product my hands were covered with a kind of brown artificial skin. The flesh ought to grow again inside that sort of glove. My looking was horrible, face and ears were black and full of crusts, with enormous nose and dried lips.

The grand devotion of doctors and nurses saved my life. On June 7th sudden haemorrhages of both hands: I am getting weaker every day. Nightmares, even by day. On June 12th a Catholic priest is called to give me the last sacraments. I offer up my life for my dear France, but it is very sad to think that I shall never more see my poor wife, my boy and all the dear ones who are far from me. On June 13th my right arm is swelling, getting blur and very painful; the next morning, the surgeon opens it and an enormous quantity of pus goes off during several days. I am saved and from now I shall slowly recover.

From about June 20th I was given hand-baths; the artificial skin started to come off by pieces, uncovering a new skin on the palm and some flesh on the back of my hands; in the meantime, I was given medicines to cure my face. My ears were very painful and prevented me to sleep on the side. I was six weeks without leaving my bed, both hands confined in bandages, fed by the nurses as a baby. The back of the hands is the part needing the longest time to be healed because there the skin must be extensible and the sores of my right hand are only healed now, 29th August, three months after I have been wounded…

Another soldier to experience the desperate retreat to the sea was Major Peter Hill, a fellow reservist, who was called up to serve with the Royal Artillery Ordnance Corps. His letter, despite its cheerful optimism and faith in the British fighting spirit, certainly sheds some light on the perilous days of May 1940 when soldier and civilian alike was seemingly at the mercy of the Luftwaffe.

Major P.R. Hill
'F' Corps Section
2nd Ond. Fld. Park
B.E.F.
25 May 1940

My Darling Wife,
When this letter will reach you if at all I don't know but like good British troops we always hope for the best.

The last few days Betty have not been pleasant and my dear it is no use my pretending otherwise. This continued fine weather favours the blasted German air force whilst ours is attacking his lines of communication or sitting at home kept there by windy politicians. Tell John Sully we want fighters and yet more fighters. If they appear the Germans simply can't stand up to them. I saw two yesterday go into about six bombers bringing them down like chaff. But our pilots can't fly 24hrs of the day. Try to impress on your friends the words of the King that we are fighting for our very existence in the world at all and that our downfall, if such a thing could be thought of, would be final and everlasting.

Every conceivable form of foulness is used by the Germans. The farmer on whose farm I am now has a son who was taken prisoner by Germans in Dutch uniforms. If any of our conscientious objectors don't like to fight the German people but only the Nazis let them do the sort of job we had to do yesterday when the few men I have who know anything about first-aid and I had to attend to dying and injured refugees after they had been bombed. My first dead was a child of five and her grandfather. I don't want to try and be horrific Betty and soldiers expect terrible things in war but when we see the pitiful plight of innocent people we have only one idea – carry the same total warfare into Germany and smash them in pieces for ever. The spirit of the soldiers I came across will blow things to pieces if ever a Gast tries to restore Germany as a power.

I have slept in my clothes for several days now and was up at 4am – this mainly to find a new place and hope I have chosen a nice quiet farm… The other day an officer of ours arrived with a truck full of provisions of wines and spirits. Then I picnicked in an orchard the other day on bully beef, tinned potatoes & champagne…

The weather continues to be perfect and I long for some of those gloriously happy days we have had quite alone and look forward to raising a family with you in a better world God willing. I feel sure you will take the necessary steps in this direction, it would be very encouraging if you did. If you have time dearest look around for the ideal little house you would like after the war in Barnstead, Chipstead, Epsom Downs districts, nicely in the country don't you think. Of course it is also very nice up the river in some places. It would be better than a flat and a cottage, but what do you think?

This afternoon I think the weather is going to break. It is like thunder and will keep les avions away…

Well my darling I often look at your photo and gain courage from you. I must say that in these days a firm belief in the Christian faith goes a long way also.

Goodbye for the present dear, don't worry, we always get away with it.

As ever
Your loving husband,
Peter
P.S. The BEF was never more alive & kicking than now.

Lionel Baylis kept a diary throughout the retreat to Dunkirk and referred to this when he wrote to his brother to tell him about the tumultuous weeks that had preceded the evacuation of the British Expeditionary Force. Baylis was at this stage serving as a signalman in the 48th Divisional Signals.

> No 2528408 Signm Baylis L.G.
> 'F' Section, No 2 Company
> 48th Divisional Signals
> Hampton Park Buckwater
> Hereford
> Tuesday 25th June '40.

> Dear Cliff and May,
> Well this letter has been a long time coming, but still, better late than never. I hope you're both going on alright, and not being as pessimistic as the majority. I hear you had an air-raid last night. Did you hear any eggs come down or did you sleep it through? I don't think an air-raid would fetch me out of bed unless things got extremely warm.
> I don't know whether you are still sufficiently interested to hear an account of my travels. If you're not, swear for five minutes for me, for wasting time and paper. I will try to make it as interesting as possible and promise not to exaggerate in any way. Some of the things you will already know, but I've got to mention them to keep things clear...
> Tuesday 10th [May 1940]. 0400hrs we were wakened by all the air-raid alarms in the district going. A.A. fire was continuous and planes droned continuously overhead. Needless to say we all tumbled out of bed and stood watching our first air-raid in pyjamas and shirt as the case may be. We didn't see any planes brought down, but several made off with smoke pouring out of them. Well we knew or guessed something was up and at seven we heard on the news that Holland, Belgium and Luxembourg

had been invaded. Bang went my leave and we prepared for an immediate move…

Thursday 16th. Ordered to move at 0330, but was cancelled. 0730 subjected to our first dive-bombing attack by German fighters. Very few casualties in our regiment though an infantry battalion marching past suffered badly. 0830 moved to our position 2 miles south of Waterloo. 48th Div supposed to act as reserve for 1st and 2nd Div, the three comprising 1st Army Corps. It didn't turn out this way 'but the idea was good'. Throughout the day German planes went over in groups of 50. No British planes seen and A.A. fire not too hot. Our positions were bombed again with very few casualties. Late tonight our first 'Tactical Withdrawal' was made…

Friday 17th. Battalion in action all day. Bombing attacks continuous. From bits of information passing over wires etc, we were beginning to appreciate that things weren't as easy as we had thought they would be…

Saturday 18th. Reached our destination at 0430 but our stay was short lived. At 0630 the main body began what looked to me like a general retreat. I had to stay behind with our officers to destroy two wagons which had been ditched. When we had finished at 0830, rifle and machine gun fire could be heard less than half a mile away. We were moved right back to a place called Houtain and by this time were half way back into France, nor were we to get any peace here. We moved yet another 5 miles back, the Btys [batteries] opened fire and during the night we seemed to be in the middle of a circle of fire. It appears that the order to advance should have been cancelled as by the time we moved the German motorised columns had already penetrated beyond the given point…

Anyway by this time the whole British Army was on the retreat. It was simply a case of get back as fast as was possible. We travelled back to Tournai. All available transport was used to pick up the infantry. Half the blokes got separated from their units and fought the rest of the time with others. It seemed a ghastly tangle. Well the orders were to hold the canal round Tournai at all cost. We heard the news on the wireless that the battle round Sedan wasn't going too well. Despite this and the retreat from Belgium, we didn't have any pessimistic feelings…

On Wednesday night we were ordered to move back. Now understand this – at no point had the Germans crossed the canal but the situation elsewhere compelled us to withdraw unless we wanted to be trapped… On Monday 27th refreshed by the last 2 days we moved back to slightly west of Ypres. By this time we knew we were trapped in the north of France and Belgium. Fighting seemed to be all around us and was bitter. Artillery fire turned the sky red at night while bombing & shell fire blackened the countryside by day. Even so the worst blow was yet to fall. Early on Tuesday 28th we heard of the capitulation of Leopold.[*] I admit at this time none of we common soldiers appreciated the dangers. Those in command did and we set about destroying all extra kit, wireless sets, exchanges, telephones and every other bit of equipment. I should think we burnt £5,000 worth of technical stores that afternoon… Well we began to move back to the coast late at night. The journey took all night and was a nightmare. Villages and towns were bombed and machine gunned as we passed through. The roads were jammed with vehicles. Well to cut a long story short we got to within 12 miles of the coast about 0430 Wednesday 29th. I immediately fell asleep over the wheel. At midday we had orders to destroy our wagons as best we could. We daren't fire them for fear of attracting enemy bombers which were like hornets in the sky. At 1300 hours we began our march and reached Lapanne just inside Belgium, a few miles north of Dunkirk, at 1800 hours. I was absolutely dead beat. Imagine carrying about 56lbs of potatoes on your back for 5 hours and you can guess how I felt.

---

[*] King Leopold III of Belgium.

Well we slept that night on the beach and with luck still with us, the morning of Thursday 30th was very cloudy. I eventually got into a boat, soaked from head to foot, at 1100hrs and was rowed out to a drifter, which left the place soon after. By this time the Germans were shelling the beach and the boats as they left. Apparently half an hour after we had left, German places machine gunned that very beach and killed and wounded 700 men. In addition they bombed and sunk a destroyer a little lower down. Well we got to England (Dover) at 2030hrs, wet and in a sorry state. A cup of tea tasted like champagne, while the railway carriage was like a feather bed…

Well I've tried not to let what I've learnt since getting back have anything to do with my tale… I will say this much, that Dame fortune followed our section. We brought every man back and only one, who lost a finger, needed medical attention. As a contrast one other section in our div signals brought 4 back out of 32…

In conclusion I'm not one of those who is eager to get back, I never want to go through another 16 days like those. I think the army is a shower of ——, badly organised and generally wants a thorough clean out. If this war goes on much longer I know I shall turn socialist and a most progressive conservative which is the same thing.

Cheers for now & all the best,
Lionel

I suppose the news of the last few days shook you a bit. It did me. Perhaps we finally realise what the German Army etc is like. Thank God we've got a navy and pray that the French fleet stays on our side.

Harry Calvert served in No. 149 Field Ambulance, Royal Army Medical Corps (RAMC). In June 1940 he too described the danger from German bombing as the troops desperately awaited evacuation from the beaches at Dunkirk.

RAMC
Beaminster
Dorset
28.6.40

Dear P. and A.,

Many thanks for your letter which arrived this morning. You will be relieved to hear that we got through all right except for a few minor wounds. I am glad to say I am OK now.

Eddie Ritchie and young Teddy Crooks are here – the unit was very lucky at times over there and we just managed to scrape through by the skin of our teeth.

I've had a few of the boys killed and also a few are missing. We went through quite a lot of action in Belgium and Northern France in quite a short while and this is not an idle boast – but the British soldiers beat the Jerries every time and must have killed a half million of them on Vimy Ridge and took about two thousand prisoners.

But the French let us down badly by letting him break through and then the Belgians packed in and there we were, hemmed in on three sides with Dunkirk the only way out, so that is where we made for and <u>was it hot</u> I'll say, he seemed to fill the sky with his bombers and they just played merry hell on the beach.

Well, that is where Eddie and I lost young Teddy – you see somehow or other the three of us were lost from the unit the day before by our lorry breaking down and when we got it away again the rest of the unit were miles away. So we made our own way to Dunkirk. Well we are about two miles away from there when all the excitement started – one of the Jerry bombers came flying very low along the road and he dropped a pill just about 6 feet in front of us. It just lifted that wagon as if it was a balloon and we thought our end had come and young Teddy got a nasty knock on the arm so he fell.

We managed somehow to get him off the wagon and dived into a ditch and lay there till the planes cleared off – most uncomfortable I can assure you with the machine gun bullets splattering on the road.

But never mind, we managed to fix young Teddy's arm and we made our way to the beach. It was like jumping out of the frying pan and into the fire. The beach was like Blackpool on a Bank Holiday – it was black with soldiers. Well, we made our way to the port and got young Teddy seen to – and Eddie and I were detailed to carry the wounded on the boats.

We saw young Teddy aboard one ship – it left the port and it wouldn't be a mile out when the bombs started to drop again. That ship was hit 5 times and I said good-bye to Teddy to myself because I thought there would have been an awful lot killed on board her – but young Teddy will tell you all about that himself when he writes. That was about the longest day I've ever spent in the army – we thought that night would never come. Our shoulders were aching with the wounded and about 12.30pm the officers decided to evacuate the Aid Post as there were some fresher men come to relieve us.

Well, we worked like devils in the few hours of darkness that we had but not enough time for at 4.30 just as we were making for the boats over came the Jerries to start it all over again.

I don't think I've ever said my prayers as many times in one day as I did then but the Jerries got more than they bargained for this time when a dozen Spitfires came out of the blue and did they make short work of them Germans and did the lads give them a cheer – it's a wonder you didn't hear it over on this side.

Well, it was all over in about half and hour and Eddie and I managed to get on board a destroyer and it wasn't long before we were making for England. Except for a few shells from the shore and two more Jerry planes it was like a pleasure cruise – thanks to the Navy – they were great – they treated us like lords coming over.

But we were pleased to see those White Cliffs – well, I ask you, were we pleased?…

Throughout the Dunkirk evacuation the RAF had only played a limited role due to the limitations of the range of the aircraft at their disposal as well as the urgent need to protect the home front. Nevertheless, their contribution played a large part in the success of the operation, their valour being officially recognised by Churchill in a speech. In total the RAF lost over 100 aircraft during the evacuation. But throughout the months of July and August the RAF would be at the very forefront of the defence of the British Isles.

Many soldiers, sailors and airmen were confronted with their own mortality on an almost daily basis. Some chose to compose a final letter home to be delivered to their loved ones if they were killed in action. Pilot Officer Michael A. Scott wrote the following to his parents in August 1940.

Torquay
21/8/40

Dear Daddy,
As this letter will only be read after my death, it may seem a somewhat macabre document, but I do not want you to look on it in that way. I have always had a feeling that our stay on earth, that thing we call 'Life', is but a transitory stage in our development and that the dreaded monosyllable 'Death' ought

not to indicate anything to be feared. I have had my fling and must now pass on to the next stage, the consummation of all earthly experience. So don't worry about me; I shall be all right.

I would like to pay tribute to the courage which you and mother have shown, and will continue to show in these tragic times. It is easy to meet an enemy face to face, and to laugh him to scorn, but the unseen enemies Hardship, Anxiety and Despair are very different problems. You have held the family together as few could have done, and I take off my hat to you.

Now for a bit about myself. You know how I hated the idea of War, and that hate will remain with me for ever. What has kept me going is the spiritual force to be derived from Music, its reflection of my own feelings, and the power it has to uplift the soul above earthly things. Mark has the same experiences as I have in this though his medium of encouragement is Poetry. Now I am off to the source of Music, and can fulfil the vague longings of my soul in becoming part of the fountain whence all good comes. I have no belief in a personal God, but I <u>do</u> believe most strongly in a spiritual force which has the source of our being, and which will be our ultimate goal. If there is anything worth fighting for, it is the right to follow our own paths to this goal and to prevent our children from having their souls sterilised by Nazi doctrines. The most horrible aspect of Nazism is its system of education, of driving instead of leading out, and of putting State above all things spiritual. And so I have been fighting.

All I can do now is to voice my faith that this war will end in Victory, and that you will have many years before you in which to resume normal civil life. Good luck to you!

Mick

Scott survived his initial training and deployment in 1940 and so the letter was never delivered. In 1941 he chose to draft a new version.

Royal Air Force Station
Bildeston 261. Suffolk
7/5/41

Dear Mother and Daddy,
You now know that you will not be seeing me any more, and
perhaps the knowledge is better than the months of uncertainty
which you have been through. There are one or two things which
I should like you to know, and which I have been too shy to let
you know in person.

Firstly let me say how splendid you both have been during
this terrible war. Neither of you have shown how hard things
must have been, and when peace comes this will serve to knit the
family together as it should always have been knit. As a family we
are terribly afraid of showing our feelings, but war has uncovered
unsuspected layers of affection beneath the crust of gentlemanly
reserve. Secondly I would like to thank you both for what you
have done for me personally. Nothing has been too much
trouble, and I have appreciated this to the full, even if I have
been unable to show my appreciation.

Finally as a word of comfort. You both know how I have
hated war, and dreaded the thought of it all my life. It has,
however, done this for me. It has shown me the realms where
man is free from earthly restrictions and conventions; where he
can be himself playing hide and seek with the clouds, or
watching a strangely silent world beneath, rolling quietly on,
touched only by vague unsubstantial shadows moving placidly
but unrelenting across its surface. So please don't pity me for the
price I have had to pay for this experience. This price is
incalculable, but it may just as well be incalculably small as
incalculably large, so why worry?

There is only one thing to add. Good luck to you all!

Mick

Tragically this letter was delivered following Michael Scott's death on 24 May 1941 while serving with No. 110 Squadron, Bomber Command. He was one of seven children, four sisters and three brothers. His brother Mark, who is mentioned in the earlier letter, was also killed during the war when he was lost at sea in 1942.

With the success of the German *Blitzkrieg* and the occupation of much of mainland Europe by 1941 the Phoney War seemed a distant memory. Although the Battle of Britain had thwarted any tentative German plans for an invasion of the British Isles there had been few other successful Allied actions and with the continuous bombing of the Blitz the war was fought as much on the home front as it was on the front lines. Many British soldiers were desperate to do their part to help to turn the tide and Ernie Probst of the Royal Artillery was no exception.

My own sweet Winifred,
Sunday afternoon and I am writing this in the sitting room down-stairs listening to Leslie Sarony on the radio.

These last two days have been horrible, raining all the time. It has made everything very miserable but I guess it is nowhere near so miserable as it must be in London.

I heard that the last few days have seen the Jerry over London very early and I have been rather worried about you not being home before they started. I pray every night that you may be kept safe and unharmed because I cannot bear to think of you hurt.

Things seem to be stirring up in this war business and the sooner we can have a good crack at Hitler the better I shall be pleased, so that we can be over with it all as soon as possible.

Sometimes I think that all this war makes life only the more worth living. The future holds forth such hopes of peace and security that it almost becomes an honour to have participated in the great struggle. I hope I live to see the end of it all and I'm not being miserable in bringing that into it.

I get impatient waiting for the time we can set up house together again and the very prospect of it almost justifies the war.

Well, I've been philosophising long enough… I love you, so looksee after yourself.

Yours forever & ever & ever,
Ernie
xxxxxxxxxxxxxxxxxxxxx

Probst's wishes were only partially fulfilled. He continued to serve with the Royal Artillery and rose to the rank of captain until the landings at Salerno in 1943 as the Allies launched their first amphibious assault on mainland Europe. The operation was a success but tragically Ernie Probst was killed and he did not live to see its successful outcome.

A key defensive position within the Mediterranean prior to the invasion of Italy was the island of Malta. With Axis and Allied armies battling for control of North Africa, British control of the island ensured that Axis supplies from Europe to North Africa could be attacked en route. The German High Command was quick to realise Malta's strategic significance and from 1940 until 1942 the island came under sustained aerial attack. Flying Officer Geoff Stillingfleet was a British pilot based on the island as part of the defence contingent. In a detailed letter home to his parents written over a two-day period he described the virtually daily attacks to which the small island was subjected.

26/6/41
148 Squadron
RAF, H.Q., M.E

Dear Mum and Dad,

In addition to the numerous letters, cards and airgraphs I write, I usually send you a long letter once a fortnight. They, unfortunately, will take considerably longer to reach their destination, but nevertheless, I know, be very welcome.

I am going to start this letter with a few words about Malta. It is no secret that Malta has been very heavily bombed and it is about this that I am going to talk. I am told that the tiny island of Malta has received more air-raids than any other place in the war, this I can quite believe, indeed, we had an average of four a day. Before leaving England, my attitude, as you know, was one of reckless contempt towards all air-raids. However, after a few days in Malta contempt changed to respect. After six weeks there I have been an exceptionally fast runner, indeed I believe I could have rivalled even the Italians. I was capable of descending the air-raid shelters with an amazing speed and agility if not exactly with dignity (that came later with practice).

Jerry had a very unpleasant habit of, without warning, sending over sixty or seventy 'Stuka' dive-bombers, complete with a very large and very necessary fighter escort. Those fearful aircraft would then proceed to hurl their screaming missiles earthwards, causing considerable smoke, noise and dust, the former chiefly coming from the remains of burning German dive bombers. These attacks were annoying. Firstly, they scared us badly, exceedingly badly I might add; secondly they were always followed by a particularly long 'alert' caused by Jerry seaplanes searching for survivors round the coast of Malta, and finally bomb craters on the aerodrome had to be filled in and shrapnel removed from the runways.

My first experience of dive bombing was a very unpleasant one. I was caught in the open, the only available 'funk hole' being a sand-bagged machine gun post. Out of the sun there came formation after formation of bombers. I saw the first one enter its dive, saw its air brakes come on, and then saw the bombs leave the aircraft. I didn't wait for more, but ran. It is impossible to describe the next twenty minutes adequately. The sky above us was filled with white puffs of hundreds of exploding shells. Nothing you thought could fly through it, but down they came one after the other, unloading the deadly bombs. Many came down but never pulled out, hitting the deck with a load crash (one narrowly missed us), another I saw exploded in mid-air showering wreckage and flak over a large area. Would they never stop, everywhere there was flying and falling shrapnel, whizzing stones and the whirr of machine gun bullets, and above all this whistling, screaming, shrieking above all noise of our gunfire the never-ending, ear-splitting explosion of heavy bombs. Suddenly the gun-fire eased off, no longer could we hear the screech of diving aircraft or the higher pitched scream of falling bombs, the last aircraft had dropped its load and to our amazement we were still in one piece. In our proximity the only casualty was a gunner with a shrapnel wound in the shoulder. German losses we learnt later were twenty-three aircraft.

27/06/41

… During the moon periods Jerry and sometimes even the Italians honoured us with frequent visits. Our hospitality was such that he often came to stay. No, Jerry definitely didn't like Malta and he was only too pleased to jettison his bombs as soon as he possibly could…

I had a friend in Malta, a kind hearted, contented orange grower, a man with ill-feelings towards no one, yet a low flying Messerschmitt thought otherwise, he dived on him, as he was working and machine gunned him. A few days later he showed me the holes in the wall and a bullet; fortunately the pilot's aim was bad. The following day I saw the charred, mangled remains of a German pilot; the awful sight did not make me sick. I had very little pity towards him, the unmerciful. Sorry to have kept to one subject, but there are plenty more letters following.

Your loving son

Geoff Stillingfleet's squadron was evacuated from the island in 1941 after suffering high losses, although in his opinion his subsequent posting to North Africa was no easier with the trials of desert warfare. But it was to prove a brief sojourn and he was soon back on Malta. In April 1942 King George VI awarded the George Cross to the island 'to bear witness to the heroism and devotion of its people' in the face of the sustained assaults by the Axis forces. The siege itself would not be over until May 1943.

148 Squadron
RAF, H.Q., M.E
19/8/41

Dear Mum and Dad,
A friend of mine will very shortly be returning to England so I am writing this special letter for him to take with him. I say 'special letter' because as this will not be censored I shall be able to give you a good deal of information which otherwise I could not write.

In a letter written previously (it's enclosed with this) I have described the Malta air raids. Well these air-raids eventually drove us from the island; our squadron suffered more from air-raids than probably any other squadron in the war. It has been estimated that over 600 tons of high explosive was dropped on our tiny aerodrome. Anyway, March 26th saw us embarking on HMS *Bonaventure* bound for Alexandria, incidentally this was the last voyage she completed before being sunk.

We had six or seven days in which to settle down at Kahit which was to be our main base shared by 10 Squadron. On

April 5th a squadron detachment was sent out to form an advanced base in Libya. Eight lorry loads were sent out on the 100-mile journey; we followed several days later by air. I soon discovered that desert life was no picnic, drinking distilled seawater, which was hot and salty; it didn't quench our thirst but just kept us alive. There was nothing we could get that would quench our thirst, in fact we had a perpetual thirst which at nights almost drove us crazy. Thirst is a terrible thing, but the imagination is the worst; we would lay awake at nights thinking of milkshakes, lemonades, cider and ice cold water from mountain streams. In the day time we were nearly driven crazy by the terrific heat and thousands of flies. At night the lice, bugs and cockroaches tormented us and the sandstorms arose covering our mouths, noses and hair with fine sand... Our worst experience was when we force landed at El-Adim. El-Adim was an Italian aerodrome situated in a no-mans-land somewhere between an advancing enemy and retreating British forces. Actually most of the fighting was going on further north, but nevertheless there were plenty of Jerry patrols active. The situation wouldn't have been so serious but for the fact that we had smashed the tail wheel on landing. We stayed there two days, and a night, before we were able to get our kite in the air... We spent the time doing as much destruction as possible, shooting at the mess crockery with Italian rifles, and spraying the windows with machine gun bullets. We also painted rude pictures of Hitler and Mussolini on the wall.

After a week's rest we again went on detachment but this time back to Malta. We first flew to Alexandria where we spent the night. The following afternoon we flew via Crete and Sicily to Malta. We spent a very enjoyable fortnight in Malta, during which time we were raiding Tripoli. Tripoli was an interesting target inasmuch as it had as much A.A. fire as any place in Germany. A great deal of it was tracer; there was so much of it that one marvelled that anyone could fly through it and not get hit. On our first visit we bombed too low and we came back more in the nature of a flying pepper pot.

On May 8th we started and are still doing what must be the longest operations in the war; the operations I refer to were those on Benghazi, they were over four hours longer than the famous trips to Venice, Milan and Turin. These Benghazi trips took twelve hours flying broken by a brief halt at an advanced base for re-fuelling.

Just before the invasion of Crete we did a number of long operations to concentrations of enemy aircraft in Greece. These trips were ten hours and another two hours returning from the advance base. During the Crete invasion we were particularly busy, each night would see twenty heavy bombers over there. We had a terrible mission, to bomb then machine gun the enemy positions and also to drop medical supplies and ammunition to our troops. Of course these were not our only targets, we have raided Searparto, Rhodes Island, Derna, Gazala, Benino, Bardia, Bairut [sic], Allepo. Since leaving England I have flown over fourteen countries.

I am in a new crew at present, and it's one of the best crews in the squadron. Our captain has done 40 raids and has a DFC for a low level attack on the Kiel Canal. His speciality is dive-bombing. Slowly flying over a target is not so much a thrill as a strain, you just sit, make yourself as small as possible and watch the 'flak' coming up at you. Dive-bombing, however, is not such a strain but is just one minute of intense action and excitement. After dropping the flares, we approach the target at say 10,000 feet; the pilot suddenly shoves the stick forward and we hurtle earthwards at between 300 and 400mph. We pull-out of the dive at about 2,000 feet, sometimes much lower, and of course its then that we meet the trouble, every gun in creation seems to be firing at us. In a bright moon they can see us [at] the bottom of the dive so we gunners retaliate by firing at these ground defences and if they are Italian gunners they immediately stop firing and dive for shelter…

Operations are like many other things, when going out or over the target, I feel a little uneasy and I make up my mind that I hate it, and that I will give up the whole game as soon as I can, and yet on the return trip and when on the ground I decide I want to continue doing 'ops' as long as possible. Actually they must have a certain hold on me, they act rather like a stimulant or drug for when-ever I am on the ground for a few days, I start getting irritable, depressed and discontented…

Just a few final words, <u>don't worry</u>, it's not half as dangerous as it sounds. On the Corinth Raid, which was considered an exceptionally dangerous one, there were forty aircraft operating, thirty-two were dropping bombs and making low-level attacks to draw the fire away from the mine-laying aircraft. Total casualties, two people slightly injured by shrapnel. Remember also, if we ever should get hit, I can bale out in twenty seconds. Another thing, should I be reported missing the chances are I shall be a prisoner of war, or at any rate safe.

Well I don't think there is anything more to say. I hope you are all as well and happy as I am.

Your loving son

Ever since his arrival in North Africa in February 1941, Erwin Rommel, later known as the 'Desert Fox', had sought to go on the offensive against the British and Commonwealth forces. At the end of March 1941 he made his move. The Afrika Korps drove the British back and isolated and surrounded the Libyan port of Tobruk, starting what was to be an eight-month siege. Captain Gordon Clover served with the 149th Anti-Tank Regiment, Royal Artillery, and recorded life under siege in a detailed letter to a friend.

149 A. TK. Regt, RA
M.E.F.
14 Oct 1941

My dear Bill,
Your letter dated 5th September arrived safely. Thank you so much. It is grand to hear from you at any time and especially so under the present circumstances of my existence. I was very glad to hear that you and Rosemary are well and happy. I'm in the same condition of body and mind myself as a matter of fact!

Every condition of one's life that I have experienced so far has its [redeeming], amusing and enjoyable parts. I have come to find it a rule of life. Every time that things get worse life still remains humorous and even enjoyable when you think it is not going to be! Experiences such as this damned well help you not to dread anything.

Let me describe shortly my immediate surroundings. I am sitting at a [rough] table in a deep dugout built of sandbags and old ammunition boxes and covered with a great variety of scrap… It is dark. There is a hurricane lamp on the table giving a dim light and throwing strange, dark shadows on the walls [of] the canvas, indeed nothing can be seen clearly a few feet from the lamp. Rats are scurrying around the sandbags, sending trickles of sand down the earth walls… I am warm (winter is beginning)… Jerry Jones (who sends you his love) sits on the other side of the table playing what he calls 'golf' with a pack of cards. I have a packet of 'Woodhams' beside me (I have had a weakness for 'Woodhams' since about 1920 when I used to smoke them…) and my rum ration. The rum is good and strong and makes one tingle all over. Now doesn't that describe a happy situation for a fellow who is making himself live from day to day without worrying about the future?

We are 'in action' somewhere in a desert (I mustn't say which!). There are a variety of explosions – not near enough to cause any anxiety – there are machine guns going off intermittently. When things 'hot up' a bit, as they probably will in an hour of two, I shall pop my head out of the dugout to watch the streams of flames and coloured lights and tracer bullets. The firework display is often worth seeing and it is interesting to know in which sector it is happening (if not in one's own!) and then speculate what, if anything it signifies.

Now let me reassure you, if it is necessary, this may all sound alarming, but it isn't really, even to me, and I should know! It is amazing how few casualties there are, even when things are hottest. You are as safe in a dugout as slit trench as anyone can expect to be, and (I have <u>seen</u> it happen as well as heard of it happening numerous times) shells and bullets can be all over the place causing a great deal of noise, and yet no one [is] even hurt…

The things I do find a bit alarming, especially at night, are the landmines. They are everywhere and no one [here] knows exactly where they are. The anti-tank ones are not <u>supposed</u> to go off if a man treads on them. The British ones are probably fairly safe in this respect. But there are a lot of fancy ones which our troops hid in haste … and if you are near them they say it is unwise to breathe heavily!… Another of our lads volunteered to guide a truck loaded with some of our 'foreign allies' through a minefield close to us. He led it straight into a mine which exploded. He was knocked flat on his face, the truck was blown up and all the 'foreigners' jumped out, shouting and cursing in about six different languages!… Well, old boy, you know the rest…

All the best Bill, old man. See you both, I hope, before too long. The war can't last forever and we are bound to win! Cheerioh!

Your ever,
Gordon

LETTERS FROM THE FRONT

While the British position remained perilous in the Middle East, a new threat arose in Asia: Japan. Manchuria was occupied in 1931, followed by the outbreak of war with China in 1937 and border clashes with the Soviets in 1939. Following the outbreak of the Second World War in the west, Japan sought to take advantage of the colonial powers' weakness by occupying all of French Indochina in July 1941. The relentless Japanese advance had provoked an American embargo on supplying oil to Japan, a position followed by the British and Dutch authorities in the region. Japan had been pushing aggressively outwards in the region in search of the natural resources needed to maintain her growing empire and, deprived of access to vital raw materials, decided to take what they needed by force and launched a concerted attack on the US naval base at Pearl Harbor and Dutch and British colonial possessions in the region in early December 1941.

Lance Corporal John Wyatt served with the 2nd Battalion, East Surrey Regiment, as the British struggled to contain the Japanese invasion of Malaya.

L/C J. Wyatt
D Coy
British Battalion
Malaya
Dec 21-41

Dear Mum & Dad & Elsie,
Hope this finds you as safe & as well as I am at present... Well mum before I start I would like you all to give thanks to God at church for the mercy he has shown not only to me but to the whole Battalion. 3 times I have just waited for death but with God's help I am still here. I have felt all along that with all your prayers God would keep me safe. I will only give you one instance of it. 10 of us were in a trench in a little ... village in the jungle, we were told last man last round, for we were

surrounded by Japs and as they were closing in on all sides some of the chaps were saying good-bye to each other, and I was really frightened at the thought of dying but as the minutes dragged on I resigned myself to it, then all of a sudden 3 aircraft came over, was they ours?…

Down came the bombs all round us, all we could do as we crouched there was to wait for one to hit us, but that good old trench saved our lives for it swayed and rocked with the impact, about one minute after they flew off believe it or not 4 tanks rumbled up the road, and [gave] our position hell. They flung everything at us, grenades, machine guns, but still we crouched in that little trench. We could not return fire for if we had showed our heads over the little trench the advancing Japs were machine gunning us, all of a sudden we heard a shout 'run for it lads', did we run, but the last I saw of the brave officer who said it, I shall never forget him, as we ran past him I saw him pistol in hand pointing it at the Japs holding them off while we got away. I haven't seen him since.

Anyway we waded through about a mile of padi, bullets whistling past all the time, but we reached the jungle and safety, then on to find the British lines, we tramped 30 miles that day living on jungle fruits. The fight started at 7 in the morning, we reached safety at 5 at night. Then for sleep, food, clean clothes, shave, for we had been at the front for 8 days without sleep or clean clothes, for we have lost everything, the Japs have got everything, all my personal stuff, photos, prayer book, everything, but thank God I am still here. Most of the Battalion reached safety but a lot of poor chaps are still missing, some of my friends too… Excuse pencil as this is the first chance I have had to write in a fortnight, so please make do with this. Keep smiling Elsie & I hope to see you next year xxxxxxx.

Well mum our worries are over, we have just been told that we are moving back, and our job is to stop looting so all our fighting is finished… We certainly knocked the old Japs about while we [were] there did we, we are miles better than them and we are sorry we wont be able to get another smack at them, I will have to hurry as the candle is burning out. So I will say good-bye for now, Dorrie xxxx. Jimmy, George, Mrs Ward, Church, rest of family and neighbours, please don't worry, God bless you all and keep you safe.

Your ever loving son,
John
xxxxxxxxx
xxxxxx
xxxxx

The Japanese steadily advanced down the Malayan peninsula until they came to the city of Singapore, the 'Gibraltar of the East' and a major British naval base. The city came under siege on 8 February 1942 and fell to the Japanese on 15 February 1942, described by Winston Churchill as the 'worst disaster and largest capitulation in British history'. Lieutenant Colonel Tim Taylor was one of the lucky few who managed to escape just before the fall of the city.

Colombo
10 March 1942

The thought of how much I have to tell you rather appals me. You know that I want to tell it to you and I love writing to you, but this will be a volume before I finish. I'll say straight away very briefly how I got here and then I'll go into details of the story.

I was ordered away, quite unexpectedly, on Friday, 13th February, heading for Java. We were bombed at sea next morning and made for the nearest land… We crossed that by slow stages, in various forms of transport and left the [*censored*] in a warship, and arrived at Java on the 22nd February. We had a few days there and then came on here – were 'torpedoed-at', but they went underneath! and I'm now awaiting orders for the next stage. A month ago I was resigned for what seemed inevitable – being a prisoner of the Japs – and now things are altered completely.

That's the bald outline and I'll try and fill in the details. I'd better start way back when I moved out of the Adelphi and went to share a house with Braithwaite and Shean…

We were getting a fair amount of bombing at night just then as there was a moon out and there again we were well off, as the town was the usual target and we could lie in bed and feel that we were reasonably safe. By day the bombing was increasing and they had an almost daily visit to the docks area. I spent many an hour in the Railway Station shelter waiting for things to clear.

Those evacuations! The more I saw of them the more I was pleased you got away when you did. As soon as I had finished my job of getting people off ships we were hard at it putting women on, usually by night to avoid what raids we could. The scrum of cards and people in those docks was indescribable and when an alert went I had many anxious moments before all was clear again. Bombs in those crowds would have caused absolute chaos, but we were fortunate and nothing happened till the last afternoon I was in Singapore, when there were some casualties unfortunately. Three of us were on a big ship when one went right down an open hold, but again we were lucky and merely felt a bit shaken…

February crept on and every day seemed more and more unreal with the Japs getting closer and closer to Singapore. Soon we had to leave the house as it was getting near the front line and we all lived in our offices after that. Shelling started then and the war was right on our doorstep. Our batteries fired all day and night from positions around Canning and the Jap used to bomb and shell them in return… Meanwhile my job was slowly closing down as all ships were getting away and if you ever got a couple of letters I wrote hurriedly and sent to you in those last days you'll have realised that it looked as if I was going to put people on ships until there were none left and then sit down and wait for the Japs. I didn't expect to go myself as there had been no talk of any of us leaving up till then.

Then on Friday evening at six o'clock Brig Lucas sent for Palmer, Brown and me, the three A/Qs, and said, 'the hunt is nearly up chaps and before it all ends I want to thank you for your work and help. I'd like to get decorations for you, but I can't do that, but what I can do is to order you away.' I'll always remember that. The suddenness of it and the ray of hope that it brought. One felt that it was unfair for some to go and not others, but we couldn't help feeling that a chance was there for us to take and the thought of all it meant was simply wonderful. Anyway he went on to say that it was the General's order. Certain people had been selected, mainly specialists and some staff officers, and there was no question of refusal and we were to tell no-one else anything... We were only to take with us what we could carry ourselves, which meant leaving practically everything behind, but that mattered very little in the circumstances. I already had my kit packed, ready for incarceration!...

Leaving Canning without being able to explain one's orders to those who were staying were very difficult... Poor Janak... He would arrive next morning to clean my buttons and find me flown and of course he would feel that I had hopped it and left them to fend for themselves. Only that morning I had gone round to the troops' camp near the station to talk to them, as the camp had had a stick of bombs on it that morning and some of them were feeling shaken and wanted to leave the camp and I had told them to stay put and that I would tell them if it was necessary to leave – and what must they think now?...

We assembled at the rendezvous in the Harbour and a party of us were sent on board a motor launch... The last sight of

Singapore was unforgettable. For days the sky had been covered in a black pall from the burning oil tanks on the island and that night it was handing low for miles about. All around was the glow of fresh fires, some in the harbour itself, making the scene as light as day, and here and there were the sudden flashes of our guns firing, or enemy shells bursting.

Java was our destination and there was conjecture as to how long our little boat would take over the journey. Our skipper later told us that he intended to run by night only, and to lie hidden by day, and that he thought we should be seven days on the trip. Water and food were limited and we should have to lie down where we could on the ship, so the trip looked like being anything but a pleasure cruise.

We slept somehow that night… In the morning we felt quite cheerful and enjoyed our coffee… Not long afterwards we saw the first planes and realised that we were far from being out of danger yet. We were amongst some islands, but showed no signs of lying up to hide, as the captain had said. Several more formations of planes went over us, but all left us alone. Soon, however, we realised from sprouts of water that our nearest neighbour in the convoy was getting it and after a while we went alongside to take off her casualties.

While alongside another formation came for us and we had the nastiest fifteen minutes I hope to experience. We cast off and went off from the other ship as fast as possible and thereby missed the first packet dropped by yards only… We were all ordered below to the cabin and there we lay on our tummies … listening to stuff coming down and feeling the boat zig-zagging as hard as she could… There [were] no life jackets on board and one hit would have put our cockleshell right under us, but we came out unscathed…

Back in the Middle East, a British attempt to relieve Tobruk in November 1941 proved successful, but the exposed British positions in the Gazala Line proved a tempting target for Rommel and he attacked once more at the end of May 1942. This attack broke the British position, sending them in a headlong retreat towards the Egyptian border; Tobruk fell on 21 June, and the whole British position in the Middle East appeared to be under threat.

Reverend Don Siddons was the Staff Chaplain at Eighth Army HQ during the retreat and this letter home to his wife, Edith, reflects his fears for the future.

From Rev V.D. Siddons C.F.c/aA.C.G. Eighth Army M.E.F. to Mrs V.D. Siddons
No 61. 25/6/42

Dearest,

Things are looking pretty serious here, and no-one knows how things are going to turn out.

It seems quite possible that at some stage or other I might become a prisoner. I hope it won't happen, and there may come a turn of the tide, or a stabilisation of the position, but we have to face possibilities.

If it does happen I shall do my best to stick it out and come home to you all in the end. If the enemy get Egypt and especially if they get Baku the war might last another 5 years, and how many people would survive 5 years in captivity is [the] question, as the food and sanitations are often poor, especially if the country we are living in is itself starving, and I imagine it is difficult not to get depressed in such conditions. On the other hand I should always have my work to do, whether prisoner or not, and I am not normally subject to depression, and am physically fit though 50…

You might not hear for some time if I became a prisoner but you must try not to become too worried. I am much more likely in this type of warfare to become a prisoner than any other type of casualty.

Whatever happens I know you will do splendidly for the children and will face life bravely. Don't in those circumstances wish for the end of the war without victory. That would be of no use to us for life would be worthless. Rather ten years of captivity and victory than an immediate return and defeat or an inconclusive result. Better to die a prisoner than that.

You have been wonderfully good to me; much better than I have deserved; and I have been completely happy with you, Darling. I want nothing better, when this job is over, than to finish my days in company with you; you have been the best pal a man could have.

I think the children should have all reasonable chances in regard to education, even if it means drawing on capital a bit. Remember that if we win the war you have ultimately fairly considerable resources. On my death you would get £1300 from my life insurance, or if I survive we get it in 1951. On the death of both my parents I think you should get between £2000 and £3000 but am not sure of the exact figure. You could always borrow from the bank (i.e. overdraw) on the security of either of the above, preferably and more easily the first… Barbara ought to get a good scholarship if she is to go to Cambridge, you ought not to have to pay a large proportion of that expense. Miss Jennings, Bill's headmistress, and Bill herself would all advise you well if a choice of university is open with various corresponding expenditures*… Education expenditure cannot always be met out of income and should be regarded as an investment…

It is useless to suggest anything for Anthony at present until we see how he is going to develop. An architect would be a

---

* 'Bill' was Edith's sister. Her name was actually Muriel, but was christened 'Bill' by her two older brothers who had wanted another brother. 'Bill' was Vice Principal at Cheltenham Ladies College.

pleasant, valuable, and I should think, prosperous career after the war for there will be much rebuilding to do for many years…

Now that is all, my Darling. Things may be all right and all this rigmarole for nothing, but it is as well to be prepared for all eventualities. I trust you absolutely, and love you entirely and always, my Beloved.

Your very own,
Don

While the British were in headlong retreat in the Far East and struggling to survive in the North African desert, the main way they were able to strike back at the Axis powers was through the strategic bombing campaign over occupied Europe and Germany.

Flying Officer Ron Williams flew as the navigator on an Avro Lancaster with Nos. 106, 61, 57 and 617 Squadrons, RAF, from October 1942 onwards.

Officers Mess
RAF Syerston
NOTTS
23/4/43 1.30pm

Dear Mum and Dad,

I have received both your letters now for which thanks. I am very sorry about the gap in mine – I was clear in my mind that I had written sometime over the weekend – until I woke up on Tuesday!…

I've got another trip done since I wrote – we took part in the varied attacks on Hitler's birthday. It was quite a nice trip as we could map read in the bright moonlight once we had crossed the sea. We did slightly different tactics which caused some fun on the way back (which I'll tell you about later) – but nothing dangerous. Bob has now only 13 more to do, and I hope to do the same – we have got to the stage of counting how many to go now, instead of how many we've done…

There is a new stunt on this afternoon, and we've all got to be in a running kit at 2pm to do a bit of a x country, so I'd better go and change.

Love to all,
Ron

Officers Mess
RAF Syerston
NOTTS
28/4/43 1.30pm

Dear Mum and Dad,
Here we are … lunch eaten, and time for a short letter before the post goes. Your letter and the *Guardian* arrived yesterday tea time, for which thanks. Regarding the 'number of trips' query, it is usual, when pilots complete their tour by doing 30 trips, to finish other members of the crew also if they are only two or three short. It is pretty well the rule in the case of navigators anyway, so, being two behind Bob, I hope to finish on 28. With these last two, it now needs only eleven – should be in single figures soon.

Friday afternoon saw us doing a cross country of two or three miles across the drome and down by the Trent. Having a hot bath on return alleviated some of the stiffness next day. Bob and I were changed in time for the bus and a short quiet evening in Notts…

Sunday was again a quiet night. In the afternoon the crew did a bit of clay pigeon shooting – it's the first I've done since ITW – and then Bob and I changed to go down to the WAAF officers' mess, to which we had been invited for tea. We stayed there until about 8.30 when we all went along to the dance in the NAFFI.

Monday of course there was considerable activity. The ace crews from each squadron were attacking first and I am almost certain we were the very first to bomb. Of course that means we get all the stuff at us as we go in. Some was close and we even got one hole in the mainplane. However, we were also first back! I don't suppose you'll see anything about last night's effort in the papers – very quiet, very short, but it counted as a trip!

Now they've given us a day off – a quiet afternoon is indicated and then probably out this evening.

The leave is still OK and I should be coming home Tuesday week. At the moment Vera and I are trying to arrange a couple of days at Bournemouth – at the weekend; but I expect she'll tell you if and when she prices it.

Time for food now,

Love to all,
Ron

Officers Mess
RAF East Kirkby
LINCS
18/7/44 9.30pm

Dear Mum & Dad,

I have just returned to my billet for an early night, having waited in the mess to hear the 9 o'clock news first. You will have heard it, or, if not, by some other means by the time you get this, and of the great offensive this morning. We were one of the thousand aircraft that 'attacked at dawn' this morning in 41 minutes. It was a marvellous sight to look all round and see Lancs and Halis everywhere; to see where your bombs were going for a change, and to look all round the cattle area (we did a circuit of Caen)…

We had an American Liberator crew up on liaison last Tuesday and they came to briefing and interrogation… On the Tuesday morning we flew with them in their Lib… I was in the waist gun position – a very good view. On taxying [sic] after landing their front wheel burst, so we flew them to their drome in our Lanc to pick up a new tyre, and had lunch there…

Yesterday morning we took the Group Captain up for practice bombing – he dropped the bombs – and then we went on to the American drome to pick up our crew that had been down there for liaison, and have lunch. Their boys were returning from a mission, and we went to the interrogation…

So long then,

Love to all,
Ron

In the month after he wrote this letter Williams was transferred to the famous 617 Squadron who had carried out the Dambusters raid in May 1943. He was promoted to flight lieutenant and took part in the first raid on the German battleship *Tirpitz* in September 1944 before being shot down at low level and killed during a raid on the Kembs Barrage near Basle on 7 October 1944.[*] He is buried in Durnbach War Cemetery in Germany.

The RAF's Bomber Command suffered some of the highest casualties of the war in proportion to the number of men involved, and the thought that they might not come back was never far from the minds of the men flying the heavy bombers over Germany. However, they

[*] Both the Dambusters raid and the raid on the Kembs Barrage were Allied missions to destroy the dams along the Rhine. The Dambusters famously used Barnes-Wallis' bouncing bomb in order to flood the Ruhr Valley, while the Allies attacked the Kembs Barrage in order to prevent the Germans from using it to flood the American troops who would be approaching the area.

had a job to do. Sergeant Reg Fayers, who flew as a navigator on Halifax bombers with No. 76 Squadron RAF, records these feelings in an unsent letter to his wife from the summer of 1943.

From Sergt. R.J. Fayers,
Sergeants Mess,
RAF HOLME ON SPALDING MOOR
To Mistress Phyl Fayers,
Ploughlane Dairy,
SUDBURY, SFK
SUMMER 1943 (Not posted).

Darling,
I've occasionally felt lately that should I not come home on leave next week, you would think it rather inconsiderate of me not to say a farewell and an excuse, so herewith both. (It's a grey evening and I've nothing to do but write and read, and I've already read.)

Lately in letters I've mentioned that I've flown by night and that I've been tired by day, but I haven't said that I can now claim battle honours – Krefeld, Muhlheim, Gelsenkirchen, Wuppertal and Cologne, I suppose I've been fighting in the Battle of the Ruhr.

But it hasn't felt like that. It doesn't seem like fighting to climb aboard an aircraft with your friends and climb to a space where the sunset seems infinite; to sit in a small space, and on the engine-noise background hear the everyday commonplaces spoken to you while you juggle with figures and lines to find God's intentions in the winds; to sit for a few hours at 20,000 feet working hard so that when Tom eventually says 'Bombs gone, photograph taken. OK Steve, fly away,' it doesn't seem anything more than part of the job, and a fresh course to be steered, this time for home. It's aloof and impersonal, this air war. One has no time to think of hell happening below to a set of people who are the same as you except that their thinking has gone a bit haywire. It's a fair assumption that when Tom dropped our bombs the other night, women and boys and girls were killed and cathedrals damaged. It must have been so. Were it more personal, I should be more regretting [it], I suppose. But I sit up there with my charts and pencils and I don't see a thing. I never look out. In five raids all I've seen is a cone of searchlights up by Amsterdam, with the southern coast of the Zuider Zee – where poor Ben Dove was found – and a few stars. And as far as humanity is concerned, I can't definitely regret that I've helped to kill German people.

The only thought that comes from the outside is when occasionally Gillie, the mid-upper gunner, says 'Turn to starboard, go…'. It might mean that out there in the darkness which you cannot even see, somewhere there is a night fighter with a German boy in it; and he may kill you. When Gillie or Reuben says 'Turn to starboard, go…', that quick weakening thought comes in – 'Maybe this is It.' But you never can believe it. It doesn't seem possible that what is so orderly and efficient a machine one second can become, within the next minute, a falling killing thing, with us throwing ourselves from it into a startling world of surprised chaos. But it can happen, and, I suppose, does happen to a lot of us. So far we've had two small holes in 'H' for Harry and nothing more. We have been very lucky. We have flown straight and high, dropped our bombs and come home to bacon and eggs, or maybe only beans on toast. But, so far, we have come home.

Should you ever read this, I suppose it will mean that I haven't. I can't imagine that. If I really could imagine it, I suppose I wouldn't fly. Or would I?

I really don't know.

But, darling, I could never live easy with the thought inside me that a struggle is going on in the world without me helping good old Right against the things so wrong that have got into our system. This world is a swell sort of place even now; there's

LETTERS FROM THE FRONT

so much beauty in it, such thrilling beauty. If a thing is really beautiful, through and through beautiful, it seems to me it is good. And it could be so much more so. I suppose really that is why I sit on our bombs and fly with them until we come to one more of Jerry's cities. Instinctively it seems I've come to help, first in destroying the bad old things, and then in rebuilding.

If you read this, I suppose there'll be no Simon in this world. But for those other worlds that will come, there will be Simon. And there will be other worlds, darling; there will be Simon. For them, I suppose, it is that I fly. That must be the answer, I guess. I struggle instinctively to be with you, walking so quietly by Brundon fields and Barnardiston hedges, eating enough lettuce hearts so clean and green for the two of us, being together in the excitement of our love, and in the quiet moonlit night when one wonders about God. That is the beginning of my new world, of all my new worlds.

The most real and living thing in the life that I've had has been you, Phyl Kirby. I have loved you so that I haven't words left to say. And I believe it's so much in the soul of me that it will always stay with me. I don't know what heaven I'll go to (the immodesty of the man) but I fancy something simple, with a river, and lots of green. And I know you'll be there. If there be a god – and there must be – and if there be a heaven – and there must be – then, too, there must be us. I'm afraid I really believe that, darling. I hope it doesn't sound too mystic or anything, but I do believe in always having you, and in new worlds.

I suppose that is why I have no personal fear of dying. It would be darned interesting, were it not that it might mean breaking an early date with you. And I'd rather take leave next week than the alternative, of course. Life is sweet, too; I'll have as much as I can.

So, if you ever read this, darling, I'm sorry if I had to break a date. It means keeping the next one the more certainly. And please don't be too sad. Together we've had more out of living than most people can reasonably expect. And if we had to stop sharing those wonderful things, perhaps it was better that it ended when our love was so strong and firm and young, and while we both had our own teeth. If I have to go to heaven, I'd rather go attractively, and still be able to play soccer.

Love me till then, darling,

Toujours a vous,
Reg

Reg Fayers was shot down during a raid over Frankfurt in November 1943, but luckily survived and spent the rest of the war in Stalag Luft 1.

Thoughts of mortality were not restricted to the air crew of Bomber Command; a common theme running through letters home is concern for the well-being of wives and children should the worst happen. Lance Corporal Fred Baker served with the Royal Corps of Signals in the Mediterranean. He wrote the letter below to his four-year-old daughter Patricia, full of words of advice for her should he not survive.

Sunday 4th Oct. 1942

My Darling Little Pat,
I have been thinking things over while waiting for my boat, & as I might not return I think it is only right that you should have a letter from me which you can keep, to remember me by. I am writing this assuming you are now grown up, as you will not receive this till then. I can picture you as a lovely girl, very happy with plenty of boy friends. I am finding it very hard to

write this as I may never see you in this stage. You have always been the pride & joy of my life. I have loved you more than my life at all times. As mother has told you perhaps I was always afraid of losing you. Now the tables have turned the other way & I might be the one to get lost. But do not let this upset you if this is the case, as the love for a father only lasts up to the time a girl finds the man she wants & gets married. Well darling, when this time arises I hope you find the right one & he will not only be a good husband to you, but will also make up for the fatherly love you have missed. At all times lovie be a pal to mother & look after her, do what you can to make her happy, as she has been, & always will be I am sure, the best little mother you will find on this earth. Don't be selfish or catty, remember there are others in the world as well as you. Try not to talk about people as this get you disliked. When the pulling to pieces start, walk out or turn a deaf ear, it will pay in the long run. Above all I want you to be a sport, to take up swimming, dancing & all games in life you can get so much fun out of. Mother, I am sure, will do her best for you & see you get all the instruction she can afford.

Always try to be a sister to Peter & John, they may pull your leg about different things but the best way after all is to ignore them & do what you can for them. You will win in the end & be the best of pals. Well darling there is no more I can say, but to look after yourself where men are concerned, be wise & quick witted & only believe half they say, of course, till you get the right one.

Remember me as your dad & pal who worshipped the ground you walked on. Please don't do anything that will upset mother, & I shouldn't like you to, I will close now my little ray of sunshine. Always loving you,

Your loving Father
xxxxxxxxx

Sadly, his premonition was to come to pass, and Baker was killed in the Dodecanese campaign of September–November 1943.

Reinforcements were flooding in to North Africa to make good the losses of the disastrous Gazala campaign and its aftermath. Although the British troops had held the line, large numbers of extra men and a great deal of materiel would be needed before Eighth Army could assault Rommel's men.

One of the divisions despatched to North Africa was the 51st (Highland) Division, which had been rebuilt after its loss in the Fall of France in 1940, and amongst its numbers was one of the better poets of the Second World War, John Jarmain. He served as an officer in the 61st Anti-Tank Regiment, and wrote the following poem that serves as an evocative description of his departure for the war in the desert. He sent the poem home as an addition to a letter.

Embarkation, 1942
In undetected trains we left our land
At evening secretly, from wayside stations.
None knew our place of parting; no pale hand
Waved as we went; not one friend said farewell.
But grouped on weed-grown platforms
Only a few officials holding watches
Noted the stealthy hour of our departing,
And, as we went, turned back to their hotel.

With blinds drawn down we left the things we know,
The simple fields, the homely ricks and yards;
Passed willows greyly bunching to the moon
And English towns. But in our blindfold train
Already those were far and long ago,
Stored quiet pictures which the mind must keep:

We saw them not. Instead we played at cards.
Or strangely droppèd asleep.

Then in a callow dawn we stood in lines
Like foreigners on bare and unknown quays.
Till someone bravely into the hollow of waiting
Cast a timid wisp of song;
It moved along the lines of patient soldiers
Like a secret passed from mouth to mouth
And slowly gave us ease;
In our whispered singing courage was set free,
We were banded once more and strong.

So we sang as our ship set sail,
Sang our own songs and leaning on the rail
Waved to the workmen on the slipping quay
And they again to us for fellowship.

He also wrote to his sister Kate about his arrival in Egypt and his feelings for the pregnant wife he left behind.

From Capt. J. Jarmain
(No 137983)
61st A/Tk Regt. R.A.
c/o Army Post Office
No 2005
June 30th 1942

Kate my love,
A new address for you to write on my letter at last as you see at the head of this sheet. In fact I have not arrived there yet but am on the way, and in any case I do not know where it is. At least the journey is a very pleasant and unwarlike interval between one job and the next, and as it lasts so long, with all its days alike and no change of

scene to show that we are moving, it is quite difficult to believe that I am bound for anything or anywhere. I suppose I do believe it in fact, but that seems not to affect my enjoyment of the trip, its warmth, amazing luxury, and above all its hours and hours of leisure…

If I thought that this isolation that I am enjoying now was to go on forever then I should immediately cease to enjoy it. But as it is I am loving it, loving the hours of the day, at last really able to see them as the [riveting] sheets of a notepad, clean and immaculate, and ready to receive whatever I may wish to put upon them. Strange how people are affected differently: many of those travelling with me are already impatient of the empty days, stretching before them… For me just the opposite is the case, the very emptiness of the days is their precious delight: what shall I fill them with? What shall I do? What shall I write poems about? War? Or flying fishes? Or English fields? – What shall I read? – Montaigne? Or Lewis Carroll? Or Shakespeare?…

I have said that I am happy on this ship, and maybe you have wondered, do I not mind leaving Beryl then? Leaving her, the goodbye, was like something happening under an anaesthetic. Travelling away from her in the train was the awakening, very miserable… Afterwards, when I get to shore and I know that she is out of reach, it will not be good. Being separated is one thing, bearable at any rate because it must be borne, but being so far that I know that I am in no way [near her], that is not pleasant.

And she is to have a child about August 8th. That for her is good, I think: it gives her a very definite hold on things and will give her duties to perform.

I wish I had not started writing about her. It has made me think about her and about the good years we should have had together, which now we will be missing. How many millions [of] lives this war has taken from their just causes and appropriated wholly to itself!

Funny, for I have, before beginning this to you, written eleven pages to her, without that bitterness against fate re-arising.

And that bitterness must be in nearly every one of us, German or Briton, Italian or American: only the Jap is incomprehensible…

God bless, and write to me, my love,
John

These new arrivals were joined by a new army commander, Lieutenant General Bernard Montgomery, and were destined to be blooded in the climactic battle of the Desert War, El Alamein. Montgomery spent the next two months training his new command for the task of breaking through Rommel's defensive positions, and on 23 October he launched the battle of El Alamein with Operation *Lightfoot*. The four infantry divisions of XXX Corps advanced against the well-prepared Axis defences, while to the south the armour of X Corps struggled to break through the German minefields.

Following a week of bitter fighting, Montgomery reorganised his forces for another push, Operation *Supercharge*, with the 2nd New Zealand Division tasked with carrying out the first attacks. Attached to them were the men of the 8th Battalion, Durham Light Infantry, part of the 151st Brigade. Private John E. Drew, who served with the battalion, wrote to a bereaved family about the death of his friend in the battle.

Pte J.E. Drew
5442875 M.T. Sect
H.Q. Coy
8 DLI
M.E.F.
21/5/43

Dear Friend,
Just a line in answer to your request for a little information in regard to you late brother Joe.

As you already know I was with him on that night, well, let's not bring back a sad moment but just imagine he's still with us and try to describe a little of what happened before.

Joe and I were both in the Cornwalls until we came out here, and then we were drafted into the Durhams with whom we went up the blue* and as soon as we got up there we were allotted trenches which as you can probably guess were next to one another and in which we would sit and talk during the day and from where I learnt quite a lot from him about your family...

Joe and I were on guard when we first got any inkling there was a push about to begin, and I cannot put into writing the excitement there was...

At last dawn approached and we stopped to get breakfast, and it was after breakfast that we were informed of the job that was before us and, I must admit that the officer who spoke to us spared us no details in telling us what to expect and what was expected of us, and I can say that by then, and not without reason [we were] beginning to shake a little in our shoes, it was here that we were told of the Barrage the RA were going to put down and this news I am sure helped us through the next few hours.

Now comes the part of my letter that has kept me so long from writing to you.

We were now dressed ready to move to a forward position and from where we were to have what was to prove our last meal together, actually it was Bully stew with Biscuits with jam, which we ate sitting together behind a mound of earth at about four o'clock in the afternoon, then after a short rest we got dressed again and were once more on the move, we seemed to have been marching miles in thick deep sand and it is a march I shall never forget for Joe and I both shared a Bren Gun between each of us carrying it for about a mile and a half at a time and with the load we were carrying it sure was hard going.

---

* Going 'up the blue' was British slang for going on operations in the desert.

Well at last we halted and were formed ready for the big push which we knew would be the turning point of the war, we layed [sic] there for quite a while and after the sweat of the march we were beginning to shiver… We only had KD on, so we cuddled up together to keep warm, and you can believe me Sardines had nothing on us.

It was here we had an issue of rum and nothing was ever more welcome, in fact we felt ten times better for it.

As we were lying there the order came to take up positions and everybody was keyed up, and it was a surprise when we were told to fix bayonets.

We moved up a few yards and then the next thing we heard was a crescendo of guns which shook us at first, we were now off and though we had to keep apart Joe and I kept in touch with one another till we were held down by machine gun fire.

Things looked pretty grim here and it was only the audacity of an NCO that got us out of it and which cost him an arm, by this time Joe and I had got our gun going again and we began to advance with the section, the next thing I knew was a tremendous crash behind us and as I fell forward I caught a glimpse of Joe going down, picking myself up I discovered that except for a few scratches I was OK. I then walked over to Joe and found much to my regret that there was nothing I could do for him and looking around I found what had been the cause of it all, one of the Jerry Panzers had feigned dead and was just going to move off. I then picked up the gun and though I must admit I was pretty mad by this time I let him have a full magazine and I am pretty certain he never lived to tell the tale.

After we had finished with our little part in the great scheme Montgomery had so successfully planned we came back to a few miles behind the front and my platoon officer informed me after we had been there a few days that he has been back and seen where our boys had been buried but though he tried, he was unable to let us go to see their graves, but I am sure they had a decent burial.

I am afraid this is all I can tell you at present but I will try to write you some more later on.

I will now close hoping you will understand and forgive me for not writing sooner.

I remain yours
Truly,
J.E. Drew

Trooper John Bassam, who served like John Jarmain in the 51st (Highland) Division, was wounded in the battle and wrote home to his family about his experiences.

10602041
Tpr F. Bassam
(A) Squadron
51st Recce Rgmt
Recce Corps
M.E.F.
2-11-42

Dear Father,
At last after such a long time I have found time to write a few lines to let you know that I am still <u>OK</u>. Well you will I suppose have been following the ME news with a lot of interest wondering if I happened to be in the battle or not, well our Squadron were right in [it] at the start [and] before we had time to realise what was on we were fighting it. Is just hell out here although all is going to scale. I am resting at present and am going to base tomorrow. I have heard nothing of the other Whitby boys but

say nothing to their people… I am deaf in my right ear but thank the Lord the only thing like a wound was on my seat, just a scratch so don't worry. The MO says my hearing will come back, at any rate my left ear is OK now. I was blown up time after time and lost my speech for a while. Quite a lot of our boys were lost but most of us live to fight another day. We hope to make this the end out here, the chances are good, we hope to be home by Spring. Well I must close and don't worry more letters for you when I get time. Cheeryo, keep smiling.

Your son,
John

Flight Lieutenant Chadwick served with the Desert Air Force during the Tunisian campaign, and describes his reactions to the victory at El Alamein after all the hard fighting that had taken place in the desert over the previous two years, as well as the aftermath on the battlefield.

F/LT E. Chadwick
107968
HQ, RAF, ME
211 Group
24th May, 1943

My dear,
From time to time in my letters I have said I would write my experiences during the recent campaign from Alamein to Tripoli or to what we later found out was our final destination – Tunis. Actually in these early days we had Tripoli the target as this [was the] prize, and had been before the eyes of the Eighth Army, from the early days when the Desert Rats first

whipped the Wops. Although my experiences date earlier than Alamein I will leave them until later as the grim days of the retreat had been put behind us and we had stopped the enemy. We were all ready now to hit back and hit him good and hard, it had taken us four months to do this – months and weeks of dreary life in the desert with the usual bombings by night and occasionally when Jerry got perky a party or two during the day. But for now it was the 23rd of October, the day we had all been waiting for. The day had been almost normal, nothing extraordinary had happened and the dusk came on with the sun dropping into a dark cloud that spread over the western horizon making a blood red flame that died away to a cold dark blue as the moon rose in the east to shed its white light on the scene which we were all expecting to begin. I remember as I saw the night draw on thinking what thoughts are in the minds of the men in the desert at this time. As zero hour approached we all listened to hear the barrage and dead on time it began and rumbled and crashed to wake up the silence of the limitless darkness of the desert... The following day the RAF took a hand and bombed and strafed with good heart all doing our best to help to give Jerry a licking just to change his continual run of success. At night the artillery opened up again pounding a way for the infantry to lever out the Hun who was still soft from the day's bombing. During the night rain fell and we all wondered if our efforts would be diminished by its effect ... but I think the Army were too full of fight to stop for the rain...

In our unit there were a matter of 300 men with about 30 officers and the whole lot could move off at about one hour's notice and travel any distance and set up in the same time. This mobility was a splendid effort by both the organisers and the men who had the carrying out of the move... Our unit was, furthermore, divided into two parties, so that one party could move forward, become operational and then the rear party could come up to us or leapfrog over us and thereby be in a position to continually control the planes and hammer the enemy without let up… During these days and nights the Army had been pounding and nibbling at the enemy's positions and we were anxious to hear that his line had been broken, so we could start away after him. This happened on the 3rd November, we were giving all we could from the air and the line was breaking slowly but surely. The advance party were on two hours' notice to move and we were all ready to go. It was not until the 5th November that we moved… Everyone was light hearted and happy to be doing his bit in the show that was to repay us for the ignominy of the recent retreat… As we went along we gradually came upon the signs of war, guns and troops moving back up, and it was here I saw the body of some high officer being brought back from the front. Modern war deals hardly with high and low, front line troops and headquarters staff are all subject to instant attack… As we passed out of the defences we came upon the war in all its horror. Apparently the Germans and Italians had made a desperate attempt to close the gap here but had been wiped out by our guns and stiffies were lying about all alongside the road and deep in the desert. To us of the RAF who had been accustomed to death in less numerical severity the widespread ghastly scene was appalling and shook us somewhat. War is like that, one gets callous and indifferent by degrees…

The following morning we were roused at dawn and moved off hoping to get to our destination [where] we could have a meal in comfort. On along the road we went until we came across tanks and vehicles which were still burning, at one point the road was blocked by an Italian vehicle which had been newly shot up as the crew were still lying around on the road. This was after we had been travelling an hour and seemed to me to be rather near, in fact too near, the battle … however we continued until a Bren gun carrier came rushing over the desert to head us off … and I never saw vans, lorries, wagons and trailers turn around quicker ignoring the danger of mines alongside the road and head back like 'the clappers of hell'…

Well, that is my story of the desert which I hope you enjoyed. It was tough in parts but one met some grand fellows during the war. Some did not complete the show & some will never see their homes again but the best of the people I have known in the service have been in the desert.

Despite the British success at El Alamein, there was still a great deal of hard fighting left to do in North Africa as the Axis troops slowly retreated across Libya and Tunisia, fighting rearguard actions all the way. At the same time a joint Anglo-American expeditionary force under the command of General Eisenhower landed in Vichy French Morocco and Algeria on 8 November 1942, in an action known as Operation *Torch*.

By 7 May 1943 the Allies had entered Tunis, and eight days later the Axis forces in North Africa surrendered, with some 230,000 men going into captivity. David Philips served as an officer with the 7th Battalion, Oxfordshire and Buckinghamshire Light Infantry, and wrote to his mother describing one of the victory celebrations following the successful conclusion to the campaign.

7th Oxf & Bucks Lt. Infty
M.E.F.
2.6.43

Dear Mummy,

Many thanks for several letters recently received; I have answered some of them in a longer letter which may take some time to reach you. As you can see, the faithful typewriter still flourishes – although under fire it was hot touched – and although a few small springs are broken and one or two screws missing it still works almost as well as ever.

Today we had a big parade in the local town for the official celebration of the King's birthday. We sent a contingent of about 80 from the Regiment, with 3 officers, of whom I was privileged to be one...

Then while the salute of twenty-one guns was fired, I thought how strange it was to be standing there as conquerors, surrounded by the symbols of Roman might, and how hollow now seemed Mussolini's boast of eight million bayonets to defend his Empire. I could not but feel awed by the circumstance, and not a little thankful for the opportunity of participating in the exposure of that hollow boast: how truly has Nemesis followed hubris once more! But perhaps the strangest part of all was the reception accorded to us by the populace. They clapped. At first I was overcome by a sense of the ridiculous, and could scarcely control my laughter: do you remember how Peter Fleming comments on the strange impressions created by seeing the citizens of a South American town clap their soldiery? In the same way I felt there was something ludicrous in this applause: as if they thought our ability to march, and present arms, were something wonderful. But afterwards I was the more struck by realising that applause from a conquered populace for their conquerors was surely an odd phenomenon, and even now we ask ourselves why it was accorded: was it just excitement at the pageantry? Perhaps; or was it fear of reprisals if they remained silent? Hardly likely: or are we genuinely welcomed? I do not know the answer.

The march past which followed was impressive – I am told – and successful, and many of my men were as thrilled by it as I was; and a very important general has given the Regiment high praise for its prowess and smartness...

Love to all from
David

However, the war in the Mediterranean was far from over and on the night of 9/10 July 1943 the Allies launched Operation *Husky*, the invasion of Sicily, and then from 3 September British and Canadian forces began landing on the Italian mainland itself, with the Americans following on the 9th. Despite the initial success of the landings, and the Italian surrender, the Allies became bogged down in front of the German defensive lines that stretched across the Italian peninsula, the most impressive of which was the Gustav Line that contained the town of Cassino as its key position. This town, dominated by the famous Benedictine monastery above it, was the scene of bitter fighting from January 1944 onwards, as the Allies sought to break the stalemate and take the city of Rome with a frontal assault on the Gustav Line and an amphibious landing behind the German front line at Anzio. After months of hard fighting at both Cassino and Anzio, the British Eighth and American Fifth armies finally broke through the German positions and beyond the bridgehead. The US Fifth Army pushed on to Rome, which was captured on 4 June 1944, instead of pursuing the retreating German forces. There was to be plenty more hard-fighting in Italy, but the first stage of the campaign was at an end.

Following the Allied invasion of Italy in September 1943, the Italians signed an armistice with the Allies which was announced on 8 September. German forces rapidly disarmed and took over the positions occupied by their erstwhile allies, but the armistice also gave opportunities to escape to the many Allied prisoners of war who had been captured in North Africa and were now held in camps across Italy.

Gordon Clover served with the 149th Field Regiment, Royal Artillery, until his capture at Tobruk. His letter describes his arduous journey to freedom.

28 Sept 1944

My dear Bill,

I have been thinking of you, of all three of you, and wondering how you are. I'm going to try and give you in this letter a short account of how I got back after the armistice with Italy, as I expect you want to hear a few details. There are plenty of others who had a more exciting time but what happened to me was quite exciting enough for your ears. I got clear of the camp after the armistice without incident. The Huns came to take us once but we had wind of their approach and got clear with a few minutes to spare and they hadn't enough men to scout the whole countryside for us. That was in northern Italy within a week's walking of the Swiss [portion], which I was much tempted to make for. However, I set out to walk south with another officer. We walked and walked and then some, always in the mountains ... across county roughly south west. We swapped uniforms with some filthy ragged civilian clothes, begged food as we went from the peasants and lived mostly on bread and [grapes]. After about six weeks we must have covered about 500 miles and with a zig-zag, cross country course...

On the whole the peasants were friendly and helpful though fearful (penalty for helping ex-POWs was death). I could speak the language fairly well but of course with my accent and appearance could not very well pass for an [Italian]! Then twenty miles from the line, we got caught again by the Huns. They were getting more and more numerous as we got close to the line and it was hard to dodge them and the line being stationary made it harder to get through. We spent some very unpleasant days staying in a dungeon well south of Rome and of course got covered with lice. Then we were put on a train for Germany, locked in cattle trucks with a bucket and a bale of straw. We took a poor view of this and a poor view still when the RAF came and bombed the train. However, there was a spot of confusion and … I managed to nip off and hide in an air raid shelter with a lot of civilians. Then I got into the mountains again alone and spent a couple of [nights] on a pile of bracken in an old shack high up in the mountains hoping for the line to move a bit. With the winter it was getting terribly cold so I continued … to Rome. There I wandered from refuge to refuge till I found a permanent cellar where I hid for few months like a troglodyte until the Allies arrived in Rome. That time in Rome was the worst of all. I had a bed but food was scarce and I had to stay hidden almost the whole time… However it all ended well and here I am, still on leave, after two months!…

We'll have plenty to talk about when we meet… Love to R. Look after yourself, Bill, and come back home as soon as you can! It's nearly over! Another letter soon to follow.

All the best, yours ever,
Gordon

In the Far East, the British had been forced out of the majority of their colonial possessions by the Japanese onslaught. Hong Kong, Malaya, Singapore and Burma had all fallen, and only India was left, but was under threat of Japanese invasion.

The British sought to rebuild their forces in order to wrest back their colonies from the Japanese occupier, which resulted in the formation of the famous Fourteenth Army in October 1943.

Freddie Ranken was a sergeant in the Royal Army Pay Corps based at Meerut in India, and wrote back to his wife's family in England full of anxiety about the situation at home.

British Army Pay Office (RA Sgts Mess)
Meerut, Indian Command
26th August 1944

Dear Willie,

This is a letter that has been about to be written on a number of occasions but although I received yours on 23 July it is only now I am sitting down to write this as I have a day off on medical grounds. I was off duty Wed and Thurs as well. I have worried badly over the past couple of weeks since hearing of poor old Edie's new trouble, being bombed out and have not had any details yet to ease my anxiety…

Your sample of summer weather, no rain till the end of May and then tons of it with cold as well is just like England at its most inconsistent worst. So you had your overcoat on for the 21 June and a fire too. Here we are in the worst part of the Indian summer, August, September, when we get the rains (monsoon) well and truly upon us and the heat still continues, so we are in a stifling atmosphere at times.

Glad you have enjoyed my various descriptions of places I have been to… Of course since your letter was written the whole course of the war has changed completely and Jerry may well be out of the war before the end of the year. The Russians are doing well now with Romania changing sides and Bulgaria packing in, while our two campaigns in France are both making wonderful headway.

I see you mention big changes on the White Hill … there certainly will be some changes to see when I get back but the one concerning me most at the moment is the loss of our home, or rather waiting to hear how much is lost. I have not had any details from Edie yet. Dad I hear is incapacitated from writing as he has his right arm in a sling, but I have written to him telling him I don't expect any replies from him for a while. Your hours of work don't give you much chance for a week-end, and fire watching duties don't help a bit. I guess you fall asleep at all sorts of odd times when you can... I certainly agree with you that the sooner this bloody war is over the better... Let us hope it does not go on much longer... I must get rid of this wretched letter or I will miss the mail.

Cheerio,
Freddie

The Fourteenth Army became popularly known as the 'Forgotten Army' owing to the lack of recognition its exploits received throughout the longest land campaign of the war.

Harold Upton served as an NCO in the 1st Battalion, Seaforth Highlanders, which was based in India and Burma throughout the war. He wrote a series of letters to his girlfriend, later fiancée, expressing his hopes for 1944.

2828228 L/Sgt H.E. Upton
M.T. Section
1st Bn. The Seaforth Highlanders
India Command
January 1st 1944

Dearest Jenny,
I have been disappointed in my expectations to find several letters of yours waiting for me on my return as none have come for three weeks. However Jenny today I received your airgraph greetings which brought me much happiness and I feel sure that there will be letters on the way; mails for everybody have been very poor lately. I have not had any other letters either.

Well Jenny the New Year celebrations were a vast improvement on the Christmas do and everybody seems to have had a good time. I did not go to bed until about four o'clock this morning but did not have to be carried to it; I must confess that I was not feeling too good this morning.

There is so much I would like to say to you Jenny and I hope that you will not think I am still under the influence, I am as sober as a judge. I hate hinting at things and in my recent letters I have not done anything else, mostly due to the fact that I am afraid that your answer may be no. I confessed to you before that I loved you but was not a free man but now that I am free of all promises I find it difficult to tell you just how much I love you. Can I hope dear Jenny that you may be able to care enough for me to marry me when things get back to normal? We have not been able to see much of each other but we have exchanged many confidences in our letters and think we have a pretty good idea of what the other is like. Will you make an old man happy Jenny and say yes? I know your heart was elsewhere but perhaps in time you could forget and I know I would do all I could to make you happy. It is a lot to ask you to risk and marriage is said to be a gamble but I am sure that you would not find the life we would have to lead very trying; it may be a bit lonely at times but it has its compensations. Don't think that you are second best, it was just bad luck that I didn't meet you sooner and I don't think you would hold this against me. You have no idea Jenny how happy you make me with any little endearments in your letters, think how much happier you will make me if you say that you will marry me; I promise I will never give you cause to regret it.

If only this war would end soon and I could see you perhaps I could tell you better how much you mean to me but all the same I do believe you have a good enough opinion of me to know that I would not love you just to pass the time and that if you can't return it you will not let it make any difference to our friendship.

Perhaps this is a very poor way of telling you how I feel about you but I am no poet Jenny and what I lack in words I make up for in feeling. Do try to make 1944 the happiest year ever for me dearest one, I know you want to see me back but it would be a much better homecoming if you were waiting for me with open arms. I will write again soon Jenny and hope some of your letters arrive tomorrow. All my love and many kisses,

Yours ever,
Harold

Sadly, Harold Upton lost his life during the battle of Imphal in April 1944 as the Fourteenth Army repulsed a Japanese attempt to invade India.

Ever since the evacuation from Dunkirk in 1940, the Allies had been looking for a way to return to the Continent and by the summer of 1944 preparations for this second front were complete. A vast Allied armada crossed the English Channel on 6 June 1944: D-Day.

Bob Connolly served as an NCO with the 8th Battalion, Rifle Brigade, part of the 11th Armoured Division that landed on Juno Beach on 13 June 1944 and took part in the vicious battles around Caen between June and August. He wrote a series of letters to his wife both before and after his departure.

6969573 Cpl Connelly, R.W.
'H' Coy, 8th Rifle Brigade
A.P.O. England
9-6-44

My own darling wife Sheila,
Hope sweet that my letters wont take too long going through the various stages, and if a few days elapse between them don't worry honey. [It] will no doubt be rather difficult at times,

but believe me dearest I'll write as often as possible, please sweetheart write as often as you can, for hearing from you will be such a grand tonic, doesn't matter if they are very short, any little thing you do will be refreshing and interesting news to me.

Everything is OK honey, food good and plenty of kip, all the boys are in the best of health and spirits are very high…

Sweetheart we have been very lucky the last few weeks, [I'm] so glad that we saw so much of each other, I've been wonderfully happy and have been walking on air, our marriage has been and always will be such a marvellous partnership. Lucky Connelly they call me, I certainly have been in love, thank you so much honey for deciding to spend your life in partnership with me. Five years now dearest, and I am more in love with you now than I ever dreamt was possible in my wildest dreams.

Just in case my letters get held up, I'll take this opportunity of wishing you all the very best on your birthday, such a pity we can't spend it together, but honey you know I'll be thinking of you whatever the circumstances I'm in, loving you with all my heart, soul and strength as always. Please buy yourself something very special for me, don't think of the expense, for on your next birthday after this we will be together I feel certain, the war will be over and I'll be able to select you something really special myself.

Must say cheerio now honey, look after your dear self, my heart is with you, and don't worry about anything, everything is going to be OK. Forgive this being rather short, I'll be able to give you more news soon.

God bless you my precious, all my love and kisses are for you only,

Bob

xxxxxxxx

6969573 Cpl Connelly, R.W.
'H' Coy, 8th Btn. Rifle Brigade
A.P.O. England
15-6-44

My own darling wife Sheila,

Had a great surprise today, two lovely letters, really sweetheart, they have done me the world of good, [I] now feel in the very best of spirits, such a lovely tonic to hear from the girl I adore, so soon after landing, please do write as often as possible my precious, hearing from you will keep me going and make me so much happier and bring dear old England lots closer.

The RAF are doing marvellous work and it's most heartening to see how they rule the air. Swarms of fighters sweep the skies from dawn to dusk, and equally terrific amounts of bombers fly in formations through flak so thick that it seems impossible for them to reach their objectives but believe me they do.

I naturally can't tell you what we are doing, but we are all in the best of health and spirits, and doing extremely well for food, cups of char and cigarettes, and of course all the usual trimmings.

The French people are very pleased to see us and most friendly, we are having lots of fun trying to understand and making ourselves understood with the help of cards and books. [I'm] beginning to pick up quite a bit of their language, and think I'll study a foreign language properly when we get this lot over, and I'm once more back in civies with you my precious better half.

Its such a crime that some of these lovely little villages have suffered so much in the cruel blows of warfare, there is plenty of beautiful countryside still to be seen however, green fields, hedges and fields, stand out beautifully and defiantly as nature's reply to mans' wilful and wicked destruction. The weather is super now and we are all getting very brown, would love to spend a holiday with you here when peace once more reigns, feel sure you would love it. Passed a lovely old cottage in most romantic settings yesterday that would have pleased your artistic eye and made your dear fingers itch for a paint brush or sketch book…

Trust my other letters have arrived OK and haven't been held up too long, also that you received the birthday greetings in time; you will get yourself something new from me wont you dearest? The old account can stand a few 'quid', [I] only wish I could be with you and buy something myself, but never mind sweetheart, I have a very strong feeling that by your next birthday we will be together in our own little home, with the world at peace at long last.

Sweetheart thanks a lot for the beautiful little enclosed sentiment, am looking forward to more, you are a darling, in every way and make me so very happy. Oh my dearest one I love you with all my heart, soul and strength and always will, stay just as sweet as you are honey, you're marvellous, and I'm the luckiest devil on earth to have such a delightful partner. With my luck and a couple of million other helpers this blasted war should soon be over. Honestly though dearest, don't worry for I promise you I won't be taking any unnecessary risks.

Well my darling Sheila must say cheerio for now, and try to get a spot of sleep, nights are a trifle hectic here, and owing to having a little job on last night didn't get much shut eye…

Look after yourself my precious one.

All my love & kisses are for you only.
God bless,
Bob
xxxxx

On 6 June Captain Gordon was part of the enormous fleet that crossed over to France. A doctor at No. 24 General Hospital in

Scarborough, Yorkshire, he spent the week leading up to D-Day, as well as the day itself, on board an American Landing Ship Tank (LST) that was earmarked for casualty evacuation.

Captain S. Gordon
24 General Hospital
15.16 **
Scarborough
20/6/44

Dear Roy and Jan,
Now at last I can tell you of my adventures. On 29th May I went to Southampton and immediately went on board a special ship. We were 3 doctors and 33 men. It was what we had been practicing for at the Isle of Wight. Our job was to bring back casualties: Easy isn't it. This is what happened.

The organisation was amazing... It was gigantic and also in flaming technicolour. There were thousands of ships of all shapes and sizes, each shape and size to do a special work. You may have seen pictures of some in the papers or on the newsreel. Ours was a landing ship for tanks and someone has a brainwave and decided that they would be useful to take vehicles over and bring back casualties. It's a large ship with a flat bottom and 2 big doors in front... The tank deck which is 3 decks down is like a huge hall and is big enough to take at least 50 large tanks. Above that is the sleeping quarters for the crew and troops galley (cook house). The top deck was flat and was for carrying lorries and also had the cabins for the officers and the dining room. Above that of [course] was the bridge...

The first few days were spent unpacking the boxes of medical stores and putting them so that we would get at them easily as while vehicles were on board they had to be packed away... The patients themselves (on stretchers) were [fixed] on special racks which had to be fitted up and taken down and when these were full the remainder were laid on the floor (on the stretchers) in pairs or lashed together to prevent the stretcher from moving if the ship got into heavy seas and my goodness it certainly could roll. It didn't pitch at all but it certainly could and did roll from side to side until it was almost impossible to stand and all loose things rolled also. Walking wounded went up to the troop deck where they slept in special bunks.

On Saturday we loaded up with lorries of all kinds, ducks (… which go on land or water) and a variety of different other vehicles, with their drivers and officers – about 400 men and that evening we were told all about the invasion – when, where and how and our place in it. It was due to start on Monday but it was postponed until Tuesday.

We set sail on Monday night at the end of the assault convoy and went along a lane through the mine field which had already been made for us by mine sweepers and marked out with flags. The sea was very rough and the crossing took about 15hrs and we anchored about a mile off the British sector of beach about 12 noon, about 4 hours after the assault had started and apart from some wrecked ships and assault boats and some firing from enemies there was very little to be seen of the actual battle. The Germans had just been pushed off the beach. I did see a tank and pillbox having a direct hit from a battle ship.

In this section the casualties were comparatively small on either side and we saw quite a number of German prisoners and every so often a mine would blow up on the beach. Because of this the ships were unloading on to special carrying craft which went from them to the beach and was rather a slow process. The number of ships had to be seen to be believed. The place was black with them and it seemed that one could quite easily walk from one to the other as far as the eye could see.

By the following day they had made the beaches comparatively safe and ships (flat bottomed ones) could be run aground on the ebb tide and be left high and dry for the vehicles to be run straight from the ship onto the beach. This we did and while they were unloading we three MOs went for a little stroll … to stretch our legs…

When the tide came in again we floated off and anchored about a mile off shore where we eventually had about 40 casualties brought to us in the ducks. These load on shore drive down to the beach into the sea and swim out to the ships and actually come on board through the doors. After being unloaded they roll out again and swim back to the shore with a load of empty stretchers and blankets…

We stayed there that night and the following day took on about 200 more casualties then had to wait for the convoy to be formed to return to England, arriving in Southampton on Friday night…

I suppose it all sounds dangerous and exciting, in actual fact it wasn't anything of the sort. Thrilling yes – and I'm glad I was in it and wouldn't have missed it for the world. We saw our enemy ships, and aeroplanes, although the latter used to come out at night when they would get a hot reception; as one of the Yanks said it's like the fourth of July…

Of the 3 beaches there's no question at all that the Yanks had the worse job and suffered the most as a consequence. It seemed amazing that they were able to land at all and push off the beach as they had to face fairly high cliffs with guns all over the place. That's why their move forward was delayed quite a few hours. They eventually did their job and are still continuing to do good work and incidentally letting everyone know about it. Good luck to them, they've actually earned it this time.

Our work finished because the medical arrangements are going along fine. 200 beach hospitals are being established all over the place. Hospital planes and proper hospital ships are running…

The things that left the biggest impression was the [success] of shipping; the organisation and smoothness with which things go … as opposed to the petty restrictions of ordinary [times] and the kindness and hospitality shown to us by the crew of our ship and the keenness and coolness of the British Tommy with his joke and grin under all circumstances…

No more news.

Best love to both

Even before the first wave of troops hit the beaches on D-Day, there were already Allied troops in action in occupied France. As a prelude to the invasion, three Allied airborne divisions – the British 6th and US 82nd and 101st – were dropped over Normandy to seize key objectives and protect the flanks of the invasion beaches.

Gerald Ritchie was a company commander in the 12 (Yorkshire Battalion), Parachute Regiment, part of the British 6th Airborne Division.

Major G. Ritchie
12 Para Bn
BLA
Sunday

My own dearest sweetie,
I shall try and write you a proper letter tonight as I have a bit of time. My last few effusions have been rather poor efforts I am afraid. But we have been rather busy just lately.

It has been an extraordinary party these last few days and a very queer mixture of extreme unpleasant moments and some quite happy ones. The most touching and most gratifying thing about it all has been the extreme joy and pathetic gratitudes which the local inhabitants have heralded on arrival. I have never before been treated as these French peasants are treating us, and it is rather an amazing sensation and rather brings a lump in ones throat. Everyone without exception waves to you, flowers are thrown into the vehicles, and I remember particularly the sight of one oldish man standing up at his gate with his family waving his arms and shouting '*merci! merci!*' At every little cottage I have stayed where the inhabitants have been there, they have produced everything of the best, wine, cider etc and given it away liberally to the troops, this appears to be the true spirit of France.

Most of the country is unspoilt and untouched; but here and there where the Boche has stood and fought, where there has been a good defence line, everything is smashed and horrible. I have seen a little town, complete and unspoilt in the morning, a blazing inferno in the evening and a mass of smouldering rubble, full of evil smells by the next morning...

Well my darling I think that is just about all for today, so will close now and go to bed.

All my love darling, mine is yours alone.

Your very loving and devoted husband,
Gerald

Though he was wounded and evacuated following operations in Normandy, Major Ritchie returned to his battalion and took part in the last great airborne operation of the Second World War, Operation *Varsity*, the crossing of the Rhine in March 1945.

Major G. Ritchie
12 Para Bn
BLA
Easter Day

My dearest Sweetheart,
At last I have found a few moments to write a proper letter

to you to let you know how I am getting on. I hope you have got all the various field post cards I have sent you, they are very useful for just letting you know I am well…

Well my darling, I seem to have lived through such a multitude of experiences since I last wrote that it is difficult to know what to say and where to begin. Most will of course have to be kept until I see you I'm afraid. The initial party was a bit hectic for a time, but it might have been a lot worse and it was a real success, as I expect you read in the papers. My company have done magnificently and I feel very proud of them all; all my officers are ok…

It is rather an extraordinary experience being in this country, the people are very docile and polite, and in most cases seem very pleased the war is for them over, particularly because of the RAF bombing, which is pretty devastating. The thing that has surprised me most in this particular part of the world is the fact that the populace are very well provided for food and most other things too, but it may be only on the surface. There is no doubt though that they are fully aware now that they are beaten.

This morning we had a wee church service, but it was only a very short one, but it was at least something being Easter Day. I wonder if you were at church this morning… Well my darling, I think I will close now, my thoughts are always with you…

All my love comes to you with this as always, your very loving husband,
Gerald.

Another officer who took part in the Allied airborne operations in Normandy and beyond was Captain Chris T. Cross, who was part of the 2nd Battalion, Oxfordshire and Buckinghamshire Light Infantry. Cross had wanted to be a paratrooper, but at 6ft 4in was deemed too tall and instead joined the 2nd Ox and Bucks, which was an airlanding battalion dropped onto the battlefield by glider.

Lt C.T. Cross, C Coy
2nd OXF & BUCKS Lt Infty
A.P.O. England
June 23rd 1944

Dear Folks,
At present I'm lying in the sun in a very pleasant orchard in N. France and a force of about 500 Fortresses has just gone overhead, most encouraging… I have just changed my underclothes and washed my feet for the first time since I left England. And today we bought a few bottles of wine, and intend, if all is quiet, to have a little dinner party this evening because when we are busy we get a bit split up and the officers don't get much chance to see one another… What we would really like is some bread – getting awfully tired of these biscuits, but the army bakers are not here yet and the local French don't have any to spare.

My platoon is in very good form and we all get on very well together. The five new blokes I had shortly before we left are pretty good and with one exception fitted in well. The exception is now no longer with us – Jerry saw to that. But he has not dealt with us too severely – touch wood.

Being now at liberty to talk slightly about D-Day here you are for what it is worth. For quite a long and very tedious time before the thing began we were cooped up very tightly in a tented camp opposite an operational aerodrome near Oxford. It was incredibly hot while we were there but they stretched a point and allowed us out of camp to go across to the RAF mess

& have a bath. ENSA* sent a show down one afternoon – held in plain air – quite amusing. And occasionally we packed a few sweaty men very tightly into a tent and showed them a film. But it was a trying time and a lot of money changed hands at cards. Meanwhile the officers and NCOs were very busy learning the story of what we were going to do, memorizing maps, studying models, air photographs, intelligence reports and all that sort of thing. All done in the near nude Nissen hut, whose doors and windows had to be kept shut! And throughout this time about half the company were within a dozen or so miles of their homes. And they had great temptations. However, all was well. The whole business was a bit nerve-wracking though, because we were not told exactly when D-Day was to be, and then, when we <u>were</u> told, the whole thing was put off for a day just when we were about keyed up to go.

The glider flight was bloody! It was of course longer than most we've done before because of the business of getting into formation, collecting fighter escort and so on. After about ¼ hour I began to be sick and continued until we were over the channel where the air was much calmer. The channel was a wonderful sight – especially the traffic at this end – Piccadilly Circus wasn't in it. We were not over the coast this side long enough for me to be sick again, and we were pretty busy thinking about landing. The landing was ghastly. Mine was the first glider down, though we were not quite in the right place, and the damn thing bucketed along a very upsy-downsy field for a bit and then broke across the middle – we just chopped through those anti-landing poles (like the ones I used to cut myself!) as we went along. However, the two halves of the glider fetched up very close together and we quickly got

---

* Entertainments National Service Association (ENSA) was established in 1939 to provide entertainment for serving British personnel during the Second World War.

out ourselves and our equipment and lay down under the thing, because other gliders were coming in all around and Jerries were shooting things about at them and us so it wasn't very healthy to wander about. Our immediate opposition – a machine gun in a little trench – was very effectively silenced by [another] glider which fetched up plumb on the trench and a couple of Huns – quite terrified – came out with their hands up! Having discovered that we were all there and bound up a few scratches we then set off to the scene of the battle. I shall not tell you about that, except that apart from a bar of chocolate and ½ the contents of the whisky flask I had no time to eat or drink for a very uncomfortably long time – too much else to do, but it seems incredible now. From my last meal in England to my first cup of char and hard ration in France was very nearly 48 hours! But I've been making up for it since.

Somebody once said that war was composed of intensive boredom relieved by periods of acute fear. This is it, in a nutshell. The boys used to hate digging themselves trenches on Salisbury Plain, but you should just see how fast they do it now. And we've had a good many to dig in various different places since we came here. My hands are not as beautiful as they were!

The French people I have met have been marvellous – very pleased to see us – pleasure mingled with apprehension because they knew that when we arrived it might mean shelling, it might mean that we should have to raid their homes to protect ourselves, and it would assuredly mean the death of a lot of their livestock. This is a horse and cattle-breeding district, and one of the saddest things is to see their carcasses lying about, nobody having time to deal with them and fields full of very scared animals, some of them wounded. The local drink is cider – rough but very good and I hate to think what goes into the making of it. However, the alcohol in it makes it safer to drink than the water hereabouts. The civilians used to give us cider if we asked for a drink. Recently though we have not been near any places with inhabitants about…

It is now time for the party, and Jerry seems to be giving little trouble this evening. So that's all for a while.

Love to you all,
Chris

Lieutenant Cross also took part in the airborne operations across the Rhine, though by this point he was the battalion's Intelligence Officer.

Lt C.T. Cross
2nd Ox & Bucks Lt Infy
BLA
Germany. 27 March 1945
Dear Family,

It seems incredible that we've only been here three days, seems like weeks. But I'm all in one piece and the morale is sky high.

I've seen no newspapers since we were first shut up in the [town's] camp. But unless there is a security blackout, I expect you know all you should know about our activities.

The Regiment has covered itself in glory – a really first class show… I've been feeding on Benzedine but it looks as though I'll be getting some sleep today. Also food. The German farmhouses around here are very well supplied … and we are at present winking an eye at looting of hams, eggs and preserved fruit! In fact we are organising it, so that everybody gets the same share!

This <u>can't</u> go on much longer, I only hope I never have to get into a glider again! The first three and half hours of that flight were wonderful – I was not a bit sick. But I put on five years in the last five minutes of it.

That must be all…
Love Chris

Lieutenant Cross stayed with the battalion right through to the end of the war, and wrote to his family at home describing the somewhat chaotic situation following the German surrender.

Lt C.T. Cross
Regtl HQ
2nd Ox & Bucks Light Infantry
BLA
4.5.45

My dear family,
I have just heard the 9pm news broadcast, containing the official news of the surrender to 21st Army Gp. As such dates go, this I suppose, will be an important one. For us, it's not any different from yesterday or the day before.

I have missed all the fun of the 'link up' with the Russians – that has been left to the Divisional Staff, who have ceased to take any interest in us, but are concentrating instead on Vodka. Meanwhile it has been left to the likes of me, and there are not enough of us, to try and cope with 1 Surrendered armies and 2 Civilian refugees.

Yesterday was the worst. At 10 o'clock in the morning I had a belated breakfast after doing the final night advance – during which incidentally, the beautiful BMW was written off. From 1030am until 1130pm I had time for one cup of char and a sandwich brought to me by Richards. All that time I was dealing with German soldiers. I had to use a reception camp for rather more than one German division. Here the soldiers were searched for arms, organised into bodies of 200 approx and marched off. Many were wounded, many had marched so far that they would go no further. Their own medical services had to be organised to cope with these, transport arranged for them and so on. We are miles ahead of supporting troops, having rushed at full tilt over and beyond the Elbe, so we have no facilities for feeding the blighters. Furthermore we have civilians to cope with, of which more anon. So at all costs we had to keep them moving back. During yesterday I had something like 10,000 through my place. By the end of the evening I had no voice left at all, having been shouting orders in German at them all day. This I did mainly from the back of a horse…

Well anyway, this bit of the war is over. I suppose I should feel elated, but I feel tired and disgusted, and I can't get the smell of Germans out of my mouth and nose, no matter how much I clean my teeth. Disgust, contempt and a little pity mix ill. What now I wonder?

Now I think is the time for you to send me some books. The Huns don't keep English books in their houses and everybody is crying out for light literature for the days.

Love to you all,
Chris

At the same time as British forces were struggling in Normandy, and the Fourteenth Army was driving back the Japanese in India at the battles of Imphal and Kohima, a very different force was fighting its own battle way behind the Japanese lines in Burma. The brainchild of the unorthodox Major General Orde Wingate, the Chindits launched their first long-range operations behind Japanese lines in early 1943, and in early 1944, after Wingate's death in March, a second more ambitious operation was launched. Twenty thousand men in six brigades, broken down into a series of individual columns of 500 or so men, were inserted behind enemy lines to seize vital airfields, and disrupt the lines of communication to the rear of the Japanese forces.

Colour Sergeant Tom Proudfoot was one of the Chindits, and served with 2nd Battalion, Queen's Royal Regiment during the operation.

888437 C/Sgt Proudfoot
2nd Queens Royal Regiment
India Command
12.5.44

Dear Bobby,
At last I am able to write and tell you of our expedition.

I am now out of Burma, and recuperating after a most thrilling, hazardous and gruelling trip. We were members of the 'Special Force' until recently commanded by the late General Wingate. We set off and marched behind the enemy to the extent of 300 miles. At the initial stage of our trec [sic] we had to cut away every yard of jungle growth, we walked, or I should say, crawled 21¾ miles over mountains, in 69 marching hours, and climbed over 14,000 feet carrying a pack weighing about 70lbs so you can see how we at times could only do three miles a day.

We crossed rivers which were often waist high. After crossing the Chindwin without much trouble we then settled down to do some really useful commando-cum-guerilla warfare. We blew up bridges, roads, railways, damaged airfields, laid a few ambushes and we were in turn ambushed ourselves, but managed to escape. Our policy was to harass the Jap so that he did not know where or when we were going to strike, and because we in our party were small we fought the Jap when it suited us not when it suited him. Our last ambush was very successful. My guns caught the first trucks loaded with Japs, and cut them to pieces. He brought up reinforcements and put in a counter-attack which looked rather 'sticky' for a time, but we managed to slip away, only losing five men killed, and several wounded for the Jap total of 60 killed, and many wounded. In all we walked during our operation behind the enemy lines to the extent of 500 odd miles. It was a great strain mentally as well as physically as you can well imagine. Every track and village held for us the possibility of being ambushed and shot up so we avoided these, except when we travelled in the dead of night.

We were hunted as criminals. After we had been 'inside' for several months we were flown out in heaven sent planes. We were also supplied with food, clothing, equipment and ammunition which we needed by air, and we all pay tribute to the pilots, and crew, because they never once let us down. They also lifted our wounded after a battle, and flew them to hospital. I am in a rest camp for the moment and expecting a leave soon.

Since we came out people have [been] doing everything for us, giving us what we have missed in the way of luxuries during the last few months. I hope Bertha and new arrival are both well, I expect it will have happened before you have this letter, or have I forgotten the date? However good luck to her... You know I don't think that it will be too long now before I come home … in my opinion we should be home by this time next year. Today I have had a thorough medical inspection, and strangely enough I have turned out one of the fittest men in our bunch as well as one of the oldest. Our physical category was A1 plus higher than that demanded by any other force. We had a commando with us who said commando work was a 'piece of cake' to ours!

Cheerio Bobby. I am trying to catch the post. Excuse horrible scribble. Regards to Bertha and (children?)

Tom

Captain Norman Durant of the South Staffordshire Regiment, who also served with the Chindits, reflected on the very different nature of the war in the Far East compared to the situation in Europe.

… And that's all that there was to it, and on reading it through, very dull in comparison with the Press version. But this is a true account and I hope I have not overstressed any one angle. I have purposely left out descriptions of scenery, the rising sun, bird-life and native dress and habits because had I begun this would have turned into a 50,000-word book. I have purposely left out descriptions of rotting bodies, spilled blood and dangling guts because that is a constant factor in fighting a war. I have purposely left out criticisms because I wish this to pass the censor, and I have purposely left out the glory and the joke-in-the-face-of-death angle because it should need no stressing. This is merely an account of the ordinary men in an ordinary infantry Bn., telling what they were ordered to do and recording briefly how in every case they succeeded in doing it; and I hope it's been legible enough to show you this.

Many people in this war had worse times and harder fighting but anyone who has fought the Italians, French, Germans and Japs will say with no hesitation that the Japs are the ones to be avoided. Somehow one can imagine that under different circumstances one could have a drink and a cigarette with a German and a quite amiable talk and a cup of tea with a prisoner, but having once met the Japs one can only imagine kicking their heads in. They look like animals and behave like animals and they can be killed as unemotionally as swatting flies. And they need to be killed, not wounded for so long as they breathe they're dangerous. I have seen plenty of our dead and plenty of theirs, and whereas ours look bewildered, as though someone has taken an unfair advantage of them, the Japs have their lips drawn back over their prominent teeth in a last snarling defiance.

Captain Durant, though somewhat dismissive of his own actions, was obviously held in high regard by the men under his command as a letter to his parents from his platoon sergeant confirms.

Dear Madam,

First of all I will introduce myself. I was Capt. Durant's platoon sergeant in the last 'Wingate' show. I have just received a letter from him thanking me for paying you a visit while on my disembarkation leave. I did say I would see you for him, but before I knew I was home my leave was ended. However, I think I can tell you more easily by mail than in person what the men, NCOs and myself thought of him while we were together.

When he first came we were a platoon of old soldiers, my fourteen years service was well down the roll, most of them were tough ones too. Pte Robinson for instance joined up in 1925 has served three or four terms in 'Aldershot' for striking. If I ran through them all you would think they were a savoury lot. The first words they said were 'who has put this boy in charge of us?' At the same time I think Capt Durant had his doubts. After three weeks together every man was satisfied with him. He could rough it as well as anyone. I tested him myself on his drinking. I cannot tell you how the night ended because I was carried to bed.

Well the night came for us to go to Burma, and of course our test was to see who was worth his salt and who was not. I think he was the first one to fire a shot. It was just after 'stand to' there were five or six Japs about two hundred yards away. I am afraid he missed, but from then until six o'clock at night it was one long fight. That was the day he got wounded. This is how it happened. About four-thirty over half of the men were killed or wounded. Brigadier Mike Calvert ordered an attack. The first time only six made the dash up the hill, lieutenants Day and Karns were killed, Major Jeffries shot through the mouth and your son through the fat of the calf, just above the knee when he was jumping over the side of the hill. I was the sixth and didn't get touched. I think the only reason Major Jeffries and myself went up the hill three times was to find the 'boy'. When we had control of the hill and still could not find him I gave up hope and came back and there he was getting the stragglers together. He had jumped over the wrong side of the hill. I put a bandage on his leg. We both went down to our own lads to get things fixed up for the night. I have been awarded the Military Medal for that day and everyone there thinks that Capt. Durant should get the MC, if not for his own bravery then for his platoon, he got them fighting mad.

Well weeks went on until we came out. I can honestly say he never showed the least bit of fear, either to [the] Japs or to his tough crowd of men who would do anything for him. It was the best nine months I have known in the Army. We could always find something to laugh about. In fact there was never a dull moment with him.

The last week must have been terrible for him, the marching was through deep mud and flooded rivers. One day he made twelve crossings on one river which was nearly a hundred yards wide. Every man, mule and our kit was over before he would rest. The last day I was lucky enough to meet an American. After bargaining with him I got twelve bottles of beer, but Capt. Durant was too ill to drink one, and still he carried his own pack.

Mr and Mrs Durant I notice this is the sixth page. I have tried to tell you what a great man your son is in action. It was a very good feeling to be with someone who went there to fight an enemy, to help win this war. I was very sorry not to have said goodbye to him when I left, but some day I hope to meet him in England in a healthy condition… So I will close by hoping you are in the very best of health and that very soon your son will be home with you.

Yours sincerely,
J. Jenkins Sgt

In Europe the Allied armies had broken out of the Normandy beachheads and were driving across France towards Belgium, with the German Army retreating before them.

Cyril Charters was one of the many thousands of men who were shipped over to France to support this great advance, in his case by serving as a projectionist with 37 Kinema Section, Royal Army Ordnance Corps (RAOC). Although, given the nature of his job, Cyril was a long way from the front line, he wrote a series of highly detailed letters home to his wife telling of his experiences and describing the situation of the French and Belgian population under German rule, as well as the end of the war in Europe.

13057038 Cpl Charters, C.J.
37 Kinema Section RAOC
BLA
Letter No. 40

Dearest sweetheart,
In this letter I am going to deal with the subject of how people lived over here under German domination. Besides being interesting (I hope!), it will help you to understand many events which have happened; from the antagonistic reception we experienced in Normandy to the recent trouble re. disarming the F.F.I. in Belgium. Now Normandy is one of the richest districts in France for dairy produce and agriculture and the behaviour of the Germans in this district was beyond reproach. It paid the Germans to be nice to the farmers and in return they seem to have been well supplied with dairy produce and the goods they wanted. It is not really surprising, therefore, that after four years living peacefully and in harmony that friendships sprang up, the girls went out with the Germans, more and more marriages were solemnized, and the Germans became a part of the villages. Then

came the invasion and with it all the horror and actuality of the war that had almost been forgotten. What were the French wives of the German soldiers to do? There were a variety of answers, but the three that most concerns us are the following: (i) those who fought side by side with their husbands, usually isolated in a church steeple or similar vantage point, sniping, until they were killed together; (ii) those who took up the [roles] of their husbands who had fled, and retired to the woods, to cause delays and annoyances, sniping, at our own troops; and (iii) those who thought they could carry on as they did before, but who now walk about trying to conceal their bald heads!

It is not hard to understand their hatred for us; and worse was to follow for the Germans took with them everything they could get, with the result that there was a shortage of many things that had formerly been plentiful. Not unnaturally they blamed the invasion. Now there were also in Normandy during the occupation, a number of pro-Allied inhabitants. Two interesting cases I know of: one Victor who was doing intelligence work for us, and a cinema operator who worked one of the four great radio links for the underground. Also, after the invasion, there were those who wanted to do something big to gain the confidences of the Allies (and at the same time possibly hide their own guilt), and these grew and grew in numbers as the Allies became more advanced. Hence came the head-shavings and similar medieval practices.

But now let us leave Normandy and see what happened in the industrial areas. Now here was a vastly different case; there was no great food production here; but goods, produced by machines – and machines can be sabotaged!

This called for the SS and the Gestapo, and with them brute rule; the press gangs of men carried off for work in Germany; the questionings and beatings up, which is in no propaganda story; the lack of food and the taking of what little home-grown foods the inhabitants could raise.

It is hard to imagine the fear and horror in which these people lived, nor can we fully realise the hardships they suffered. We can only see it in the eyes of these people as they tell us; in the undeveloped state of the children, most of them suffering with rickets; in the anxiety which they cannot hide when they speak of their menfolk in Germany; and in the unexpected nooks and corners where their rabbits and other potential foodstuffs were kept, to keep them from the prying eyes of the German.

It is little wonder that this was the Maquis country. Young and able-bodied men had to hide, nor did they dare venture to a cinema or dances or entertainment, for the Gestapo kept a close watch on such places. What better then than to get their own back on this foe who kept them from their homes. And what a job they did when the time came!

Belgium presents another case again. As I told you in previous letters there exists a strong bond between England and Belgium created by intermarriage during the last war, and by the great exchange of tourists between the two countries. They never fully submitted to the German yoke, although of course there are individual cases, and there always seems to have been that silent antagonism, which the Germans could not break down. Food was rationed to such an extent that it was impossible to live on the meagre allowance, and there were many cases of starvation. Then came the blackest black market ever known, and one that makes the world stand still and gasp at its immensity. Fabulous prices were paid to the fortunate few who could get the urgently needed commodities. Starve or pay up.

Business men sold all their businesses, the wealthy spent all their money, and the poor – well, another alternative arose, starve or steal! Steal! But from whom?

Meanwhile underground movements had sprung up. Not one but dozens, assuming all sorts of names. The most popular

LEFT
Pilot Officer Michael A. Scott photographed here wearing his RAF wings. Like many pilots and servicemen during the war, Scott wrote a final letter home, to be delivered if he was killed in action. © IWM (Documents 431)

BOTTOM
Reverend Don Siddons, Staff Chaplain at Eighth Army HQ, conducting a communion service in the desert during the Second World War. © IWM (Documents 9143)

TOP
Defence of Tobruk: the Royal Artillery utilise their guns to repel the Germans in the desert, 1941.
© IWM (E 2887)

MIDDLE
In a posed photograph, British infantry are shown rushing an enemy strong-point through the dust and smoke of enemy shell fire at El Alamein. © IWM (E 18513)

BOTTOM
El Alamein, 1942. A mine explodes close to a British truck as the infantry move through an enemy minefield to new front lines. © IWM (E 18542)

Support troops of the 3rd British Infantry Division assemble on Sword Beach, 6 June 1944. The soldiers pictured here include engineers and, in the background, medical orderlies preparing to move wounded men off the beach. © IWM (B 5114)

Field Marshal Sir Alan Brooke, Winston Churchill, Field Marshal Sir Bernard Montgomery and Lieutenant-General William Simpson walk across a Bailey bridge over the Rhine on 26 March 1945, marking the success of the Allied sweep across Europe. © IWM (EA 56602)

TOP
Men of the 1st Battalion, Dorsetshire Regiment, with South Korean soldiers during the hand-over of the 'Lozenge' position to the 4th Republic of Korea (ROK) Infantry Division, c.1954. © IWM (CT 1908)

MIDDLE
During a lull in the fighting in Korea, British soldiers enjoy a game of football, c.1952. © IWM (BF 10081)

BOTTOM
A trooper of the 8th Battalion, King's Royal Irish Hussars writes a letter home while serving in Korea. © IWM (BF 522)

Lieutenant Robert Gill, photographed with Doreen, his then girlfriend. He wrote letters to her from Korea, detailing his movements. © IWM (Documents 13204)

A Bren gunner pictured here in a concealed ambush position while on patrol during the Malayan Emergency. © IWM (MAL 171)

British troops from 1st Battalion, King's Own Yorkshire Light Infantry, are shown here on patrol through a Malayan jungle, c.1952. © IWM (BF 10387)

TOP:
HMS *Sheffield* on fire after being hit by an Exocet missile fired from an Argentinian aircraft. © IWM (FKD 64)

MIDDLE:
Heavily laden British troops during the land campaign on the Falklands. Here they are waiting to board a helicopter in 1982. © IWM (FKD 2124)

3rd Battalion, Parachute Regiment, pictured here with the battalion flag in Port Stanley after the Argentine surrender on 14 June 1982. © IWM (FLD 364)

A British Army M110 self-propelled gun in action during the first Gulf War in 1991.
© IWM (GLF 1280)

An RAF Tornado F3 in flight over the burning oilwells of the Gulf in the 1990s.
© IWM (GLF 762)

From a vantage point at Basra Technical College, a sniper of 1st Battalion, Irish Guards provides covering fire for Royal Engineers as they attempt to extinguish an oil well fire during the battle for Basra City in 2003. © IWM (OP-TELIC 03-010-34-003)

Four British soldiers of 3 Division Headquarters and Signal Regiment conduct a foot patrol on the outskirts of Basra during Operation *Telic 2*, September 2003.
© IWM (HQMND(SE)-03-053-009)

was the White Brigade, so called in opposition to the Black Brigade (collaborators with the Germans). Their main job was sabotage and this they did well. But there was no uniting bond between parties. Consequently, when the advance of the allies swept past and there was no further need to sabotage, many (and I regret to say, the majority) [degenerated] into nothing more than hooliganism. But, as the need, or rather excuse, for hooliganism ended, and all the collaborators had been beaten up, another opening arose – the Black Market!…

The real big suffering of Belgium during the occupation was the food shortage. I have seen photos of people, taken before the war, fat and plump and sturdy. To see those same people today is incredible: thin and wan and meagre. Mummy used to laugh about giving me sausages whenever I was home on a 48hrs; but what would they have given for those same sausages here in Belgium!

Well this was intended to be a four page letter but it has turned out nine, and I could still write another nine but – pity the poor censor – I'll continue it later!

So cheerio for now darling,
And all my fondest love,
Cyril
xxx

13057038 Cpl Charters, C.J.
37 Kinema Section RAOC
BLA
Sat. 5th May 1945

Hello darling,
Isn't the news grand! The announcement of the surrender of the armies in Denmark, Holland and N.W. Germany has just been made, or rather, it has just come into effect from 8.00 this

morning. And as I write this I am just half a mile away from where Monty accepted the surrender.

Everybody looks decidedly happy and cheerful but very little has been made of it so far. I think all the prisoners coming in and the general decay of the German resistance foreshadowed the news so that it was accepted more as a matter of course than anything.

It is Sunday as I continue this letter. It is nearly dinner-time and I have a few minutes to spare.

Last night I gave the grandest show of all. It was to men who had not seen a show for five years – our xPOW's [sic]. The show did not start until just after eleven and it finished just before one in the morning. They were absolutely fascinated during the performance, and as they left afterwards, one after the other as they passed thanked me. It was very touching.

Today, darling, I had the satisfaction of crossing that last river barrier, the Elbe – now for that other water barrier and home, peace and you!…

Now, cheerio once more and all my love darling.

Your ever loving husband,
Cyril
xxxx

The collapse of the German positions in France led to the liberation of Paris in August 1944, and the Allied armies continued their rapid advance across the Belgian frontier, reaching Brussels at the beginning of September.

Captain Michael G.T. Webster was the commander of the Reconnaissance Troop, 2nd Battalion Grenadier Guards, part of the Guards Armoured Division. His letters home to his family from this period give an impression of the exhilaration felt by both the liberators and the civilian populations of both France and Belgium.

1 September 1944

We are all making history, I am writing this in my tank, on paper captured from a German officer who I took prisoner, personally; in fact we had rather a field day yesterday so I captured myself a German half track motor bicycle, you may have seen pictures of them. However, that is all very small fry compared with everything else. If only I could tell you where I am, how we got here and all the thousand other things which have added up to what has been the most exciting and exhilarating days of my life, but I mustn't, I must simply be content in telling you that I'm more than alright and I'm in the best possible form anybody could be. That I've actually had tears coming to my eyes through sheer joyous excitement during the past two days. This might seem a bit exaggerated, but if it is, it is because the whole conception seems so...

11 September 1944

... This is to thank you for a lot of things, your letters, the soap, razor blade, saccharine, powdered milk and above all the last pair of socks. Imagine my quandary. You know something of the four hundred mile advance of the Guards Armoured Division to Brussels from Normandy.

It was my unfortunate lot, just before we started, my own tank broke down and I had to transfer to another one. This is always inconvenient, at the best of times, but normally one is either able to transfer one's kit into a new tank or the original tank turns up again having been repaired in, say, a couple of days, but this time neither conditions apply... The result of all this was that I had not got with me the amount of reserve clothing that I normally budget for to carry on my tank. So it was an answer to prayer that your parcel turned up with the immortal pair of socks. Socks, however, and their replacement have been of minor interest in what has been the most exciting 10 days of my life. The battalion was virtually in the front the whole way and it was, along with Timothy Tufnell and his boys, the first brigade into Brussels; racing the whole way on a centre line parallel with the rest of our brigade. They only just got in before us and this even though they had a dead straight road the whole way, while we had an extremely curly and narrow one.

The job of a liberator although thoroughly enviable is also pretty exacting. As you can imagine, throughout France and all the way up to Brussels we received a rapturous welcome. Each successive village that we passed invariably stood out to wave us through. Nine times out of ten they were not simply content with waving; flowers, apples, beer, pears, plums were literally hurled at us, as we sped by… As for when we stopped in a village, or worse in a town, the tank would be swamped by animated Frenchmen, women and children who simultaneously wanted to kiss you, shake your hand, photograph you, give you a glass of cognac, explain in voluble French, or, hopeless for us, Flemish, how glad he was to see you and what his experience was of being at the hands of the Germans. This greeting, generally worked to a formal, rapid and incomprehensive patois, would be followed by what seemed to be three entirely ritualistic gestures.

1. General agitation of hands and arms as description ensued.

2. Realistic play of throat cutting plus appropriate noises in throat. To the un-initiated this appeared to be what the Germans had tried to do [to] the Frenchmen or women, but in point of fact it was intended to show what the particular native wanted to do to the Germans as a whole and Hitler in particular.

3. Pointed an imaginary rifle at an imaginary enemy and with cries of pop, pop, pop, showing how he decimated hundreds of 'les Boches'.

In Brussels itself of course, this was multiplied by the hundred fold…

Despite the apparent ease of the advance in August and September 1944, the fighting in Normandy had been hard fought and bloody, with the British suffering particularly heavy casualties in the repeated attempts to take the strategically vital city of Caen.

Lieutenant Brin Francis was serving with the 8th (Belfast) Heavy Anti Aircraft Regiment, Royal Artillery, in the Far East when he learnt of the death of his brother David during the fighting around Caen.

21/8 (Belfast) HAA Regiment
SEAC
Sept 5th 1944

My Dear Mum,

I heard tonight from Joy – I should say Joy wrote to Jack Williams who came here and in a very kind way told me about David. I can only hope and pray that you, and Billy, learnt in as gentle way as I did.

When David went we <u>all</u> feared bad news, but when it <u>comes</u> it is a terrible thing, especially for <u>you</u>, who had been through all this wretched heartbreak before in this war.

I've only learnt of this a matter of hours, and I can't believe it yet; to say that I'm very sad and very sorry would be a poor way, all I <u>can</u> say is I'm completely at a loss to say just how much this news hits me.

My thoughts flew to you and Billy, and I can hardly bear to think of you suffering all this agony again. It doesn't seem fair that one family should be hit twice. All I can say to this is that whatever life holds for us, or for <u>ours</u>, we must not allow ourselves to grow either bitter or hard; and although this news does seem so hard to bear, we must never lose faith for a moment, and God will help us. Life may be difficult to understand, but we must go on the same way as we can be <u>CERTAIN</u> Dad and David would have us going on, doing our very best to be <u>HAPPY</u> and making others happy too.

It seems hard that this second loss to us should happen so near to the end of the war ... but if we remember 'where and when' David died, we can be proud.

I will write a letter to Billy now, poor Billy, she will be suffering now, and we must do all in our power to help her, although I know that anything that can be done to help her in any way will be done by Mrs McLaine and Dolly. I'm afraid Billy will be heartbroken and nothing we can do will help her over her grief, as <u>you</u> know from bitter experience.

Try to be brave, as you can be; I know you will put on a 'brave show' for the world, and to relatives too, but try with all your might to be brave <u>inside</u>, because that's the one I love.

God bless and help you,
Lots and lots of love,
From Brin

Following the advance into Belgium, and the failure of Operation *Market Garden* to gain a foothold over the Rhine, the German defences stiffened and the winter of 1944/45 saw a great deal of hard fighting as the British battled the German defences of the Siegfried Line and the Reichswald Forest.

David Sheldon was posted to Belgium in December 1944 and went on to serve as a platoon commander in the 5th Battalion, Coldstream Guards, part of the Guards Armoured Division. He took part in most of the major combat operations through to the end of the war, and described them in some detail in his letters home.

Somewhere in Belgium
15 December 1944

My dear Bob,
It may surprise you to hear at the moment of writing I am only about six yards from the Germans! That may sound startling but of course they are behind barbed wire! As a matter of fact the pieces of wire between me and them is terribly weak and it would be as easy as winking for them to slip through in the dark and if they took a disliking to me they could easily cut my throat if they wanted to. Luckily the night is over, but naturally I didn't sleep too heavily and only had about a couple of hours of dozing.

The night before last about seven men escaped by cutting their way through the wire, so last night I had my guard on their toes. None has escaped under me so far and they are not likely to in daylight. One of the reasons for their probable plans of escape not being fulfilled last night, was that some searchlights were used for the first time which aided the sentries job considerably. Last night I had my revolver fully loaded and [it] is still on me at the moment ready to shoot.

The prisoners are pretty desperate chaps believe me and at the first opportunity would kill you. Some are very young boys (about your age of 12). It is said that some of them are tied to a tree, given food and water and a rifle and told to shoot any enemy they see. When prisoners arrive here they have only just been captured. None of them seem to shave and they look so shabby in their huge long coats but also they look terrible fighters and look as though they are born to fight...

Well, not so very long now, I expect to come into contact with them not behind wire. But still don't worry, it is my job as an Englishman and as a member of the good Sheldon family to return the blows to those who create evil…

At the moment I hear the guns firing at the doodlebugs* in the distance. I saw the old familiar flame of one this morning, but it is much less dangerous here (in that way) than at home.

A very happy Christmas and it may be New Year by the time you get this but I am told all our letters go by air.

Much love to you all,
David

4 Coy, 5th Bn
Coldstream Guards B.L.A
19th February 1945
Somewhere in Germany

My dear Mum and Dad,
I expect my address will be the first thing that surprises you. Well if only I could tell you. I've had the greatest experience of my life and you know what that is. It is very difficult for me to know what I can say and what I can't, but we certainly are on the winning side and never could that have been illustrated more than a few days ago. I was slap in front of everything, leading section, leading platoon, leading company and it was 'hot'. Somehow I didn't feel a bit frightened except before the battle, [and] then I was too busy to bother much. I am sure the thought of so many people praying for me helped me no end.

The support we had was terrific. I can't over emphasize it and the air support was the closest the battalion has ever had.

---

* The 'doodlebug' was the colloquial name given to the German V1 flying bomb. These unmanned bombs were first launched in June 1944 and British citizens on the south coast were subjected to their terrors until March 1945. The Germans also developed the V2, a ballistic missile, which again was used to target Britain from September 1944 until March 1945.

The orders I had to give out for the attack were detailed and one of the hardships was to go 24 hours with only one piece of bread and a little bacon fat for breakfast and some steak pie and one peach for lunch. From lunch onwards, after being very energetic, as even to carry full battle orders in action is pretty great, we had nothing until six o'clock the next morning, except a bar of chocolate which I ate in the night. I for one hardly knew how to stand up.

As I've always told you, it's one thing to take a place and it's another to hold it. We got it all right but we dug in and we were safe, that is the whole platoon. There were only a few casualties altogether, but the Germans came in, in many groups. A very rough estimate, for security reasons, was we captured over 150 prisoners. Once I was within about 15 or 20 yards of a Spandau when I was in front of my leading section. Luckily he didn't fire accurately. I can't tell the whole story but we killed him before long.

A great prize, there were plenty of them, was to get a German revolver as we disarmed them. Mine is in a very good condition and some day perhaps it many hang on a wall at home as a souvenir. German resistance was very poor considering they had so much kit. There was one chap, who when asked his age, said he was only fifteen and he only looked that too.

How I have enjoyed seeing so many German houses burning to the ground, as I've always wanted to have my revenge for the blitzes on England and for the V1 and V2. I am glad to have contributed to routing the enemy from his own grounds and the Sheldon family can say it was responsible (in a tiny way) for driving the enemy back.

Yesterday I got a letter from you Dad. Grand it was too and such a contrast to such a tremendous event in my life. My platoon is full of very experienced fighting men and all are very good chaps, practically all older than me. I've got lots of censored envelopes for you, but won't send them all at once.

I don't know when this letter will be posted, perhaps in a few days' time, as the circumstances are rather awkward.

Much love,
David
P.S. Have eaten many animals recently.

4 Coy, 5th Bn
Coldstream Guards B.L.A
12th March 1945

My dear Mum and Dad,
Never before have I wanted to be able to tell you about my experiences recently which now, thank God, are over. Suspense for the last battle was terrible as it lasted for about three days and we knew it wouldn't be pleasant. However, I was brought through with God's help, unharmed, and I do feel it was something to be thankful for. I was not in front again, at least not to start with, but my name and yours is very ill omened. I have read in the paper about our sector as being described as 'absolute hell' and for a few hours it certainly was.

Now things are all right again and I've never felt so happy in my life to get away from recent events. I myself have been extremely lucky. I shall be able to tell you later, in another letter, in what way. I was lucky, as my steel helmet got blown off and my slit trench partially filled in. I had a rifle or something on top of my head when it was over, but still I was unhurt in any way except for a slightly sore head and slightly deafened. Still I had the practice in training of being run over by a tank and that was about the same!

You can imagine my relief now, although all along through everything I didn't seem to be frightened as I had so much to do and other people to think about. The 'Stonks' sometimes were terrifying.

Now I believe all trouble in that part is over, as it ought to be. I have now changed into a clean shirt, the first time for about six weeks and shortly I hope to have a 'bath'! Although it is a rest to come away (from the line), there is not the fun of doing what you like to a totally unoccupied fully furnished house!... The thing now is to sleep of course, but although I can't say at this stage, I have, at the moment, rather a special job...

I must end now, all is well and I feel grand now especially having had a good wash and shave in comfort. I am sure your many prayers from home and Crowborough have comforted me tremendously under rather difficult times and I know you will rejoice at my being brought out totally fit and happy.

Much love to all,
David

As the Allied armies advanced into Germany they began to come across the many prisoner of war camps that housed men such as William Hymers, who had been in captivity since he was taken prisoner in France in 1940 while serving as a Lance Corporal with the 5th Battalion, Buffs (Royal East Kent Regiment).

He spent most of the war in Stalag XXA near Thorn, in what is now Poland, before being marched back to Germany when the Russians neared the camp and was eventually liberated by the British near Hamburg.

18 April 1945

Sweetheart,
Am writing this in the hope that I shall be able to post it. We are still waiting to be sent home as patiently as we can and still trying to grasp the wonderful fact that we are once again free men.

What a day that was when we made our own guards prisoners and met up with some of our own lads with the tanks. They gave us grub and fags – all they had in fact. Our chief regret is that we are not at our best just now after the terrible time we have had but I bet you will soon feed me up to fighting pitch once more. Not that I'm too bad dear compared with many poor devils.

Went for a haircut yesterday and sat down right beside Gary. He looked a bit different owing to the fact of losing his teeth by getting a bang in the mouth with a German rifle butt. They were full of such tricks – setting large dogs on to us, whacking us with rifles as sticks, shooting some, stopping the food, what there was of it, and so on. Still they are paying now. Give my love to all and tell 'em I'll be with you all soon.

Always Your Bill

All across the world, British and Allied prisoners were forced to wait for their release as the war in the Far East dragged on until August 1945.

William Innes-Ker was captured at the fall of Singapore while serving as an NCO with the 1st Battalion Straits Settlements Volunteer Force. His diary takes the form of a series of letters to his wife and describes his last Christmas in captivity and the disintegration of the Japanese position in the Pacific.

24.12.44

Christmas Eve! The shops all blazing with lights – full of good things, glittering tinsels, lovely silks and mountainous hams. Butchers with their shop fronts hidden by rows of turkeys, ducks and fat geese, and the flower shops with their little pots of white heather and early hyacinths – I wonder when we shall see those dear sights again? It's extraordinary how infectious this Christmas

Spirit is – even here in a Jail, hemmed in by walls, bars and dumb looking Nip Guards, the Spirit is abroad in no uncertain form. Jokes, ragging and general gaiety are order of the day. Plans are published for an immense feast tomorrow, and the cooks will work like madmen to turn out rice and veg in 10 different shapes and forms. Everyone has purchased 50 cent cheroots to smoke and a bulb of garlic to mix in with the food! What a stench there will be! And wonder of wonders, our temporary masters have notified [us] that all British born may send a 25 word radio to their next of kin… The Christmas pantomime here – called 'Twinkletoes' – a really 'Crazy Gang' effort, was so appreciated by some Nip guards who saw it, that the next thing was the General had ordered a Command Performance, and a bus load of military and civil Nips from town came out to see it!…

I wonder what you will be doing tomorrow… I picture your midday dinner – if in the country quite probably a turkey and maybe even a pseudo-pudding. Yum! I'd scream for joy just for a loaf of bread! Fancy, I've not eaten, or even seen, bread since July 1942 – 2½ years. Stop it Tam, this sort of writing gets you nowhere. I'll close now Sweet till after the New Year – praying and wishing for you everything you can desire, which comes to the same thing as I do – namely our reunion soon – rich or poor never mind – just reunion and the freedom to live our lives together in peace.

3.2.45

Another very satisfactory visit from a great number of our friends who stayed some couple of hours and made a lot of noise. This was a few days ago, and since then every day one has called to see how we are getting on… I wonder if it will be all over by June? Things seem to be moving pretty rapidly here and there, or rather I should say there and there, NOT here! Apart from visits by B29s we see or hear nothing of what goes on around us, and while it is obvious there must be a terrible food shortage amongst the natives, we ourselves so far have not been reduced, through rumours are very strong just now. For this place to be so short of food, with its much reduced population, it may be deduced that Japan's mastery of these seas is gone – presumably most of her ships are gone too.

Perhaps the most difficult task for those engaged in the liberation of Europe and the occupation of Germany was dealing with the concentration camps set up by the Nazi regime. Many camps came to light, including Sandbostel, a notorious prisoner of war camp, which contained a mixture of POWs and political prisoners, many of whom had been treated appallingly.

For the British, the most horrifying concentration camp they encountered was that at Bergen-Belsen, which was discovered by troops from the 11th Armoured Division on 15 April 1945. Michael Carey was a gunner with 48th Battery, 4th (Durham) Survey Regiment, Royal Artillery, part of XXX Corps who liberated the camp on 29 April 1945.

… But to conclude this epistle, here is an account of the camp we are now having to guard.

Situated in a tract of open countryside, largely bracken covered and black sandy soil, think of a huge tract wired off by an 8ft wall of barbed wire – an area of about 30 acres! All round the perimeter are high watch towers with search lights [fixed] on high. The inside area is <u>quite</u> bare of all vegetation and is now dry, very dusty and dirty with the black sandy soil. The area is laid out like any army camp – roads, huts and administration buildings, built for the greater part of wood. The normal population was 25,000, composed of <u>all</u> European nationalities… The fellows (and a few women) now in the place were marched for 2 months a distance of 600 kilometres, sleeping in barns and [haylofts] during February and March of this year. A few did part of the journey by rail – 100 men to a wagon built for 40 – but ¼ were dead on arrival at the destination.

The dead were thrown into miniature railway trucks and tipped into a common burial spot. The daily ration for the march was 3 potatoes and hot water – the rest had to be scrounged for. So the present inhabitants arrived on March 25th. For each hut, such as in our [camp] would house 100 men, there were 400 of the luckless people: in the hut they had to live for <u>all</u> purposes. There [is] a small area around each hut for [excrement] – perhaps 20yds wide. Water [is] laid on, but sanitation and hygiene is of <u>the </u>most primitive nature. Dysentery, typhus and general physical decay are rampant. I have had experience of dysentery myself in the Desert … but <u>never</u> have I seen anything as awful. After 5 or 6 years of captivity, bad treatment and little food you can form a slight impression of the state these creatures are in. Many of them are walking death – and during the first few days of our arrival they were dying at the rate of 400 a day! Even now we get 35 a day who die of starvation, typhus, dysentery or….! The Poles and Russians appear have been worst treated, and are in some cases almost not human! We have to guard our lot who are cannibals! – having cut out and eaten raw the heart and livers of their dead comrades. One party are German political opponents of the Nazis and they are in an awful state. They wear concentration camp uniform – i.e. a pyjama like outfit of blue and white stripes. No hair, and no real footwear. They live in dark cells and are too weak to be moved. At the moment all the people are being slowly fed up on better food – it is a great strain on their digestion – and tended by the doctor for whatever treatment is best. The poor beggars hobble about like frail ghosts and take ages to get up, move and settle down again. One man aged 42, was found to weigh 36 pounds! They are of all ages – from 13 to 85, living together – and yet there are many who remain fairly reasonable. The French, Belgians and Yugo Slavs are the quickest to recover and appear to have fared best during the past years. A few speak English, they still laugh and chatter among themselves, one fellow I have heard singing and a few have been kicking a football around. But the saddest of all is to talk to the Poles about their future. They are a party [who] leave the camp each day to go home, but several have asked us 'where can we go?' The Russians intend to hold on to [their] 'homeland' – and nearly all the Poles I have spoken to dislike the Russians as much as they do the Germans. Unless a big compromise is quickly reached on the question, Poland is to be a problem of the first magnitude. But to get back to the camp description. For the last two weeks German men and women labour corps have been brought into the place daily to clean it up, and you can not conceive the muck and mess they have had to clean up. The huts have been quite unsanitary and unkept, and the only thing to do has been to empty the huts lock, stock and barrel. Burn the whole stinking lot… Really, Kay, the filth and stench is indescribable, and unless experienced cannot be really conceived. However, one soon gets hardened to it and we get every other day free from the place. Now I am immune to all sights (dead, living, debased and half dead) and smell. One other point and I will finish this impression of a live real Hell. Now it is warm and dry, but what was the condition in February's snow? Huts have fallen in, owing to having been stripped of wood for fires, and their clothing is made up of all manner of gear. In fact, that is the one comic side of the place. All queer mixtures of [beards] and clothes fashions. The place is daily improving, emptying, cleaned. The fellows are recovering strength, going out for walks, washing and wondering about their future. Others are still clinging to the last straws of life and an MO has told us that he thinks 60% of the camp will be able to survive.

The Germans who are working on the place, appear to be quite unmoved by the scene and the jobs they have to do. They have to do the most menial tasks imaginable, and are full of laughter and talk as they do it. Of course, all the POWs say we treat them in far too generously a manner. They want us to be more brutal and severe with them. Two days ago I saw a distribution of Red X parcels. They were delighted to have them, and are obviously vital to their survival. The Russians do not get Red X parcels and that may explain why they are in so much worse a condition than the French, for example Lolly and I went to an exhibition of art done by some of the inmates, and I asked for a painting as a souvenir from [a] Russian ... but when I called for it the next day, he had left for Russia!

Well that is a slight impression of a horror camp. It is far worse in actual fact and some of the sights I shall never be able to forget.

What would help most of all though, would be to see you again and to spend a fortnight together on the jaunt in Devon, N. Wales or......

'Au revoir' blow out a match for me,

All my love is yours,
Michael

MODERN WARFARE

There has only been one year since the Second World War in which British servicemen have not been killed in action: 1968. Otherwise, British forces have been engaged actively and dangerously around the world, as the post-war letters in this volume demonstrate.

With the end of the Second World War came the beginning of the end of the British Empire. The overseas empire became a luxury for which the British, who had expended one-third of their net worth in the struggle against Nazism, could no longer afford, particularly as the Japanese had comprehensively destroyed the prestige of the British Empire in the fall of Singapore in February 1942. Many of the post-war conflicts involving British troops around the globe sprung up as a result of having to withdraw from empire, which policy makers in London understandably did not want to look like an undignified scuttle.

Yet the first major post-war conflicts involving Britain had nothing to do with empire at all, but everything to do with ideology. In February 1950, Josef Stalin's USSR signed a 30-year treaty of friendship with Mao Zedong's Communist China, which enabled China to pursue an aggressive and expansionist policy on the Korean peninsula. The Cold War had only been simmering for four years, but the Communist World was about to test the resolve of the Free World.

At dawn on Sunday 25 June 1950, China's satellite state, Communist North Korea, invaded South Korea without warning, driving southwards as fast as possible and capturing the South Korean capital Seoul three days later. A temporary boycott of the United Nations by the USSR meant that the Security Council could pass a resolution condemning the North Korean invasion of her southern neighbour, promising to 'furnish such assistance as may be necessary to meet the armed attack'. The entire war was thus fought under UN auspices, something which greatly helped President Harry Truman and the British Prime Minister Clement Attlee.

On 15 September, UN forces under General Douglas MacArthur landed at Inchon, west of Seoul, and liberated the city on 26 September. Five days later UN and South Korean forces crossed the 38th Parallel into North Korea, capturing its capital, Pyongyang, on 20 October. Yet the whole strategic situation radically altered on 26 November when Red China entered the war, forcing the UN to retreat southwards. On New Year's Day 1951, Chinese forces broke through the UN lines at the 38th Parallel and three days later they and their North Korean allies retook Seoul.

The United States, South Korea, Britain, Australia, New Zealand and Canada were then engaged in a desperate fight against the vast Chinese People's Liberation Army. Between 22 and 25 April 1951 the British 29th Brigade, including the 1st Battalion, Gloucestershire Regiment ('the Glorious Glosters'), and the 3rd Battalion, Royal Australian Regiment, helped to halt a huge Communist offensive along the Imjin River in some of the bitterest fighting of the war. In retrospect it was astonishing that the British death toll in Korea was only 1,078 and Australia's 340. The United States' was far higher, with around 40,000 killed and 103,284 wounded.

It was not until 27 July 1953 that delegates from the United Nations, North Korea and China signed an armistice at Panmunjom, after an estimated 3 million people had perished, and a 2½-mile-wide demilitarized zone across Korea was accepted by both sides, which has remained in place ever since.

Throughout this period, indeed from 1948 to 1960, the British Commonwealth was also fighting a guerrilla war against the Communist Malayan National Liberation Army (MNLA) in the jungles of Malaya, which involved some 40,000 British, Malayan and Commonwealth forces trying to hold down a Communist insurgency of between 5,000 and 8,000 fighters. The Commonwealth forces, under General Sir Gerald Templer, adopted a 'hearts and minds' strategy designed to win over villagers and ordinary Malayans from Communism, which was eventually very successful. In all 519 British soldiers and 1,346 policemen lost their lives in what became known as the Malayan Emergency, against over 6,000 insurgents. The fact that Malaya did not fall to Communism, in the way that Vietnam, Cambodia and Laos were to – and is today a successful democratic country – can be largely explained by the imaginative, proactive tactics adopted by Templer and his senior commanders.

Fought simultaneously with the Malayan Emergency was another insurgency operation in Kenya known as the Mau Mau Uprising. For many years Kenyan nationalists had been pressing the British for political rights and land reforms, but in 1952, as no action was seen to be taken, a significant part – but by no means the majority – of the Kikuyu tribe began to adopt terrorist techniques to try to force the British out of Kenya. The result was a guerrilla war that was fought there until 1960. Since many Kikuyu fought with the British against the Mau Mau, modern scholars tends to see the conflict largely in terms of an intra-Kikuyu tribal civil war. Although the capture of their charismatic leader Didan Kimathi in October 1956 marked the turning point in the campaign, it was not truly over until nearly four years later, by which time some 200 British and African servicemen had been killed, as well as nearly 12,000 Mau Mau and 1,817 Kenyan civilians. The independence of Kenya in December 1963 came in part because Britain refused to continue to shoulder the burden of colonialism, but would probably not have happened so soon had it not been for the war.

Cyprus had become a protectorate of the British Empire in 1878, and during the Second World War some 30,000 Cypriots had fought against the Axis. After Britain withdrew from Egypt in 1954, however, a Greek Cypriot nationalist organisation named Ethniki Organosis Kyprion Agoniston (National Organisation of Cypriot Fighters – EOKA), which wanted Cyprus to enter into political union with Greece, began fighting for a total British withdrawal in a campaign that was to cost the lives of 371 British servicemen. By November 1955 a state of emergency had been declared by the British governor, which continued until Cyprus became independent in August 1960. Yet EOKA did not get what it ultimately wanted, and the disputes between the Greek and Turkish communities on the island eventually led to a Turkish invasion in 1974, and the partition of the island.

Another post-war dispute over British rule occurred in Aden, a British Crown Colony. After the loss of the Suez Canal in 1956, Aden had become the main British base in the region, and was an important link for the British trade routes and oil. In January 1963 the colony was renamed the State of Aden, falling within the Federation of South Arabia (FSA). That same year, a grenade attack launched by the National Liberation Front against the British High Commissioner resulted in one person killed and around 50 injured. A state of emergency was declared. The following year Britain announced their intention to grant independence to the FSA in 1968, however over the following years the situation deteriorated and rival factions fought for control of the area. The Aden police were unarmed and in many instances reluctant to get involved, so keeping the peace fell to the British Army, who patrolled as best they could. 1967 saw mass riots and the intervention of British troops did little to quell the situation, but instead the troops found themselves caught in the middle and attacked by both sides. It is estimated that 90 British soldiers died during the conflict. On 30 November the British pulled out of Aden and the People's Republic of South Yemen was proclaimed.

In the Malayan, Mau Mau and Cypriot emergencies it was at least debatable about the extent to which local people wanted local nationalist leaders as opposed to British governors to rule them.

That was certainly not the case in the next conflict to cost a significant numbers of British lives, in and around the Falklands Islands, whose 1,813-strong population were 97 per cent British. Yet on 31 March 1982 the head of the Argentinian Junta, General Leopoldo Galtieri, who had seized power the previous December, ordered an invasion of the Islands 250 miles off Argentina's coast. The Argentinians landed on the Falklands on 2 April. At a meeting with the British prime minister, Margaret Thatcher, the First Sea Lord, Admiral Sir Henry Leach, argued for 'sending every element of the fleet of any possible value', which he felt required a powerful force, not just a small squadron, with an amphibious capacity and a full commando brigade. He concluded that it should also include two aircraft carriers HMS *Invincible* and *Hermes*, as well the a number of destroyers and frigate as escorts. Enough, in short, for a war rather than just a 'police action'.

These were very much Margaret Thatcher's own views, so a 'Task Force' was sent on the over 8,000-mile journey to the South Atlantic, to wrest back the Falkland Islands by force. Early on in the conflict the British had announced the creation of a 200-mile Total Exclusion Zone around the Islands, inside which Argentine vessels could not sail. On 2 May the Argentinian cruiser *General Belgrano* was sunk with the loss of 323 lives even though it was outside this exclusion zone. Since she had already made no fewer than three major changes in direction over the previous 19 hours, there was no telling whether she might not make a fourth back towards shallower water, where the British submarine HMS *Conqueror* might have lost track of her, so she was sunk. The sinking of *Belgrano* ensured the removal of the Argentine naval threat, as after her loss, the fleet, with the exception of one submarine, returned to port for the remainder of the conflict. On 21 May, British troops landed on San Carlos and after some heavy fighting, including the battles of Goose Green and Mount Tumbledown, the Argentinians surrendered on 14 June. Some 253 Britons had lost their lives recovering the Falklands, and 775 were wounded, against 649

Argentinians killed and 1,068 wounded. Three Falkland Islanders were killed.

British involvement in the Bosnian conflict of the 1990s was driven neither by Cold War ideological nor post-imperial imperatives, but was simply humanitarian. The Bosnian conflict of 1992–95 grew out of ancient religious and ethnic hatreds in the Balkans that had for decades been submerged and kept quiescent in the ethnically diverse country of Yugoslavia, which had been ruled by the Communist dictator Marshal Tito. After his death in 1980, but especially after the fall of Communism in Europe in 1989–90, the country began to disintegrate and collapse into warring territorial parts, made worse by Christian–Muslim tensions, in which entire communities were 'ethnically cleansed' by their immediate neighbours. The British Army took part in the United Nations' peace keeping mission to the former Yugoslavia, known as UNPROFOR (United Nations Protection Force), between 1992 and 1995, attempting to bring relief to communities that had been devastated by the fighting. After France, Britain was the largest contributor of troops to Bosnia. The numbers killed in the fighting in the Balkans in the 1990s is still disputed, but was probably in the region of a quarter of a million. For so many people to die on the European continent half a century after the end of the Second World War is a severe indictment of Western political leadership, as well as, of course, the perpetrators themselves.

The Gulf War came about as the direct result of the attempt by President Saddam Hussein of Iraq to annex the neighbouring and hugely oil-rich state of Kuwait by force on 2 August 1990, in contravention of every rule of international law. Great Britain provided the third-largest force (53,462 personnel), after the United States and Saudi Arabia, of a 34-country coalition that began the liberation of Kuwait in Operation *Desert Storm* on 17 January 1991. The operation ended on 28 February, by which time 392 coalition personnel had lost their lives, including 47 British troops, as well as an estimated 20,000–35,000 Iraqis.

Although the Iraqi forces were in full retreat, it was decided not to overthrow Saddam for fear of breaking up the coalition, a decision that many came to regret a decade later when the British Army took part in the Iraq War.

The American-led military invasion began on 20 March 2003; 248,000 American soldiers were supported by 40 countries, 46,000 British and 2,000 Australian soldiers. Its aims were stated as being the end of Saddam Hussein's regime, elimination of any weapons of mass destruction, removal of Islamist militants, intelligence gathering, distribution of humanitarian aid and assisting in the creation of a new government. On 9 April, Baghdad fell and Hussein's 24-year rule was brought to an end. The 'invasion' phase of the conflict thus ended; the reported casualty figures were 9,200 Iraqi combatants killed, while the Coalition figures included 139 US personnel and 33 British soldiers. After the short and successful land campaign, a long counter-insurgency war had to be fought, in which the British Army was given the province of Basra in southern Iraq to protect, which it did to the best of its abilities until 2009. Unlike conventional wars, the insurgency campaign the British faced meant that it was hard to tell civilians and insurgents apart, and it became a very different battle to those previously fought by the British Army; suicide bombs and roadside Improvised Explosive Devices (IEDs) were a frequent threat. As such the Coalition began to use air power and artillery in order to strike at suspected ambush sites or mortar-launching positions, while also increasing surveillance efforts on major routes, stepping up the number of patrols and raiding suspected insurgents. At the same time, the Coalition sought to establish the country as a stable, democratic state, holding elections in early 2005.

The British Army announced its withdrawal from Iraq on 30 April 2009, handing Basra over to American forces. It has been estimated that a total of 26,320 insurgents, 16,623 Iraqi military and police, 4,474 US troops (including 66 during Operation *New*

Dawn) and 178 British service personnel and one MOD civilian were killed throughout the campaign.

On 7 October 2001, the armed forces of the United States launched Operation *Enduring Freedom*, a bid to remove the Al Qaeda terrorist organization from Afghanistan and the Taliban regime from power. The action was a direct response to the Al Qaeda terrorist attack on New York on 11 September 2001, in which nearly 3,000 people died. The United Kingdom, alongside Coalition forces including the Commonwealth of Australia and the Afghan United Front (Northern Alliance), were first deployed in November 2001, with 1,700 Marines committed in eastern Afghanistan. In December of that year the United Nations formed the International Security Assistance Force (ISAF) in order to secure Kabul and the surrounding areas.

The initial operations were a combination of air strikes and ground offensives, and by mid November Kabul had fallen to the Northern Alliance and Coalition troops, while some of the senior Taliban leadership had fled to neighbouring Pakistan. In 2004 the Afghan people held elections and Hamid Karzai, already the leader of an interim government, was elected to create a government, giving the people representative institutions. Osama bin Laden was killed during a Special Forces raid in Pakistan on 2 May 2011, however this action further strained the diplomatic relationship between the United States and Pakistan, which had been deteriorating for many years.

In 2006 ISAF expanded and the British were deployed to Helmand Province as their area of operations. A total of 3,300 British soldiers were committed to the region. As with the war in Iraq, British troops found themselves up against a long, drawn-out counter-insurgency campaign, and a battle for hearts and minds among the population. The insurgents used similar tactics as they had in Iraq: roadside and suicide bombs and IEDs. ISAF troops have spent much time building up the Afghan security forces and police in order for there to be a successful handover as and when they pull out.

While the war is still ongoing, and British forces are committed to the fight until 2014, figures are estimated to be nearly 40,000 Taliban and insurgents dead and around 14,022 Coalition and Afghan forces lost, including 445 British dead and more than 5,500 wounded. The civilian death toll is thought to be up to as much as 12,500 between 2007–11. British troops have begun to withdraw, but, as of the end of 2013, there are estimated to be 6,000 British soldiers still serving in Afganistan.

The outbreak of the Korean War in June 1950 caught British forces unprepared and, as the North Koreans poured southwards and the United States rushed forces from Japan to try to stop them, Great Britain gathered together what troops it could to assist the UN cause. The first units came from the 27th Infantry Brigade, based in Hong Kong, which arrived in time to take part in the battle for the Pusan Perimeter. The 29th Infantry Brigade followed shortly afterwards, with 1st Battalion, the Royal Ulster Rifles, amongst its units.

Lieutenant Robert Gill was called up from the officer reserve to serve as a platoon commander with the Ulster Rifles in Korea, arriving at the beginning of November 1950. They moved to the city of Suwon, just south of the South Korean capital of Seoul, from where Bob Gill wrote to his girlfriend back home.

Suwon
Friday Nov 17

Dearest Doreen,
I am on duty tonight as Orderly Officer. At the moment I am in the Orderly room which is the 'office' of the battalion, and here I will stay the night. One of the clerks is tapping away at an old typewriter and altogether things are very quiet and peaceful. Later I will take a walk around camp and check on the various guards. The night is fine and there is a moon coming up. I have too much time to think of you and home, Darling. You say the same. You like to be busy so that the days pass quicker and so do I.

We have been here ten days now and the time has been spent preparing the transport and kit before we move North. I am still waiting for three of my carriers and a truck which have not arrived from Pusan. They shall be here quite soon though now and then off we go.

The main battalion is still patrolling north of Seoul and during the last two days there have been reports of a guerrilla attack on Seoul which is to take place tomorrow the 18th. However we will soon know whether the report is accurate.

We are still on American rations and tonight there was an issue of chewing gum. I haven't felt the urge to chew yet though, Darling.

My sweet, this will only be a short letter. I haven't anything new to talk about. However, whenever I do have a chance to write, you're the one I always want to talk to. I may not be able to write often later on and so I should make the most of the time now.

My lovely Darling, I want to be with you so much. I don't know how long this bloomin' war is going to last but it has parted us for too long already.

Cheerio for now.

All my love,
Bob
PS Hope the nylons arrived!

Bob Gill was on the front line as the Chinese launched an offensive on 31 December 1950, with Seoul falling again on 4 January 1951, and the Ulster Rifles being pushed back from Suwon a few days later.

Suwon
Jan 4th

My Dearest,
Just a note to let you know that I am quite safe after our first big battle with the chinks. We were moved north on Jan 1st to take up positions covering Seoul. The next day we had a small battle with some North Koreans and drove them off the positions they had taken.

Naturally we were very pleased with ourselves but last night the American command, to my surprise gave us orders to withdraw. We did and the Chinese ambushed us. It really was a hell of a night... Our company suffered very heavy casualties, being last to leave. Seoul has now had it presumably and we are at the moment back where we started, in the silk factory...

All my love for now Sweet,
Bob

Middle of Nowhere
Korea
Wed 10 Jan

Dearest Doreen,
You see I have some posh stationary now, thanks to you. The parcel arrived safely and I was pleased with all the odds and ends.

I wrote to you from Suwon the other day after we packed up and moved further south. We have been in this position a few days now and we all hope that each day will be the last. It is rather grim with mud everywhere and now we have had a heavy fall of snow. Settled sleep is out of the question because we are expecting the Chinese to come along here anytime. Actually though I have my doubts because all the countryside is very open or with the tanks and guns we have, we're on 'home ground'. These Chinks are best at night in the hills and I am rather sceptical about them meeting us in the open. If they come along here we'll paste them!

Alternatively they may come around through the hills and outflank us. If that happens, and it is expected, we'll move south again. You see I am going all tactical at the moment dear – soldiering may be damned uncomfortable at times, but it is never dull or uninteresting.

No more news now dearest, keep on sending me these lovely letters and the cuttings for I am not really out of touch with home when I hear from you all.

Cheerio sweet.

Affectionately,
Bob

The British forces also saw considerable action during the battle of the Imjin River in April 1951 when the 29th Infantry Brigade, and notably the men of the 1st Battalion, Gloucestershire Regiment, fought a desperate rearguard action against overwhelming Chinese forces.

Julian Potter served as a National Service junior officer with 11 Light Anti Aircraft Battery, Royal Artillery, in Korea, and took part in the aftermath of the battle of the Imjin, guarding the Han River bridges to the south.

Dear Mum and Dad,

In case you did not get my last letter, my release has come through; I am to be demobbed by October 1st and in 'J' RHU by July 1st. With this Chinese Communist offensive in full swing however, one cannot be <u>certain</u> that things will work out just like that. 'J' RHU has been practically emptied in the last few days, and there is a rumour that all leave to Japan has been stopped. If the Chinese advance is stemmed north of Seoul, we will presumably carry on in our safe role of protecting the bridges. Since the offensive begun, 11 Bty has had only one sergeant injured in the way of casualties, which shows the comparative safety of our job: the infantry battalions of 29 Brigade suffered an appalling proportion of killed, wounded or missing – I don't know if the papers published the figures…

At the moment there is a general air of anticipation and excitement, as everyone is digging in for the defence of Seoul. All the gun detachments are scrounging and pilfering from the Americans' supply of sandbags, in order to increase the width and height of the walls of their gunpits. The air-strip is in continuous use, as sortie after sortie of UN planes take off, loaded with napalm bombs, rockets, etc. UN gunfire has now been rumbling in the distance for 24 hours non-stop. No more refugees are allowed to cross the river, for fear of letting through enemy in disguise. To-day one of the more nervy gun detachments complained that they had spotted Koreans digging trenches on the other side of a gulley in front of the gun. On investigation, I found that the holes they had dug were filled in. Fearing the civilians might be hiding arms for the eventual use of the Communists, I made them dig the holes out again; only to find that they had been protecting their food and clothing from any bombs or shells that might come down...

Love from Julian

Following the fluctuating offensives of 1950 and 1951, as the Communist and UN forces made great territorial gains in large-scale operations, the period from July 1951 until the end of the war in July 1953 was one of stalemate and attrition. The two sides settled into a prolonged period of trench warfare, interrupted only by sporadic major operations, while peace talks dragged on.

Lieutenant Garry Smith was a National Serviceman with the 5th Royal Inniskilling Dragoon Guards, again part of the 29th Infantry Brigade, and describes his first Christmas in Korea.

KOREA
CHRISTMAS DAY 1951

Dear Mum & Dad,
I expect you have all had the normal round of Christmas festivities, or will have had by the time you get this letter. I believe in fact although it is five minutes to five in the afternoon here, you will just be getting up on Christmas morning to go to early service. I must say we are not very cheerful here. Last night we had some Canadians who made a lot of noise up till about three in the morning. They were all very tight and had been attracted by the lights of my cookhouse where the turkeys were being roasted on our field oven which is made out of a 50 gallon oil drum and corrugated iron. The noise kept a major in HQ Squadron, who lives about 200 yards away, awake and both Dave and I who had slept through almost all of it except the last when I went out and quelled the riot, were not very popular. We did our best for the men, took them tea and rum in bed in the morning and served out the dinner which was very good, though a bit cold as we have no dining room. It started to hail in the morning, then snow till lunch, and now it is pouring with rain and we are all very damp. But the men are in good heart and have lots of sweets and nuts and beer in moderation so that's all right. I am going to Kure in Japan on about the 27th which does not please me, but I expect you will be glad to hear.

A merry Christmas and the Best of Luck,
From Garry & Dave

PS. We had a bit of a battle yesterday, I wasn't there but apparently one tank got stuck and everyone flapped quite unnecessarily, not much on today, though there was a lot of shelling on both sides last night. The doctor shot a deer which looks like a dog and has big front teeth and no horns but tastes quite good. We had a Carol service this morning.

G.

444 Field Rel Squadron
KOREA ASAPO 3
10/3/52

Dear Mum & Dad,
I am sorry I haven't written to you for so long, but as you will see from the address I am now once more up sharp, as the saying is, for the last month we have been chasing all over mid-western Korea, but we are now static once more at Tokehony where I am engaged in hewing a habitation out of the wilderness with the boys.

Luckily Boing Cho Jail which was our last stopping place had wooden floors and ceilings. These were brought with us … and now we have wooden floors and doors to each tent.

We are in a very pleasant position in a little valley opening onto the main plain up which the main road runs to the north. It is sunny and quite warm during the day, but very cold at night. My tooth water is always frozen…

Behind our camp up the hill there is a comfortable gook position wonderfully dug in and in places the camouflage is still on. They dig great tunnels sometimes right through a ridge, with deep entrenchments on the forward slope and little shacks on the other side. In this case one can follow the whole campaign that finally eliminated this position. First the American foxholes on the lower slopes, then tank tracks where tanks came up to support the advance then the blasted line of trenches, and finally then the crest, the second line of American foxholes…

More later,

Love Garry

PS. I have grown a moustache as threatened, I shall not be back until November definitely.

Indy. Guard Coy Pusan

BAPO 3.

3/5/52

Dear Mum & Dad,

The weather of late has been very depressing, we get two days of sun and then it rains and drizzles for the rest of the week. Yesterday I went round all the guards to pay them. Things have been very quiet surprisingly as trouble was expected over Monday and no one was allowed out, but nothing happened except that all the Koreans got very drunk on Sake. We have some excitement; a band of guerrillas has holed up in the middle of some very rough country outside Pusan which is also a big store area with only very scattered guards mostly Korean police; they have taken of late to coming out at night and shooting at lighted windows which is rather inconvenient…

Still no sign of this action ending, the Koreans certainly do not want it to, at any rate not down here, they have never had it so good in their lines and all will be lost if the Americans go home. There are some Americans whom I like very much, but collectively they are an awful lot of clots. We had one to dinner the other day whose rank over here is Colonel, but whose substantive rank is Corporal. I think theirs is probably the only army in which such a thing could exist, though the adjutant at Kure who is a major was a full lieut when he came out…

Your son,

Garry

At the same time as the British Army was providing troops for the UN commitment in Korea, it was also garrisoning the last bastions of empire around the globe. The post-war years saw Great Britain gradually withdraw from most of her imperial possessions, sometimes peacefully but often in the face of armed opposition from local groups. This was the situation in the British colony of Malaya, where the British Army carried out anti-guerrilla operations against a Communist insurgency from 1948 until 1960. Michael Rugman served with the King's Royal Hussars in Malaya in 1955, one of the many British regiments committed to what became known as the Malayan Emergency.

23217940 Tpr Rugman
HQ Sqn
XV-XIX K.R.H.
C/O GPO IPOH
Ipoh
Monday 19th Sept 1955

Dear Mum & Dad,
The mail this end has been arriving so fast I've hardly had time to reply before the next one comes in… I'm glad you had a good long spell of summer weather. Pity you didn't have a week or two away somewhere. My summer has lasted six and half months and time has flown. Yes, I've been in the army about a year now. And on the whole life hasn't been too bad, it's been interesting and I'm with people my own age and interests, but things get a bit niggling at times, you live from one lot of Sqn details to the next and you feel rather restricted at times. It's a bit difficult to explain, but on the whole it's passable.

The weekend before last I went into the ule [jungle] on a jungle bash. But we returned with no notches on our rifle butts.

We went into a forest reserve twenty miles south of Ipoh early Saturday afternoon, pushed into the interior, stopped just before sunset to change, have a quick meal cooked on small portable cookers and chunks of solid fuel, and laid ambush for the night. Next morning we pressed on and reached a track. We stopped by a pool of murky water for breakfast, where we refilled our water bottles making the water drinkable with special sterilizing tablets. We continued until we came out in the afternoon. All the time you have your rifle cocked and keep ten yards behind the man in front, and you can only talk in whispers. But they (CT's) must have seen us coming, for we didn't see a sign of any bandits. It rather resembled a Live Scout widegame, the type that flop…

I expect you've heard about the Jubilee celebrations of the Sultan of Johore, to what extent I don't know but it appears the Sultan made a good speech and to the point when he said if he were a Britishman he would not stay and fight the CTs as the security forces weren't getting enough info from the civilians, leading to the capture of terrorists.

As I've said before, quite a few people in our troop have been getting, or are, timex (going out soon) and the main topic of conversation these days verges on this subject and is rather disconcerting…

Keep well,
Love to you all,
Michael

The British also faced opposition to their rule in the East African colony of Kenya, where a revolt by the Kikuyu tribe, known as the Mau Mau Uprising, caused a state of emergency to be declared by the British governor in October 1952. Theodore Henry Birkbeck was the commanding officer of the 70th Infantry Brigade, King's African Rifles (KAR), which was one of the principal units deployed to Kenya by the British authorities to crush the uprising. In August 1955 Birkbeck wrote the following letter to a fellow major general, William Alfred Dimoline.

Tel NYER 76 Ext 2
Ref 800/P
15 Aug 55

I arrived here on Sunday 7th August, having spent my first night in Nairobi with General Lathbury. Coming from 'tropical England' I ran into some extremely cold and damp weather here which was rather odd, to say the least of it.

John Orr and I got straight down to the handover and a pretty busy week followed. The brigade was deployed in the forest in Operation *Dante*, mostly in the Eastern Aberdares. We visited 4 and 5 KAR early in the week and then had to go on Wednesday to a C-in-Cs conference at GHQ.

I expect you will see General Lathbury in London this week, who will give you his plan for our future deployment.

Operation *Dante* finishes today and all 5 Battalions are returning to their base camps where they will rest and refit until the end of the month. After that we shall deploy again right up as far as the Meru where I shall be sending the 7th KAR. The idea then is for each battalion to dominate a particular area of forest while the reserves are handed over to the Administration and the Police.

My first impression of the Mau Mau is that they are definitely on the run and that if we continue to hit them hard and confine them more and more to the forest the end may well be in sight. This is my personal view and I should be grateful if you would treat the contents of this letter as confidential and between ourselves.

I have not seen very much of the Battalions as yet but they seem to be in excellent heart in spite of nearly three years of continual operations.

Lieut Col F.H.W. Brind, DSO, OBE and Lieut Col C.V. Watson-Gandy are both on leave so I have not met them. Brigadier J.F. McNab, DSO, OBE is also away but I look forward to seeing him on his return.

It was most kind of you and Mrs Dimoline to give me lunch before I left and I am finding the talk we had together most useful. I shall send you 'sitreps' from time to time to keep you in the picture, but they may not be as frequent as I would desire, as I think that I shall be a bit pushed for time to start with.

With best wishes and kindest regards to you both.
Yours,
THB

It wasn't just in the far-flung colonies that Great Britain was confronting issues arising out of the retreat from empire, even in the Mediterranean there were problems that required military intervention. The island of Cyprus was annexed by Britain during the First World War and became a crown colony from 1923, however, in the years following the Second World War a national movement demanding enosis, union with Greece, became increasingly popular. This movement broke out into armed revolt in 1955 when Ethniki Organosis Kyprion Agoniston (National Organization of Cypriot Fighters – EOKA) launched a campaign against British rule.

Peter J. Houghton-Brown was a National Service officer in the 1st Battalion, Wiltshire Regiment, which was deployed to Cyprus as reinforcements following the outbreak of the emergency.

[1956]
1st Battalion. The Wiltshire Regiment
BFPO 53

… Landed safely and have come straight up here to Aghirda. It
is a tented camp on the side of the northern range of mountains,
just like any other Army camp, except that gin is 5 pence and
beer is expensive at 1 shilling.

One carries a loaded pistol with one everywhere you go. It
must never leave you. One man dying and two injured was their
bag last night. The terrorists threw a bomb into the back of an
Army truck.

In a few days I go off to my platoon at Myrtou; a village 40
minutes drive to the west. This seems a most unsavoury job. You
have orders to shoot at anyone you see who might be going to
throw a bomb, and you cannot tell if it's a bomb or a stone. I
cannot quite see how we are not going to get hateful to
these people.

B Company,
BFPO 53

… I have been blooded. Did you read in the papers that an
army Patrol had been stoned in Kyrenia (also BBC Wednesday
news). That was me. I have been going to a Court Marshal [sic]
every day for the last 3 days. This means going by land rover
along the coast road at about 9am each morning. The first
morning we got stoned badly in Lapithos, we were going under
a bank and about 30 school children hurled rocks on us. No
one was hit except me. I got a big stone on the arm and have a
large bruise to show for it. There was only me, the driver and
our guard. Not enough of us to stop and beat the hell out [of]
them as we wished.

The next day we caught it again, this time it was school children from Kyrenia. This was the incident on the news, not half as bad as the day before, not so many stones and more clumps of earth. I was in my Blues, best hat, etc, and got very dirty again. Again we did not have enough people to do anything about it.

They threw a bomb at some of my platoon last night. They were in a truck and the bomb blew a great hole in it. No one was hurt, just luck. Everything they do they seem to get away with. They killed 24 troops last year and we only killed 6.

Further east the Protectorate of Aden was the main British base in the Middle East following the withdrawal from Suez in 1956. In 1963 an insurgency erupted against British rule in the area, which ended with a unilateral British withdrawal in 1967.

Flying Officer Anne Peterkin served with Princess Mary's Royal Air Force Nursing Service based at the RAF hospital, Khormaksar, in Aden and had to deal with the casualties arising from the conflict.

Officers Mess
RAF Hospital
Khormaksar Beach
Aden
16-5-65

Dearest family,
Again, many thanks for your letters... News from the Middle East:
... The ward has been exceptionally busy this last week. We had several very badly injured men admitted having been attacked by mortar fire up country. In fact the worst battle casualties I've seen!

They were brought down by helicopter and the pilots got a terrific appraisal on the local news as they picked them up under fire.

Today there is a marked improvement in their conditions but it is sad to see a young officer of 21 and an 18-year-old so ill.

Again, as always when we're busy the air conditioning failed and we've been working in tremendous heat. In fact today is the hottest day it's been. Mind you, I am very lucky as I don't find it too bad as long as I swig plenty of fluid…

Well, think that's all the news there is for now. Sorry no photo this week.

All the best to William in his exams.

Much love to all,
Annie

The issue of the sovereignty of the Falkland Islands has been a subject of both discourse and dispute since the very first settlers landed there in the second half of the 18th century. Great Britain has held the islands continuously from 1833 onwards in the face of Argentinian territorial claims and the issue has been a source of intermittent tension between the two countries ever since. On 2 April 1982 the Argentinians invaded the Falklands Islands, sparking a conflict that involved a British Task Force being mobilised and then racing to the Islands to protect British interests.

Nick Van der Bijl was a staff sergeant in the Intelligence Corps who was attached to HQ 3 Commando, Royal Marines, for the duration of the campaign. He travelled south to the Falklands aboard HMS *Fearless* from where he wrote home to his family.

HMS *Fearless*
BFPO 666

Dearest Penny and Imogen,
It is now Saturday, the day before Easter Sunday and we have been at sea for four days. At present we are somewhere off the North-West African coast. It is beautiful and hot upstairs and the sea is a deep blue azure. It contrasts quite nicely with the grey paint of the warships that are all around. Something straight out of World War Two!...

We have been working extraordinarily hard trying to catch up on years of collation and recording. Unfortunately some of the channels of communication are suspect and so not all the information that is being produced is actually reaching us at sea. It makes one's life very hard especially because we cannot disseminate information... On the whole the Army, Marines and Air Force are working very well together but the Navy are proving very difficult – falling into line, so much so that important information is being withheld because 'they did not think you needed it'...

Today ships from the Gibraltar / Mediterranean joined us at first light and our Task Force is now in convoy configuration with warships, destroyers, RFAs and LSLs. It is quite extraordinary and I am not quite sure I believe it. In fact ... this is no exercise – it is a real operation. We continue to pick up the BBC and understand that the Government are still maintaining an offensive posture, as are the Argentinians. I expect much will depend on Gen Haig and the 200-mile limit warnings that come into force on Monday.

Sunday now... This morning HMS *Antelope*, another frigate, came alongside and a package was passed by heavy line. The Navy remain full of tradition and as the ship left the officers saluted each other and the Bosun blew his whistle. Talking about the Navy; they are probably the least aware of the problem at the moment and do seem disinclined to believe that we may be sailing to a shooting war…

Monday today… We still do not know really what is going to happen as we receive the BBC news only. Obviously our Lnt tells us a bit more but the political manoeuvring does not give us too much. The word at present on *Fearless* is censorships. We have all been told what we are not allowed to write about – [but] most of [what] I am not meant to tell you, you will obtain from the TV…

Wednesday evening and really the first time since Monday that I have had time to write. We have had a good deal of work to do, although we do not seem to be any nearer a solution as to activities or the objective. I am now beginning to feel rather tired… The trouble is that there does not appear to be any end to the work, it just seems to come pouring – mind you, I am not complaining because this is 'for real' and the way that the Government have dug their heels in it may end in some form of confrontation…

Just heard the news that Mr Haig has returned to the US to report to Reagan.* I imagine that this might be a bit depressing for you – perhaps hoping that a solution will be arrived at. It is clear that UK and Argentina are miles apart. UK has mounted a massive military and naval operation and is committed to retaking the Falklands and Argentina is committed to retaining, and perhaps defending this barren but minerally rich island. Somewhere there is a solution. Rest assured that before any amphibious forces move the naval and air battle must be won…

Miss you, love you and see you soon. Adore you both.
Nick

---

* Alexander Haig was the American Secretary of State who conducted negotiations between Argentina and Britain after the Argentinians invaded the Islands. Negotiations broke down and Haig returned to Washington on 19 April.

By the end of April the Task Force was within striking distance of the Falklands, though the threat posed by Argentinian Exocet missiles was all too real, and on 4 May HMS *Sheffield* was hit by two missiles which caused the death of 20 of her crew and the ship had to be abandoned. On the same day the first Sea Harrier was lost over Goose Green.

> 5 May 82
> HMS *Fearless*
> BFPO 666

> My darling Penny and Imogen,
> It happened. The abandoning of *Sheffield* and the shooting down of the [Harrier], tragic though it is, has finally bought it home that this is a serious situation and real live bullets are being used and this inevitably means loss of life. The 'gungho' 'we can win' spirit has gone to be replaced by a stunned realization that things are not going to be that easy. Fortunately the ground troops and those who have been to Northern Ireland, where lives are lost, are virtually unaffected by it all. There is a degree of anger and frustration but at least a few realize that we are now at the mercy of cynical politicians and that to escalate the situation might encourage a superpower clash… As you probably are aware there is no way we can go ashore unless air superiority is gained. I met a couple of the Harrier pilots during the voyage out and then they virtually claimed that they could win all by themselves. Bags of confidence and Battle of Britain stuff, but hardly the ingredients for a political confrontation…
> By the time you receive this letter I shall probably be out of contact for some time, and so there will be little, if any, opportunity for discussion… Today I sorted out my kit for going ashore… Apart from the task I told you about earlier, I shall be part of the Bde Cmd Tactical HQ, a group of six to eight people who set up a small HQ prior to the main HQ

moving ashore… My kit is quite heavy and we have still to be issued with our quota of ammo and rations. Regrettably I cannot tell you more because I do not know about any more. All that I can recommend is listen to the BBC, preferably Radio 4, which generally gives an accurate view of events, without the frills of some of the more popular media outlets…

On 21 May the British went ashore in large numbers. Around 3,000 troops from 2 Para, 3 Para and 3 Commando Brigade (consisting of 40, 42 and 45 Royal Marine Commandos) landed as part of an amphibious force in San Carlos Bay.

3 Cde Bde
BFPO 666

Darling,
A very rapid letter. Went ashore during evening of D-Day. For us ashore all is OK although we have dug in deep. The Argentinians are continuing to attack the shipping and a very predictable fight it is, Skyhawk and Mirage weaving their way through the sky, dropping bombs. So far no attack against me. Have interrogated a Sgt POW who surrendered.

Rather tired and dirty although a shower has just improved the situation. The weather, fortunately, is good – we are all hoping for rain and fog – then no flying. Learning to live in holes in the ground…

I have been under fire with four near misses on *Fearless*. A bit of a hole. But very glad to be ashore. Do <u>not</u> worry; I am well. LOVE YOU AND MISS YOU! Please tell my mother the contents of this letter, please do not become concerned. Must go – my boat awaits me.

All my love,
Nick xxxx

The landing of the Task Force on East Falkland provoked a tough response from the Argentinian Air Force, with the amphibious group and its escorts taking casualties at a level that had not been experienced by the British since the battle for Crete in May 1941.

May 82
HQ 3 Cde Bde
BFPO 666

Darling Penny and Imogen,
Air raid warning just gone. It's 10pm and it is a dark starlight night. I hope you received my scribbled letter from *Fearless*. Today I went onto LSL *Belvedere* to brief some reinforcements. I had just entered the interior when the first raid came in with no warning. Guns opened up and I literally threw myself to the floor and waited. The aircraft screamed overhead. One was shot down just in front and the pilot made a POW! While I was aboard – 4 air raid warnings in three hours. Everyone was very tense. When I was picked up ... we went to Red Beach where Cdr Log was and there was a warning. Later heard that the aircraft had attacked HMS *Coventry*. There is anger because the Argies are getting through and it does seem that the Harrier screen and warships are not between us and the mainland. Therefore they have an easy run in. At least they have not gone for us. The Bde HQ is dug in below ground... We are settled into a routine now of living below ground in trenches and deep pits. We watch all the raids going in and a very spectacular business it is. Their Navy pilots are the best and all their pilots are brave men. The odds are against them but the attacks continue. Wherever an aircraft is hit or trailing smoke everybody cheers. It is like something out of *Star Wars* ... tracers and bombs flying all over the place and the noise is incredible. We watch from the top of our trenches with tin hats on...

I am well – dirty, not tired, not hungry. Everything is going well although only half IR Section ashore. There is a lot of work, though I suppose I am rather enjoying the experience… So do not worry about anything… Meanwhile LOVE and MISS YOU BOTH and look forward to seeing you.

Love and kisses,
Nick
xxxxxxx

Glenn Canham was a radio operator on board HMS *Arrow* during the campaign. This ship fired the first shot against Port Stanley on 1 May, and was also on the scene when HMS *Sheffield* was hit on 4 May and helped to take off the survivors.

Tuesday 11th May
RO (T) G. Canham
D175294N
3 Mess
HMS *Arrow*
BFPO Ships
London

Dear Mum, Dad and Ash,
Hope all is well at home and everyone is bearing up under the strain.

Sorry I haven't written for a while, you're probably getting worried, but as you have no doubt heard on the news things have been, to say the least, 'Hectic'. I'll start at the beginning of the month as good a place as any I suppose.

1st May we entered the Total Exclusion Zone (TEZ) for the first time in a solid group. Immediately we had established a standing off area, three of our ships were sent in to bombard the Airfield at Stanley. We arrived off the coast just after dinner time… For a couple of hours the three of us sat there sending off about 50 shells apiece. We then turned tail and started heading out to sea, when out from the side of the Island came two jet fighters. They missed the *Glamorgan* but caught us right across the funnel and just aft of that on the Seacot deck. That was when Brittnell was hit by a small piece of shrapnel, you probably heard that on the news. Well that was our first piece of Action and I was scared stupid for the whole time.

After that for the next few days we kept our distance during the day, legging it in at night, bombing designated targets and rejoining the main group again by morning.

I can't remember what day it was but I know it was a shocking blow to everyone when the *Sheffield* was hit by the missile. Our ship was the first one to get near her, the only things beating us there being our own helo [helicopter] and some Sea Kings from the *Hermes*. At first we waited off sailing around her in circles because apart from the missile attack we also had a Possible Submarine Contact. Our first job was to get fire fighting equipment and Medics to her which we did by helo, we then tried to get as close as possible to her so as we could help fight the fire with our own hoses but twice we had to leg out of the way of two Torpedoes. The *Yarmouth* then joined us and we prosecuted the sub contact, the *Yarmouth* lobbing mortars into the water like they were going out of fashion. Eventually we got alongside her managing to tie ourselves ruffly [sic] together not helped by the long swell that was running … but eventually it was decided to abandon her, *Yarmouth* pulled away and we switched off our hoses and started grabbing blokes and pulling them on to our ship. As we eventually pulled away because of the danger of her ammunition blowing there were still a few people including the skipper still on deck but they were taken off safely by helo.

Since then we have been doing night bombardments fairly regularly... Yesterday, or last night rather, *Alacrity* and ourselves closed the coast hunting for ships of any sort that might be using the hours of darkness for blockade running and resupply to the shore... Well that's enough of that, in fact there's far too much trash there really... Still no news of when we will be home although I have it on fairly good authority that our relief ships sailed from home yesterday. Well I think that's about it for now. I'm feeling very tired and I'm on watch again in four hours so all at home take care, keep the letters coming, thanks again for the papers.

Love,
Glenn
xx

Back ashore, the men of 3 Commando Brigade had established a beachhead and were preparing to take the fight to the Argentinian forces. On the night of 26 May, 2 Para set out for Goose Green and Darwin, while the rest of the brigade marched towards Stanley. At the beginning of June reinforcements arrived in the form of 5th Infantry Brigade, and the British were now ready to take on the ring of mountain positions that defended the capital, Port Stanley.

Sergeant Ian McKay was the platoon sergeant of 4 Platoon, B Company, 3 Para, and he won a posthumous Victoria Cross for his heroic actions in the night attack on Mount Longdon on 11/12 June. In his last letter home, written on 8 June, to his family he describes conditions before the attack.

... Sorry this is a bit scruffy, but the bottom of my hole in the ground might not be the cleanest part of the island but it is the safest.

Mind you, things are much quieter now than for some time and finding things to occupy our time is now a problem.

Some clown has put one of our artillery batteries just behind our positions and as the Argentinian guns try to range in on them they sometimes drop one in around [our] position. Life isn't dull all the time.

Mail is taking the best part of three weeks to get here so I assume the same applies vice versa. It is quite possible we will be on the way home before this gets to you.

Personally I can't wait to get back on board. I have never known a more bleak, windswept and wet place in my life. We spend our life with wet feet trying to dry out and keep warm. The wind blows constantly but is cooling rather than drying. You cannot walk 50 paces anywhere, even on the mountainsides, without walking in a bog.

I thought the Brecon Beacons was bad, but this takes the biscuit.

One of the officers I knew in the depot was shot while standing under a white flag when 2 Paras took Goose Green so feelings are running quite high both in 2 and 3 Para.

Also the papers we get, again all well out of date, mention only Marines and Guards so if we aren't officially here we might as well come home.

Apart from that bit of grousing things aren't too bad and things should be over one way or another in a week so you will probably be [reading] this with hindsight.

We will be home hopefully about two weeks afterwards…

With the fall of the mountain positions the road to Stanley lay open and the Falklands conflict came to a rapid conclusion.

Lance Corporal Andrew Mortimore was part of the 1st Battalion, Welsh Guards, who had been shipped around East Falkland at the beginning of June and were caught aboard the LSL *Sir Galahad* when the Argentinian Air Force attacked. He was meant to be on the tank deck with the Mortar Platoon when the ship was hit by three bombs, but, luckily, he was in search of a cup of tea at the time and so survived the attack. 49 men were killed, with another 115 seriously injured.

23rd June – Town Hall – Port Stanley

Dear Kay,

Many thanks for the postcard, yes I am looking forward to seeing Exmouth again. Got to Port Stanley yesterday after being on the *Canberra* doing the POW run to Argy Island. When they came on board first they smelt just like the school house at Cusichaca! Two weeks ago, as I'm sure you know already, we were hit badly as we waited to go ashore from the *Sir Galahad*. By not being where I should be I escaped with singed hair and a large burn hole in my waterproof. Had I been where I should have been I wouldn't be writing this. Thanks to your first aid lessons at least one soldier got away alive who wouldn't have had I not known what I was doing – only two medics got out.[*] The whole thing was a mess – a mess that got 25 of my mates killed. We were left in daylight for eight hours without air cover! There was hardly any warning, just someone screaming 'Air Raid Warning Red, Air Raid' – he never finished. A 500lb bomb came through the wall about 15ft away from me and carried on through two more walls and a floor where it exploded. The guy stood behind me was killed. I didn't have time to panic or be scared. Even after I got out I had to go back again to bring some others out. The smoke was so thick you could walk on it.

---

[*] Lance Corporal Mortimore had been part of an expedition to the Cusichaca Valley in the Peruvian Andes with Captain Kay Foster, who was the nurse for the expedition. While on the six month trip, Kay taught Mortimore basic first aid.

Luckily every other man was carrying a 1 litre Hartmans Drip – these saved a lot of the guys with burns. Later on today we're going back to 'Bluff Cove' by chopper for a memorial service. The wreck of the ship will be towed out to sea and sunk as an official war grave.

I lost nearly all my kit – I got away in what I was wearing. The lads from 2 Para who put us up for the night in their sheep shed were fantastic. Some of them stayed up all night making us tea. Next day we were choppered out to HMS *Intrepid* where we rested and [were] issued new kit.

Don't know how long before we get home but in the meantime we are doing a Northern Ireland type job in Stanley – patrolling – chatting up the locals – checking possible booby traps etc. Mines are still a big problem. They won't let us use Argies to find them! Looking after the POWs was a bit like giving treatment to the people in Cusichaca who had stolen from us – crazy.

Still that's life – that's war and I've had enough of this one for the moment. Not sure when I'll be home – about six weeks they say – we'll see. Hope to see you then. Give my love to Exmouth.

Love and best wishes,
Andy

During the 1990s war broke out once more in mainland Europe as the collapse of Yugoslavia saw conflict in Croatia in 1991, and then a bitter internal struggle in Bosnia from 1992 until 1995. Foreign powers sought to intervene to protect, initially through the auspices of the United Nations and from 1995 through the North Atlantic Treaty Organisation (NATO) with a more robust mandate.

Captain Peter Caddick-Adams is a military historian who served with the British Army in Bosnia in 1996. Although initially attached to the 1st Mechanised Brigade and 20th Armoured Brigade HQ, he later became a historian at the headquarters of the International Stabilisation Force (IFOR).

HQ 1st Mechanised Brigade, Operation *Resolute*, SIPOVO, Bosnia
BFPO 538
31 July 1996

Dear Nigel,

I trust this finds you well and prospering... My latest news, as my address indicates, is that I was mobilised from the TA nearly 2 months ago, for a 6 month stint with the Regular Army in Bosnia. I landed here on the morning of the 55th anniversary of Operation *Barbarossa*, and so far, all is going well, working in a brigade HQ – so now I can see how all the nuts and bolts go together for real!...

Because of the landmine threat (6 million of 'em scattered about, we are told), movement is restricted to a very few roads, each of which have names like the trenches of the Great War, which reflect the identity of their uses. The Americans drive along routes called 'Arkansas', 'Utah' or 'Kentucky'. The Brits have named theirs 'Hornblower', or 'Salmon' but the Dutch – well they cruise along a road called 'Clog'!

I often drive past the confrontation lines resembling Ypres or the Somme in 1919–20, abandoned here only last October. It's as though *Blitzkrieg* was never invented – twin sets of trenches, and communications trenches separated by No Man's Land, crater-ridden. Bunkers with log and turf roofs are set into hillsides. Artillery positions, with horse-shoe shaped low walls of stones, turf and sandbags, are dotted around, still strewn with shell cases and ammunition boxes. Bits of equipment, helmets, a lone boot etc, litter the area. Unfortunately we may look but not touch because of the booby traps/landmine threat out here. I am reading Siegfried Sassoon and one or two other choice favourites in the quiet moments. The wanton destruction of homes and villages is initially distressing – either by battle damage, or ethnic cleansing. In Sipovo, where I am based, all shops were gutted and looted, and most houses at least lost their roofs. Now the 1st shops are starting up again – just trestle tables of vegetables or cigarettes outside gutted buildings – possibly like Normandy or Germany in 1944–5.

Stay in touch, best wishes,
Pete Caddick-Addams

In August 1990 Iraqi President Saddam Hussein ordered the invasion of the neighbouring state of Kuwait, setting on course a train of events that would lead to the deployment of over 45,000 British troops to the region as part of a vast UN-authorised, US-led coalition.

Saddam Hussein had used chemical weapons during the Iran–Iraq war of the 1980s, and there was a fear that these would be deployed against coalition soldiers, as Private Neil Robertshaw vividly describes in a letter home from December 1990.

2/3-12-90

Dear Eric & Edith,
I hope you're all fine and that Julie settles in at her new flat. At the moment I'm still at Baldrick lines. It now takes only 3–4 days for letters to get here but parcels will take up to 2 weeks...

At the moment Baldrick lines are on white alert and not yellow. Although saying that everyone's hearts dropped a beat or ten this morning when we all went to Red alert.

What happened was as our company (and other ordnance companies) was preparing for the St Barbaras Day church parade. There was suddenly shouts from everywhere and people sprinting about. People were shouting 'NBC attack, NO DUFF, there's four SCUDs on their way here' – NBC (chemicals), NO DUFF (it's for real) SCUD B's (high explosive/chemical long range missiles capable of travelling from Iraq to here in 6 minutes which is 150 miles away).

So you can imagine that everyone was frightened to say the least. I raced to my chemical suit and put it on with my heart thundering and then applied my respirator and went to my platoon's lines where we were accounted for. All this took place in 4 minutes. For the next 2 minutes we waited for the impact which never came.

Apparently what happened was 4 Scud B's were spotted on radar and the alert was sounded, but the Iraqi's were only carrying out firing tests on their own ranges in Iraq. The popular belief was that they were going to fire on Israel who would return fire with nuclear armaments!

When everything returned to normal sighs of relief were heard in every direction and some other words I won't repeat.

It's now 5.00am (I'm on guard again) so I can write some more letters.

The Yanks have 24 patriot missiles aimed towards Iraq only 150mtrs down the road and they reckon they've a 97% chance of knocking out the scuds well before they reach here.

Well that's all I can think of for now. I just can't wait to get my head down when I come off guard at half seven.

Anyway, take care and lots of love,
Neil
xxx

Following months of preparation, the assault on Iraqi positions in Kuwait was launched on the night of 16/17 January 1991, with an aerial bombing campaign targeting Iraqi air defence and command and control positions.

Lieutenant Richard Whitticase served with a Royal Electrical and Mechanical Engineers unit (REME) attached to the 1st (UK) Armoured Division and wrote home on the outbreak of war.

Some place
17 Jan 91

Dear Di & Ian,

Sorry if my writing is a bit funny – it's night and this is a LED torch job. Well it seems that we're at war. We weren't told anything officially – all I know is what I've heard on the BBC World Service – 100 cruise missiles and over 1,000 bomber sorties.

The only effect on us was an air raid warning when a Scud B was launched this morning. It was a bit inconvenient having to dive into my trench because I'd just heated the water to have a shave. However, at least with scuds their time of flight is only a few minutes so after 10 minutes it must have landed somewhere else so you can come out from under cover.

I'm losing weight which is a bit worrying. I'm always starving – the food is still good but there's never enough… If you have any spare food send it over! I find it really tiring just walking about. Walking on sand is always hard work anyway and as our vehicles are so dispersed over a large area, I'm walking miles every day.

This is my last but one bluey, so you're quite privileged…

How is all this affecting the people back home? Last time I was in England, I got the impression that most people were not very interested. It didn't affect them and it was all very remote.

John Major seems to be doing a good job. Kinnock and Kohl should be shot. At least the French are doing their bit.

Anyway keep writing.

Love,
Richard x

Although there had been fears before the start of the land campaign that the Iraqi forces would prove a tough challenge for the coalition, in the event the land battle only lasted four days from 24 to 28 February as the coalition forces outclassed their Iraqi opponents.

Sergeant Pete MacPherson-Smith of the 3rd Battalion, Staffordshire Regiment, was based in the UK throughout the First Gulf War, but corresponded regularly with men of the 1st Battalion who were out in the Gulf, and some of them wrote to him describing their exploits in the land battle.

Dear Pete,

Well we cried havoc and they let us loose. It was, I must say, my kind of war with very little coming this way, but a fucking lot going that. Actually apart from about 5 or 6 battles that we got involved with (1st Bn) the bastard tanks got into the en posn before us and we got stuck with the flaming EPW (en Prisoners of War) and what a sight. On talking to the EPW they had been conscripted ten days before and dumped in the front, where upon their officer legged it back to Baghdad. They didn't cause many problems, although they were not able to tell us where the anti-personnel mines were, but we soon found out. One of the trucks found one and then the rotten bastards made me ride around in the APC [Armoured Personnel Carrier] until I'd cleared a route. Some bloody mate. (Actually, the pressure of the tracks set them off and we couldn't feel anything.)

Then came the Rep Gt they kicked it into touch when we told them Jonny Reeves was coming.

I nearly got to fire my .50 cal one night in an ambush, but would you believe it C Coy and Milan got in first again.

The above action was where young Moult was killed, the bastards had started to surrender, but as it got dark one of them fired an RPG7 [Rocket Propelled Grenade] which got him in the upper chest. I think C Coy showed tremendous restraint because apart from killing the bastard who fired it they took the rest prisoner.

We have eventually ended up north of Kuwait City blocking their main escape route to Basra. By the time we got here there were only a few minor skirmishes. The place is a complete wreck [of] tanks, bodies, APCs, bodies, AA guns and more bodies and yes our first tank clean up! Primarily the bodies and before you ask I've got your share of teeth in my webbing.

To top it all it's now pissing down with rain and the Prats want us to stand around and listen to the PM's 'boots fit, letters from home etc etc crap'.

We wanted to play football but can't find a space without cluster bombs in it (courtesy of the RAF).

All in all we didn't do too bad only 2 dead and about 4 or 5 injured, but upon reading this it wasn't as easy as it sounds and I must admit I wouldn't want to do it again.

Well Pete, that's all for now…

See you soon,

Steve

PS Translated 'if the bastards don't get us home soon there'll be another revolution'.

Tues 5th March 9.30am

Hi there Pete,
Well we can finally shove this war right up Tony Benn's arse and pack the bastard off to Baghdad now it's over…

Well as the war went there was some hell-raising times and we spent most of the time on the move advancing on positions. But we performed brilliantly when called upon. My crew and vehicle was responsible [for] taking out the most enemy tanks/APCs in one attack, 5 in less than 5 minutes, all kills, good hey. We were out on the flanks and came in on the unprotected rear of a div position and took out the tanks from 1,600–1,700m. We were so chuffed.

We were all slightly pissed off when the cease fire was announced as we were on a high and heading for the retreating Republican Guard, it would have made my day to take out some T72s but never mind.

Well Pete you had a few drinks on us to celebrate over victory, well I tell you what mate, there [will] be some more done as soon as I get back that I promise.

You're a real friend Pete and have kept me going in the right spirit through this war and for that truly thank you…

Tomorrow we meet the Prime Minister so I'll say hello for you mate. Pete, don't write any more as I don't plan on being here to receive them by that stage.

Cheers,
Tomo

A decade later British forces found themselves in the Gulf once more as part of another US-led coalition. This time the target was Iraq itself.

Lance-Corporal Iain McMenemy of the Scots Guards was one of those who took part in the initial invasion of Iraq in March 2003, as British troops headed towards the southern Iraqi city of Basra.

Dear Mark, Alison and Katie,

Thanks for taking the trouble to write to me. You would not believe how your spirits are lifted when you receive post.

The war started in the early hours of Thursday 20th March and we rolled over the border from Kuwait into Iraq on Friday 21st at 1255. War is shit.

You live on your nerves the whole time. The rag-heads are using dirty tricks like wearing civilian clothes or suicide bombers etc. So it is hard to tell who is who. We are also confused by the fact that we are under orders to be extra nice to the civilian population. We don't know who is who.

Only 4 days ago I caught a guy passing through a checkpoint with an AK-47 rifle down his side. I caught a glimpse of the bayonet under his robes.

We are constantly missiled with Scuds and mortars and RPGs (Rocket Propelled Grenades). Pretty hairy! And if they don't get us, the Yanks will! Daft cowboy bastards (sorry Katie).

Parenthood seems to be treating you well. You probably have a tougher time than me. You'll get less sleep! I hope I can get home in time for your pilgrimage to Scotland in May. I have no idea when I will be released. It all depends how long this war phase lasts.

If I am still here I am sure Pearl and Jamie will entertain you.

Your dad has probably shot more Arabs than me but we can swap war stories one day…

Thanks again for writing, you are true friends!

Love Iain xxx

X – big kiss for Katie

Far from being a short-term operation, it wasn't until 2009 that British combat troops finally withdrew from Iraq.

One of those deployed on what became known as Operation *Telic* was Major Nick Lock, who was commander of B Company, 1st Battalion, Royal Welsh Fusiliers. He and his men were based in Az Zubayr to the south of Basra in 2004.

8 July 2004

Dear Alan,

Well we are three months into our tour and still not halfways through yet, a seven month tour is going to prove a long hot summer! I think we are getting used to the heat now as it is touching the fifties and we are still able to operate although you rapidly get soaked through. Apparently July and August are the 'Hell Months' as the locals say, so I may regret my comments above very rapidly. Aircon in our rooms give a good deal of relief when you come in off patrol.

The handover of power seems to have gone off OK with Paul Bremmer doing something right in handing over early. In the south after a quiet period our local roadside bomber is back with two bombs in three days. We were lucky again with no casualties unlike the unfortunate Fusilier from the RHF [Royal Highland Fusiliers] in Basra the other day. It is a sobering reminder that up until now British troops have been very lucky, despite a lot of battle casualties we have had very few deaths. We have now handed over responsibility for much of the security in the town to the Iraqi police so we will have to see how they do on their own. I think in many cases they may go back to their old ways. A station commander informed me today that he had got nothing out of a hijacker who had attacked an isolated police station but after a few slaps he had sung like a bird! I had to remind him that that is how Saddam dealt with people and that the people here would rapidly lose any respect for them if it continued.

Our efforts are now concentrated on stopping the terrorists blowing up the oil pipelines and stopping smuggling and hijacking. We have had some notable successes with smuggling recently breaking up an illegal fuel documentation market and making forty-four arrests. This is still the tip of the iceberg as it is believed that sixty per cent of all the fuel produced is being smuggled away.

The local elections have been on – off – on and off again over the last week. We now hope that they will take place at the end of next week. We have done enough work towards preparing the police and ourselves for the elections that we just want to get them out the way now and once in place we hope that the Iraqis will start to take responsibility for their own affairs. I will be pleased if it means that I will no longer be the stand in mayor of Az Zubayr! I am also about to be an honorary sheik of one of the local tribes whose head is also chairman of the tribal council. Apparently they have the full outfit ready to go, Lawrence of Arabia here I come, just have to make sure I don't become too eccentric in the process!

Only three weeks to go to R&R [rest and recuperation] now so that will definitely keep me sane, can't wait to see Sarah and Jack who I am sure will have really changed. No real holiday plans at present just time at home relaxing with the family which will make a wonderful change.

Once I get back I will only have a few weeks left in command of the company before I move on to be Senior Major of the Battalion. It will be very strange to say goodbye to the company after what has been a very hectic but incredibly rewarding two years. I don't think I could have wished for a better sequence of activities over the two years than I have had. I have also been very lucky to have worked with a truly excellent bunch of officers, NCOs and soldiers of whom I think I am justifiably proud. The new job will bring a different set of challenges but at least I will still be with my Regiment which is never dull and always full of good fun...

Well best close, I have a Sector Security Meeting to go to with the Police and Iraqi National Guard.

Best wishes,
Nick

During the operations in Iraq, Maurice Benton and Joanne Goody-Orris, affectionately known as Mo and Jo, sent care packages filled with both luxuries and essentials to British soldiers on the front line. They continued this operation as the Coalition troops were sent into Afghanistan, and in November 2011 sent their 9,000th parcel to the front line. In response to the 'morale' parcels a number of soldiers wrote back, mainly to thank them for their efforts, but in some cases to provide a bit of detail about their life on the front line.

Captain Kit Kyte of the Royal Gurkha Rifles was one such recipient during Operation *Herrick 9* in the winter of 2008.

Captain Kit Kyte
Recce Pl
2nd Battalion Royal Gurkha Rifles

Dear Mo and Jo
... I write this letter on behalf of myself and the men of Recce Pl who have all benefited from the 'morale' parcels and letters that you have sent... It is truly appreciated and you cannot appreciate the positive effect that it has for all of us, and myself in particular. It is the one thing you look forward to when you

have been out on the ground for a sustained period of time, and it is the one thing no matter how small that gives you the opportunity to detach from the current reality and consider the real world.

So I shall now write a small amount of news from our time out here so far. Obviously the detail will be limited for operational reasons but I hope that it might give you a small insight into what we are about. Firstly, we must consider the ground and the operating environment out here. Southern Afghanistan is the most inhospitable region in the entire country with temperatures in the summer going plus of 50 degrees Celsius! You can imagine the impact it has on men who are moving tactically with kit and equipment that at a basic level often weigh in at more than sixty pounds, and that is just for a small scale patrol. We went on an operation early on for 8 days into bandit country with each man carrying kit in excess of 62kgs! The weather has now changed though, and is more bearable. However temperatures by day reach 18 degrees but drop below 0 at night so the change is one you can never get used to.

The land here is barren rock and desert for the majority with dust and sand in the air at all times, you stay clean for about 5 seconds once you step out of the gate, your lungs are filled with it all and the sun is blinding. The only areas of green are to be found down in the main Wadis (rivers – usually dry). The majority of the population live here in accommodation that can only be described as that out of *Star Wars*, compounds of mud with walls 2 feet thick, very hard to penetrate I can assure you. The people here in particular are extremely conservative, in that they live an existence that can only be described as medieval with the exception that they have electricity, motorbikes, mobile phones, oh and obviously guns! They are extremely hostile to us, and from my perception, having spent a significant amount of time out in places you wouldn't really want to go, they are supportive of the Taliban who have an almost mob like grip on the population. The enemy are hard to see because in essence they come from the local population, they wear no uniform and you cannot distinguish them from local farmers until they start firing at you. The complexity of operations is extreme and the danger always close by. We will eventually win any fire-fight that they engage us with, they know this and so often adopt hit and run tactics and small scale ambushes, and then most cowardly of all the use of improvised explosive devices (IEDs). These devices have been responsible for many Coalition casualties, but also many local casualties with children and women often falling foul of an enemy IED. Quite why they can respect the enemy when they are also being killed by them is astounding. I suspect they are in the terrible position of living in constant fear, terrorized on a daily basis. This is why we must continue to push the enemy back, constantly keeping him guessing, disrupt his mindset etc.

The job is extremely demanding and constantly challenging, we live on the extreme end of a volatile world but this is something we chose to do and if we don't take the fight to them here then we will be doing it on the streets of London with greater consequences for all.

I hope this gives you a brief insight into the kind of existence we are operating in and why anything we can receive out here is of such benefit to us.

Once again can I thank you all for thinking of my men and I at this time, it is sincerely appreciated.

Yours aye,
Kit Kyte

Another recipient of Mo and Jo's parcels was Lieutenant Anthony Gibbs, Royal Navy, who served on the front line of Afghanistan in a different capacity to many of the other ISAF troops.

Monday 1 July 2008

Dear Mo and Jo,

I write to you today to extend sincere thanks to both of you and to all of the people who contribute in any way, however small or large, to your campaign to support troops in Iraq and Afghanistan. Of course this letter also conveys the heart-felt thanks of all the members of the unit here to whom the receipt of support and comforts from home, especially from perfect strangers, cements our belief that we are genuinely supported by the British public and our contribution to operations here are valued and recognized. This, I personally feel, is the most important rationale and gives us a reason and determination to execute our duties with purpose and the feeling that we are, ultimately, making a difference.

Here in Afghanistan, our unit works closely with the Afghan indigenous armed forces on the front line. We are a small but specialist unit drawn together from men and women of all three services. We have a different raison d'être to our esteemed colleagues in Helmand Province, who provide a highly visible military presence designed at tackling the main fighting body of the Taliban, Al Qaeda and insurgency head-on. We are charged with tackling insurgency combined with the illicit generation of monetary funds that would eventually, in the form of weapons, find their way into the hands of those who wish to de-stabilise the region and ultimately provide havens and training facilities for terrorists worldwide…

Afghanistan in the height of summer is not an environment to be taken lightly. On average, in the run up to summer the midday temperature rises to a blistering 45 degrees Celsius. This is set to rise even further towards mid-August to the truly searing region of 50 degrees. This simply has to be experienced to understand how difficult it is to exist in these conditions, let alone wear armour, carry weapons and kit and remain at the top of your game. It is, as you can imagine, severely debilitating when you are trying to carry out your duties and look out for your colleagues. Conversely, the winters here see some bases where the temperature struggles to get above freezing and snow lies on the ground for 3 months or more. It really is a country of extremes with lowlands at 2,000 feet above sea level and the mountains at 14,000 feet where the snow never melts.

Once again thank you and all of your contributors for thinking of us and supporting us in our difficult task. I look forward to meeting you and thanking you in person.

I remain your obedient servant,
Anthony M. Gibbs
Royal Navy

Mo and Jo continue to send care packages to British troops serving abroad. After sending a large number of letters and parcels to the Gurkha units posting in Afghanistan they were awarded with honourary membership of the regiment. It is clear from this letter that their contributions made a contribution to the morale of those on the front line.

Capt Kulbahadur Gurung
Op Herrick 14
30 April 11

Dear Hon Member Jo and Mo,
First of all, thank you very much for the parcel and lovely letter which you have sent us. At the beginning [I] was totally surprised, who and how this good parcel arrived in this place?… Once I opened the parcel boxes, I managed to get your letter and have a good knowledge about both of you. It's really nice to read your letter and receive a fantastic parcel. It really made our morale

high and we are determined to do our duties with pride and we will do it in a proficient manner. Now I also have a feeling that both of you are our parents, guardians and friends who are supporting us in a tough time… There is not such a word to express our happiness at the moment.

People like you two can make a huge difference in the Armed forces morale… Reading you letter made me very proud. You have great experiences in your lifetime serving in past wars and doing a fantastic job to help current Armed forces. I always salute both of you on your hard work and achievement.

Finally, my boys and I have a great appreciation … for your generous help and support. Your support made our life better and we are delighted to receive fantastic packs. Like you said, we will be safe here with God's blessing…

Thank you,
Kulbahadur Gurung.

The war in Afghanistan is the longest running conflict included in this compilation, lasting over a decade. From the letters sent home by the soldiers that we can get a sense of the conflict changing over time. This letter from Marine Mark Kemp, who served with 45 Commando on Operation *Herrick 9*, provides us with his perspective on the situation in 2009, eight years after British forces first deployed to Afghanistan, and three years after they arrived in Helmand Province.

5/4/09

Good morning,
Well the weather isn't very good today, it has been raining for nearly 12 hours so it's a mud bath outside. Better get my wellies out of my box…

A patrol to a place we call Robin was cancelled this morning because the MERT (Medical Emergency Response Team) and IRT (Incident Response Team) couldn't fly because of the weather, they can fly now it's day time but it's too late to go to Robin now, it takes about an hour to walk there because you have to go through the green zone and they would see the company coming.

I think a lot of the lads were glad because the last time we went there is when the RPG went about 3ft past me. But the OC then decided that he is going to send 5 troop on a patrol to duchess hill, which is a mine field. He wants to see where the dead ground is to our cameras (dead ground means where you can't see from the FOB). I bet 5 troop are happy about that. It's called duchess hill because a bloke from Whiskey company was killed there on Herrick 5 when W Coy were based at FOB Rob. I was talking to Reg the other day, he was on Herrick 5 with W Coy and when they couldn't even come as far north as we are because there were too many Taliban positions around where the FOB is now and they could very rarely break through. So I guess it goes to show that progress is being made even if it is a bit slow. But Rome wasn't built in a day.

It's nearly time for Bob or Mad Bob as he likes to call himself to relive me from watch. This is the last letter I'll send, because I'll probably beat this one home!

Love you both,
Mark

In his letters home, Major Simon Bradley, Officer Commanding Field Squadron 2, 24 (Commando) Engineer Regiment, often wrote to his children to give them a sense of what daily life in Afghanistan was like for the Afghan people and for troops on the front line.

23/03/11

* See if you can read this out loud to mummy *

Dearest Matthew,

Thank you very much for your last bluey – I really like getting them from you and James because they tell me what you have been up to. Have you both had my last bluey? I drew a picture of my rifle and explained what it does. If you like it let me know and I will do some more.

Your writing is really nice and neat and I was interested to read that you want to be a footballer!

There are certainly lots of boys in the world who want to be the same thing! We will have to see if we can get you playing for a club; the more practice you get, the better you will be. You might also have to get a job before you play for one of the big teams!

Daddy is keeping very busy and we are enjoying helping the people out here in Afghanistan. They are very friendly towards us – especially the children. Many of the children have little and they only want simple things like pencils and footballs. When we give them these things they are very grateful.

It's time I got back to work so I'll finish my bluey by saying I love you very much and I'm missing playing with you and James every day.

Take care, keep being a good boy and I will speak to you soon.

With lots and lots of love,
Daddy

04/04/11
Camp Bastion
Afghanistan

Dearest Matthew and James,

I hope you are both well and still being very good boys for mummy. She told me on the phone the other day that you had been very good – especially when you went swimming again. Good boys – keep it up! I am really looking forward to going swimming with you when I come home. I have visited another school this week here in Afghanistan and we are looking to help the people there build some play apparatus for the small children. Do you have any ideas for me? It would have to be something we could make from basic materials; like wood and rope. Why don't you write to me with some ideas? They would be really useful. I'm glad you like the Afghan children's hats I sent back – mummy says they look great and you enjoy wearing them.

By the time you read this you will be on half-term from school. I know you are going back to England and staying with Grandma & Grandpa, and Granny & Grandad. I am sure you will have had a great time and I know there were some fun activities planned for you... I hope the weather was good for you in the UK. It is very mixed here in Afghanistan; some days it is very clear, with blue sky and lots of hot sunshine; other days it is quite cool because of the strong winds – which also blow up huge dust storms which are horrible! It also rains here sometimes, not very much. We are expecting thunder storms on Sunday. Those and the dust storms mean we can not fly around in helicopters and are stuck on the ground.

I have also gone out a few times at night. Most nights it is very clear and the stars are amazing. At the places with no lights I have to use special equipment to help me see in the dark... I will write about that in my next bluey!

Take care, be good and I will hopefully get to speak to you soon.

With lots and lots of love
Daddy xxxxxx

One of Marine John O'Loughlin's letters from his tour in Afghanistan with Commando Logistic Regiment, *Herrick 14* (March–September 2011), recalls his first patrol of Afghanistan and encounters with the local population.

Dear Clodagh
Op Baba 3 was my first foray on the ground and into the green zone … a two day planned operation to clear a compound deserted by the Taliban a number of months ago in order for its owner to return home … a simple hearts and minds number and within view of PB Karnica so with relative safety, a good warm for a first time. It meant flying out along with a search team and combing with Karnica's team… The intel was that the compound contained up to 8 IEDs and that with the support of the locals and close proximity there would be little chance of getting into a contact… The infantry left around 530 to establish a cordon and by about an hour later I stepped out the rear gate of the base into Afghanistan… There were no nerves, just excitement and the comfort of being able to do what I'm best at doing … to flick that tactical switch and turn up the senses … scanning the world around … assessing … targeting … listening … watching for the normal or any lack thereof. The target compound was no more than a few hundred metres away but it's only a matter of metres from the cross line before you became fully immersed in this new world… You move from the haphazard of modern straight into ancient… The paths, the fields, the building's and a people

modelled and modelled on the generations before… You patrol
through shaded lanes and dusty wall and skirt along fields in full
poppy blossom… You watch the young kids running around,
their mothers peering from the compound gates. You see the
men singing in the fields weeding with no sense of hurry… The
dogs, chickens and goats left to their own interests… The pace of
life is a slow one, from morning prayers at 5am to evening every
task seems to take as long as it takes.

We patrolled along the route cleared by those in front making
sure to stay between the markers of white talc that show the safe
lane – a careless step either side has led to many an unfortunate
soldier… Even assured safety in the friendliest of areas is no
guarantee. A friendly smile out here can be genuine or just a
clever ploy… The first task was for the searchers to isolate the
target compound. They do this to ensure there's no command
wires or pulls that could be used to detonate devices when we get
close – you have to assume you're being watched at all times and
most time you are so busy isolating you know the only threat can
come from within… While the isolation was being carried out
we sat in a cleared location awaiting to be called forward and it
wasn't long before the locals started to come over… They're a
very curious people, not to mention peculiar. They approach
some time with a greeting, other times without a word, and will
just sit down a few feet or next to you and watch. Eventually one
will try [to] converse and as is universal both parties try to
communicate by repeating foreign words slowing, assuming to
be understood… But you don't need to understand to know
when they're taking the piss and it soon wears thin. I don't like
bad manners no matter the language or culture, it's just a
universal decency. The thing that really got to me was how they
treated the three women that were with us. As a culture that
treats the respect and protection of women as an almost sacred
duty, it most definitely does not extend to western women. They
would sit there and unashamedly stare and comment trying to

engage a reaction from them… Word would spread and more men would appear to stare – I got to my feet on more than one occasion with my weapon clenched to prevent them from sliding closer or pestering the poor girls. If it wasn't for the importance of keeping locals on die I'd have given them a fuck off that would be universally understood! I also had to keep telling local kids to politely fuck off… They just want to see what's going on and if you let them, they'd stand right up beside any bomb. From these encounters I can see how the local population can be trusted. They want to appear to help out, but part of you suspects they'd do the same with the Taliban…

Marine John O'Loughlin's letters provide an insight into everyday life for front line troops serving in Afghanistan and the dangers they faced from improvised explosive devices (IEDs) and from grenade attacks, as well as missing home.

It's starting to develop a pattern … or monotony only understood by the unemployed and all without the benefits of cartoons and day time telly… I've made the observation before in the UK that I didn't work for a living but instead I waited. Well I thank the lord for the blessings of patience he bestowed! I'm currently on Herrick 14 which means there has been 13 tours before I came along… 13 tours where teams like mine have been infinitely busier – so what's changed? Well seasonal factors, progressive factors but the biggest being that for Herrick 14 they decided to massively increase the number of teams sent out – more than double previous tours. Now the bad guys didn't get the memo and have failed to scale their production in accordance so in a quiet phase like this you have twice the amount of lads scratching their balls – I could use the time wisely and work on my tan but I'm bored and in a puddle of sweat after ten minutes, plus I don't have the body for it yet – I did try working on that part but my patience draws a line at standing in the shadows of brick shit houses waiting to use the weights. So 'Operation Get Massive' has been scaled back slightly for the time being ... but I'm still looking to make some gains by the end of six months... I interrupt this with the sound of mortars putting up a rapid volley of illum – ah I've missed [Patrol Base] Rahim!

I'm still working from [FOB] Price but a week's ass sitting was interrupted yesterday for a task that sounded awesome! Intel had come through of an underground bomb factory in a compound that was producing up to 60 IEDs a day... Bomb factory turned out to be false info but I did get a lovely night sleeping in the desert with the kind of night sky that had me longing for home...

There was a grenade attack on a manned compound about a km outside of the gate. Five injured but thankfully nothing worse than frag ... one grenade failed to detonate so the team was called out to detonate and clear. The mortars are still throwing up illum, the air is buzzing with the sound of incoming helos and on call apache, all around the base rushes to get men on the ground and all in the drama of darkness and red torch light... The real Tom Clancy shit was patrolling through the green zone with NVG's and infrared illum ... crossing ditches and canals and skirting along fields and walls in total blackness... Watching as man after man tried to gage a ditch jump offers a rare smile given the trouble gauging depth perception when on monocle... We sprinted the last 20 meters or so and the compound doors were shut tight behind us.

The pace of events along with everyone's adrenaline was still racing. The injured had been evacuated safely but the danger was still palpable from the scramble of radio orders and questions. Our job firstly was to deal with the unexploded grenade in the courtyard so everyone was ushered into hard cover while Rod and Fraze set up the Dem. In a tiny cupboard room I lay hunched against any number of guys ... everyone just shadows but for the flickers of red torch light. The ten minutes to explosion was given and we sat and waited. I watched as silent witness while others still processed the events, some sat with heads and ears still ringing, a few checked for injuries but all thankful for their own lucky 'it could of/should of' been me story. For them the war in Afghanistan just got real, no one gets hurt on exercise.

It was only minutes to go when it came across the net that such an attack had been forecasted on the last tour but never happened. Perhaps the death of Bin Laden and the start of the summer offensive gave them the interest to follow through… The old intelligence was for a planned grenade attack on the compound then a withdrawal as the Apache helicopters circled above. We could hear them in the skies above us and I can tell you it's comforting protection! The Taliban know the response … from the time to casevac, to the time air cover can stay on call. So they knew they need only wait out till both eyes on the ground and in the sky were on the back foot. Air cover gone, 15 Taliban would then try [and] over run the compound.

The first reaction was excitement, the scene was set for the kind of thing I'd only read about but I stopped myself short from getting carried away. This was a very real danger and I had to admit it was an unwanted one. 5 guys had been injured tonight and many more had all ready [sic] had more than their day's worth. I thought of everyone back home and of the guys huddled around me and said a prayer…

The grenade was blown and the compound was made safe again but now it became a case of waiting for an attack. The guard and sentries were doubled and every one given their positions if 'stand to' was to be called. If the Taliban did attack they would be as brave as they would be stupid. There was now 24 of us in this small compound – even a 3/1 ratio would have been suicide. My team along with the searchers with us were given a small store room to sleep in. Everyone was to sleep in armour and take their turns on sentry. We huddled in, resting back against the wall but it wasn't a night for sleep ... just snatched rest from uncomfort.

With sunrise came assurance. The night had now passed without incidence and for the first time people could assess in light what had happened and too many the extent of their luck. 7 grenades had been thrown in the attack. One failed to detonate, two still had the grenade pins attached and four had done their damage. Lads surveyed the frag marks on the walls, through kit and through a damaged pack of fags recounting what had happened and with thought of those injured. One interpreter could count himself among the luckiest men in Afghanistan. A grenade had landed less than a metre's length from where he lay. It had reduced his [mosquito] net to rags without so much as a scratch to his health. The new day put everyone at ease and normal routine endured... I sat again in the sentry looking out at what had only been darkness and shades of green and enjoyed watching the locals working in the fields and the children playing. Atmospherics as its known were good and with that came safety.

Two hours later as I still sat on guard that changed ... things had gone quiet and any one passing seemed to be passing away from us... Enemy radio chatter had rightly or wrongly put Taliban movement in the area. The reality returned rapidly. My gloves and glasses went back on, I oiled the machine gun, arranged its ammo and adjusted my fire position... Once more every one braced and waited... And once more I thought myself selfish and said a prayer...

Allah was merciful that day ... half an hour of heightened nerves eased off as kids came back to play and with news that a mix ANA patrol from Rahim was on its way to us (Afghan National Army along with our lads). People returned to the fields and everyday life continued both outside and within the compound walls. As the mixed patrol returned we attached along and made our way back to Rahim... tired hot sweaty and with a lot to be thankful for and lot more to cautious of in the coming days and months...

It's given me a taste of what danger is faced and how very real the threat can be when you roam in their back yard... And I don't want to write for the sake of theatrics and nor is it my intent to seed worry... It's just a case of wanting to tell life out here the way it is because for good but definitely not for bad the media at home never will...

20-06-11

Dear Clodagh,
... Well you'll probably be happy to hear that "Op *Certain Death*" didn't go ahead ...it kept getting scaled back further and further until it was to end with us clearing out a single compound, and then it all got put on a shelf due to a Taliban threat about blowing up some bridge or another... So that ended my fun and all the excitement on the horizon, unless we get the next call out :(and even then if the last few call outs are anything to go on, they're mostly mundane affairs... Like the last one, a ten minute trip down the road to blow up an anti-tank mine – sure it made a big bang but even blowing stuff up doesn't rock my world these days... I need a little DANGER!! (against all the advice and hopes of everyone I know). Actually, I'll rephrase danger and substitute it for a little more agreeable term – EXCITEMENT!! I'm in a country surrounded by people trying to kill me and so far the only danger/excitement I've felt was in the grenade compound and with that came the only real time where I could do some soldiering... Every day I sit here and can hear bombs and missiles and all manner of things bringing bad news to unfortunate insurgents yet as soon as I step foot on the ground it's like a stalemate ... both sides just content with watching... I'm not looking to shoot bad guys necessarily... (just like bugs I've a strict ethics policy – I even saved a wasp this morning that

was doing his best to swim in a bucket of water) everything has a right to live until they try to kill, bite or eat me and then it's safety off and whoop ass at the ready...

It's mostly just because I'm bored... It's just too hot to use the gym – you sweat just lying down so to do anything akin to activity is just messy!... And I start to burn in minutes so I'm sat here in the tent just looking out at some of the guys getting their tan on ... so I'm sitting on a wobbly crate and writing on "shabby chic" plywood table because it keeps me upright (laying down invites a puddle), I just finished a letter to Linda, she sent me a letter in the last mail bag to come in – great day – a letter AND a parcel for John! I think she wrote the letter over about a month and a paragraph or few lines every now and then but it made me smile all the same... All news from before I was last home and nothing that I hadn't heard but her take of current affairs and news headlines made for entertaining reading! It's just frustrating that post takes so long... (Although improvements have been made and shorter times have been promised.) I sent you a few letters last week but it will probably be 2/3 weeks minimum before you get them... What we need is a cross between a pigeon and a swallow – a Pigeallow! A bird that can fly half way around the world in a relatively straight line and carry a few pages of quality letter! And one of course that takes considerably less than 2/3 weeks or else that plan is kinda flawed – feck it, while I'm making animals up I'll just settle on one of those flying unicorns ... no – one of Santa's reindeer! Those feckers are good with weight and can get around the whole world in a single night so with a simple A – B route they'd be there within the hour! Just leave a few carrots in your post box!

Oh, and I made a new friend out here ... and then I lost him. When we arrived up here in Nahidullah there was a WIS (weapons intelligence specialist) guy staying on from the last team. Probably mentioned WIS before, but just in case, they come out on the ground with us and it's their job to take whatever we find and send it up for forensics. They also keep us briefed on what's gone on in the area, lately or in the past to give us the potential for threats. Anyways … when I arrived and dropped my kit in my bed space I saw the space beside me had an Ulster flag and a towel draped with "Loyal" printed on it. It put my deduction skills into practice and I assumed this guy was one of those "Protestants" you here about back home!… Politics and cultures aside he turned out to be a great craic, even if it did take him a while to grasp the concept of why I wouldn't sign the English national anthem when I served in the British forces. Folks really struggle to grasp the "she's not my queen, just my boss". Anyways, he was replaced yesterday by a new WIS and I have to say I miss the wee (tall) guy – always nice to hear a home voice, even if that's north of the border.

I miss you too kid… I used to have the card you sent me blutac'ed to a piece of cardboard beside my bed space along with photos but it gave me too much to miss. It was too constant a reminder during the long days of waiting, when my days would be spent under the watch of everything dear from home. So about a week ago I took it all down and I now keep it in by bits'n'bobs box. No point spending the days just wishing I was home when I spent so long wishing I was out here. I still take a moment most days to flick through those photos and card…

Becci has just commented on how the hell I can write so much on nothing. In fact the whole team think I'm crazy… The longest I've seen any of them write is a thank you letter and that's usually half a bluey…

But I'm going to end my ramblings for now as it's not even a week since I wrote to you last and I made a conscious thought to try and limit my habit to once every week or so… Alas, it seems I'm failing… I could write every day but even then I can see that comes about as borderline craziness – actually, there'd be no borderline about it!…

Right, take care as ever kid, and I'm hoping all's well – sorry, one last interruption! I watched Casablanca the other night and it's just reminded me of Bogart lifting his glass "... Here's looking at you kid"... so here's lifting my half empty bottle of warm water and saying the same – here's looking at you kid!

The best to you and yours,
Johno.

03-09-11

Dear Clodagh,
It's over a week since I've been here now in Bridzar and I think this week's been busier than the last month I spent in Nahidullah – and that's not to assume these last few days have been flat out busy, they haven't, but three jobs in seven days for the team is still more than we managed there. There's a constant reminder here in this PB of just how dangerous it can be out here, and it's a rare occurrence that a patrol sent out into the green zone doesn't come into contact. I spent one morning on sentry overlooking north when a few hundred metres west gun fire rang out back and forth. In the ten minutes hundreds of rounds exchanged into unseen locations. I watched and listened as two Apaches came in to circle and engage, the trees lighting up in bursts of flashes and leafs falling like confetti! Winning the fire fight can be summed up with the suppression of the enemy by weight of fire – you put more bullets over their head or into them than they can into you. With an Apache it's almost cheating. There was no confirmation that I heard of that any insurgents had been killed, but if they survived they very quickly changed plan and retreated. One Danish soldier was shot in the hand, the round having struck his rifle and gone clean through both it and his hand. I watched as two American Blackhawk helicopters came to extract him. They operate in pairs, one

helicopter covering while the other retrieves. I've never seen helicopters manoeuvre so fast and to watch them almost dance is a joy to behold. A joy with a taste of concern for those injured. For no good news follows their arrival.

I mentioned to Tony that I'd like to go out on patrol with one of the call signs some morning if it would be allowed and he said he would ask. Given my job and training he saw no problem to it and asked the two English advisors attached to the ANA if they would allow me to join in one of their patrols. They agree and with two days to wait before they next set off I was hopeful that maybe, just maybe, I would get a taste of what my drivers draft had robbed me of: that I would get to patrol through the green zone as a rifleman in a close combat section. The plan initially was for just me to join this patrol, but it soon became the whole team including searchers. It was sold to the higher powers that it would be a "familiarisation patrol" and with us attached we could deal with anything uncovered. I joined up to soldier and fight, I chose to be a Marine – others though seemed all too unimpressed with the idea of having to needlessly set foot anywhere they didn't need to. Grumblings within the team of searchers shut the door completely. Some excuse was given and that was the end of any idea of going out. I'm running out of time to experience what I wanted from Afghanistan and if I'm honest I fear it's going to be one box that I wont get to tick off.

But another box I am excited about ticking off is South America baby!! And if the best memories are the memories shared then I'm thankful I'll get to share them with someone like you! I've been looking online at what I can find about the places, looking at photos, trying to think of things I need to do… Now if I could just learn Spanish and Portuguese in a few weeks… Also on the holiday front I go an email today from one of my mates back at the unit asking if I'd like to go skiing for two weeks in January. Two weeks of "working". The Navy ski championships are on in France and it's mostly just an excuse for the Navy to go drinking and skiing for two weeks at subsidised prices... Every month we contribute about seven bucks into a sports lottery and the lottery in turn helps out with the cost of such events. I've been paying it for almost three years and never won or gone on anything like this so finally it's nice to use and abuse the system... So not only have I home to look forward to, then with luck South America, then with additional luck I'll also have a little skiing to ease myself back to the sad reality of having to go back to work!...

The whole PB has just been assembled and it was announced that a Danish soldier has just been killed and five others wounded... He was a double amputee but died back at Bastion... The brief announcement was all the more poignant as it was given in Danish, the list of names and the moments silence the only thing we understood. The silence was interrupted by a call to prayer from the mosque nearby – a reminder if ever needed of where we fight. The incident wasn't too far from here, but none of them were based with this company. It was a compound search where the unfortunate soldiers triggered an IED... One of the lads here did a job not so long ago exactly opposite the compound in question – it just goes to show that you can only be metres away from a pressure plate perhaps inches and know nothing of your danger or your luck.

But we all know my luck and I'm sure it's going to hold out the next 5 weeks although with most of us on the countdown to home any deaths or injuries will seem the worst for the proximity of home.

Right, well I'll call it a day... It's now just gone seven and I'm lying here on my bed fighting off mosquitoes and sweat so I think a cold shower is in order.

Take care kiddo and I look forward to seeing you soon.
John

As with any conflict, soldiers often became attached to their comrades and felt a strong sense of responsibility to do a good job while they were in Afghanistan. Deployments to Afghanistan for most troops lasted around six months, and very often the soldiers felt they left a job half-finished, particularly when every day proved full of dangers, as Marine John O'Loughlin explained.

06-09-11

Dear Clodagh,
I just received some good news ... and yet I'm not happy.

I've heard a lot of the guys were going home earlier than the date we had been originally given so I didn't want to find myself at short notice to move when in my mind I had days or weeks to go. Well it's now been confirmed – I'm to leave on the 24th of this month, some three weeks earlier than planned. Tony gave me the news expecting a smile on my face, it was as I said good news and everyone else congratulated me as such, but I didn't feel it that way. I was disappointed. It's not that I'm not eager to get home; it's not that six months hasn't been long enough from all I've missed. It's just that coming home early feels like leaving my job unfinished. But what's three weeks? Well, there's still a plan to move my team up into the Gereshk Valley, the Americans are pulling out of an area and the Brits are filling the gap. But it's a dangerous gap – and yes I can't deny that the thought of the danger isn't an attraction but it's not for excitement that I'm so keen to go. I just don't want my team going into danger when I'm not there to keep them safe, and that's not to say they won't be safe with someone else, it's just I'd feel safer if it was me.

So I requested to extend my tour to my original dates, to spend those three weeks with my team – much to the dismay and confusion of everyone. Request denied.

So with luck I can just hope what little time I've left is busy and to that end it appears it well may be. Tomorrow morning we have a patrol into the green zone to assist in an ANA search operation on a number of compounds. There's been a lot of assets brought into the planning of this search so they must have some reason for suspicion but I've learnt to be sceptical – if not pessimistic when it comes to jobs at this stage … so I'm going to assume we find nothing so that I may be pleasantly surprised if they do. It will be a welcome excursion all the same…

Time has progressed a bit and that patrol just mentioned was this morning.

We were up at 4am and left the gates an hour later. I've always loved patrolling at night. It's not the fearing of what lurks in the shadows it's the knowing that the biggest fear in those shadows is me. To know you have the upper hand when the imitative is yours. Out here the night belongs to us. There's also the almost unnoticed change from night to day … so gradual is the change that looking back you can't recall at what point things changed from black and white into colour.

We patrolled out from the PB down along the main track for a few hundred meters, extended in line and silent. Every one ready we stepped off the track through the wire and into the Green Zone. The first fields we crossed were used only for grazing and the rice fields of Vietnam easily came to mind. It doesn't rain here in the summer so water comes through flooding, each field runs aside an irrigation ditch and each field takes its share. So in the heat of summer you can find yourself wading ankle deep through either mud or water. We patrolled on across the fields, our sound track the helicopter above, the crack of gunfire and the distant thud of mortar … and us, we were walking ever closer towards it. At the front of our patrol are the searchers, scanning the ground and providing a safe route to follow. Left or right of their blue sprayed markers and you find a foolish man. Even on the way in they detected suspect devices but given the time they were simply marked and avoided. Some were obvious, some without trace but all no more than a foot or two from where we crossed ditches and tracks. We cleared the low flooded grass and entered into the tall fields of corn, we had crossed a number of flooded ditches knee high but some ditches required the use of a ladder bridge across. Martin was in front of me and it was always a moment to smile as a man with the agility and grace of a baby elephant stumbled, wobbled and tripped across every obstacle we came across. He would pick himself up and turn to offer me assistance across this perilous chasm only to watch me spritely bound across with possibly a surmised hint of smugness :)

Stepping into the corn is like entering the jungle, a wall of three meter greenery like the walls of a maze. You can see no more than perhaps two foot through it with no points of reference but the sky above, it has a claustrophobic feel, an unwelcome unease…

Finally we arrived at a point where we had to hold firm in a corner of a field to await another call sign to move into place to our front. Every one cleared a space and eagerly dropped their heavy kit, falling with it to take water on and rest. It wasn't particularly hot in the day yet but it was still uncomfortable, boots and combat wet and caked with mud… Five minutes later an explosion well within 20 meters reminded us we weren't in Kansas, it was assessed as a UGL round and it meant two things – either they knew where we were and they were close, or they were close and just shooting lucky into our general direction. The patrol that had been sitting in gaggles and groups suddenly dispersed and took up arcs, waiting to see what would follow. Nothing did. In the background we could hear bursts of automatic fire as another call sign tried to draw out the Taliban into firing back but again nothing…

ICOM was picking up groups of insurgents pulling out, others moving in and over head we could hear the Apache circling. We finally stopped short from our original target again still immersed and hidden in the corn, we sat in the thick mud drinking water while events higher up were co-ordinated. It only sounded like the other end of the field as the helicopters above suddenly unleashed with all fury their chain gun and 30mm cannon ... the noise of hundreds of rounds spitting out was fantastic, it was as if Zeus himself was throwing down bolts of thunder. No matter how close the enemy had been to us there was soon to be no trace of them... We had spent the morning wet, muddy and exhausted to arrive at a point we should have been hours before... The plan to search the compounds was now under review. We had lost surprise, an enemy alerted and with ample time to remove anything we would have found. It came across the radio that the whole operation was cancelled and all would return to base. Hours spent and for nothing... Finally we arrived back into the PB – exhausted, filthy and with it tempers were a little frayed...

As soon as I'd taken off my armour and kit I made a rush for the showers to cool off and clean up and no sooner was I back in clean shorts than shots rang out over our heads. It would seem the insurgents fancied a pop at us now that we were behind thick walls, it's a common tactic for them to wait until forces are withdrawing and then claim the propaganda of beating them back into retreat. Stand to was called and every one scrambled back into armour and helmets and mounted the walls. The excitement was palatable and every one had hopes of being there to repulse a mass assault...

I'd come close to danger, been shot at, come to a distance I could shout at the enemy and still finished the day without firing a single round – carrying 300 rounds of belted ammunition, four magazines, grenades, an automatic weapon and nothing!

Anywho, I'll finish now and as always wish you well, see you soon feels all the sooner these days :)

John.

The conflict in Afghanistan has been played out on TV and online and media organizations play a crucial role in making distant events seem more immediate to those at home.

During his tour in Afghanistan in 2012, Captain Duncan Fraser, of the Adjutant General Corps' Education and Training Services Branch, played host to various television crews in Helmand Province, as he wrote home to explain.

29/06/12

Dear Mum and Dad,

Hello again from sunny Helmand Province. I have had a very busy week indeed. As you know I was hosting a news team from the BBC from Tuesday until Saturday. From the moment the producer Liz, cameraman Nick and presenter Caroline Wyatt arrived I organised every interview, every meal, every road move and ensured they had a pleasant yet productive visit to Nad' Ali. Although it was exhausting it was also thoroughly rewarding: Caroline said it was one the best visits she had ever had and was at the perfect pace. The Commanding Officer even congratulated me at the evening briefing tonight for a job well done. So good news all round!

I took them to all the local places of interest near [FOB] Shawqat. I organised close protection from the boys in B (Suffolk) Company on the promise they would feature on the news this week. Soldiers seem easily pleased! We saw the district governors new meeting hall, the police HQ, then down to the hustle and bustle of the bazaar. Caroline did a 'walk through' piece there before we moved on to see the new girls school and clinic. It was a positive spread of locations and it may feature on the news over the coming weeks.

I am still due to arrive back in the UK on the evening of August 5th, I am trying to jump on an earlier flight and wangle an extra day of leave. Some fellow officers have managed it so I may arrive … with Sam on the evening of the 5th. I will keep you posted.

Well I shall leave you there. All my love and speak soon.
Duncan x

Captain Fraser wrote to his girlfriend Samantha in mid-September with news of an attack on Camp Bastion, the Main Operating Base for all British forces in Afghanistan, a few weeks before he was due to leave theatre and return home.

15 September 2012

Dear Samantha,
Last night the insurgents attacked Camp Bastion, it's all over the news. It is really strange to think somewhere we all think of as a vestige of security has been breached. It's a strange atmosphere in camp today, it's obvious tensions are high. I don't envy the Commanding Officer; the new battlegroup start to arrive over the next few weeks and keeping momentum amongst the troops is going to be a challenge.

My big brother flew out of Bastion just a few hours before all the fun and games started. Mum and Dad will be happy to have him home now. All going well I will join him in the UK for a beer on the 16th October. Just one month to push.

The weather had really started to cool down in the evenings. I have actually begun to sleep in my sleeping bag and not on top of it! In a weird way I long for some rain. Some of the other guys and myself have planned a week in the Highlands together in November. We have all spoken at length [about] how we intended to sit in the rain with a beer and forget all about this place!

I think about you everyday. I will be home soon to give you that hug I promised you. Stay safe and I will see you very soon.

All my love,
Duncan

While violence in Afghanistan continues, British troops are gradually withdrawing and handing over their areas of operations to the Afghan National Security Forces (ANSF). Britain is due to end combat operations in Afghanistan in 2014, but it is expected that British forces will continue to assist with the training, advising and mentoring of the ANSF as the Afghan government attempts to build a lasting peace for the country.

GLOSSARY

AA	anti-aircraft
ADMS	Assistant Director Medical Services
ANA	Afghan National Army
ANSF	Afghan National Security Forces
ANZAC	Australian and New Zealand Army Corps
APC	Armoured Personnel Carrier
BEF	British Expeditionary Force
BFPO	British Forces Post Office
BLA	British Liberation Army
Boche	slang for German
Bt / Btn	Battalion
Bully stew	Traditional British rations, normally a beef stew of sorts
Casevac	casualty evacuation
C.B.	confined to barracks
CC	casualty clearing (stations)
C-in-C	Commander-in-Chief
CMF	Central Mediterranean Forces
Co / Coy	Company
CO	Commanding Officer
C.O.	conscientious objector
C.T.	Communist Terrorist
Dem	demolition
DCM	Distinguished Conduct Medal
DFC	Distinguished Flying Cross
DSO	Distinguished Service Order
ENSA	Entertainments National Service Association
EOKA	Ethniki Organosis Kyprion Agoniston (National Organisation of Cypriot Fighters)
EPW	enemy prisoner of war
F.F.I.	Free from Infection

FOB	Forward Operating Base
Frag	fragmentation
G.A.D.	Guards Armoured Division
GHQ	General Headquarters
GOC	General Officer Commanding
HAA	Heavy Anti-Aircraft
HAC	Honourable Artillery Company
helos	helicopters
HQ	Headquarters
Hun	British slang for German soldiers
ICOM	radio/listening device used to listen to the Taliban's communications in Afghanistan
IED	improvised explosive device
Illum	illumination – a round fired from a mortar
Intel	intelligence
IRT	Incident Response Team
ISAF	International Security Assistance Force
ITW	Initial Training Wing
Japs	slang for Japanese
KAR	King's African Rifles
KD	khaki drill
LAA	Light Anti-Aircraft
LSL	Landing Ship Logistic
LST	Landing Ship Tank
MC	Military Cross
ME	Middle East
M.E.F.	Middle East Forces
MERT	Medical Emergency Response Team
MO	Medical Officer
MT	Motor Transport (section)
NATO	North Atlantic Treaty Organisation
NBC	Nuclear, Biological or Chemical
NCO	Non-Commissioned Officer
NVG	Night Vision Goggles

OC	Officer Commanding
OP	Observation Post
PB	patrol base
Pl	Platoon
POW	Prisoner of War
RA	Royal Artillery
RAF	Royal Air Force
RAMC	Royal Army Medical Corps
RAOC	Royal Army Ordnance Corps
REME	Royal Electrical and Mechanical Engineers
RFA	Royal Fleet Auxilliary
RHF	Royal Highland Fusiliers
RHU	Reserve Holding Unit
RM	Royal Marines
RMO	Regimental Medical Officer
RPG	Rocket Propelled Grenade
R&R	Rest and Recuperation
sitrep	situation report
TA	Territorial Army
TEZ	Total Exclusion Zone
UGL	Under-slung Grenade Launcher
UN	United Nations
US	United States
USAAF	United States Army Air Force
VAD	Volunteer Aid Detatchment
VC	Victoria Cross
VE Day	Victory in Europe Day
WAAF	Womens' Auxiliary Air Force

ACKNOWLEDGEMENTS

The letters in this book all come from the collection of the Documents and Sound Section in the Imperial War Museum. In all cases I am grateful to the Trustees of the Imperial War Museum for allowing me access to these materials and to the following for granting permission to use the various documents.

Mr D. Anderton for the papers of H. Anderton (446); Mrs Wallis for the papers of F. Baker (2521); Mrs Baylis for the papers of L.G. Baylis (7969); Mrs J.E. Overall for the papers of J.B. and W.G. Beer (2295); Major S. Bradley for the papers of Major S. Bradley (WS 0695); Mr D. Russell for the papers of Colonel G.S. Brighten (1376); Ms S. Campbell Cross for the papers of Rifleman B. Britland (577); Ms J. Marsden for the papers of Dr W. Bullock (9546); Mr G. Canham for the papers of G. Canham (2690); Mr S. Chater for the papers of Captain D. Chater (1697); Mr A. Nixon for the papers of Lieutenant Sir P. Duff (799); Mrs M. Durant for the papers of Captain N. Durant (4885); Captain D. Fraser for the papers of Captain D. Fraser (WS 0848); Ms Y. Gautier Long and Mr A. Tann for the papers of F.H. Gautier (2296); Mr R.S. Gill for the papers of R. Gill (13204); Mr P.J. Houghton Brown for the papers of P.J. Houghton Brown (15316); Mrs L. Eltringham for the papers of W. Hymers (250); Mr R. Innes-Ker for the papers of W. Innes-Ker (1349); Mrs J. Weston and Mrs J. Coward for the papers of J. Jarmain; Marine M. Kemp for the papers of Marine Mark Kemp (WS 0607); Mrs W. Stock for the papers of J.H. Leather; Major N. Lock for the papers of Major N. Lock (15501); Imperial War Museums for the papers of Captain C.K. McKerrow (2886); Maurice Benton, Joanne Goody-Orris, Antony Gibbs, Kit Kyte and Captain Kulbahadur Gurung for the papers of Mo and Jo (Misc Mo and Jo 1); Mr A. Mortimore for the papers of A. Mortimore (3922); Marine

J. O'Loughlin for the papers of Marine J. O'Loughlin (WS 0535); Mr R. Jepson and Seafarers UK for the papers of Captain R.H. Owen (748); Trevor Campbell Smith for the papers of Lieutenant H.S. Payne (196); Mrs A. Bowlam for the papers of A. Peterkin (9290); Mrs R. Philips for the papers of D. Philips (3903); Mr J. Potter for the papers of J. Potter (6882); Mr M.J. Rugman for the papers of M.J. Rugman (14435); Mrs B.J. Siddons for the papers of Reverend V. Siddons (9143); Mr J. Paine and Mme Serin for the papers of Captain E. Simeons (2808); Mrs E.A. Smith for the papers of E.A. Smith (7913); Mr L.G.G. Smith for the papers of G. Smith (1665); Mr P.G. MacPherson-Smith for the papers of P. Smith (1165); Mr B. Wynick for the 'Letter Containing the Poem *In the Trenches* from Isaac Rosenberg, 1916', the papers of Special Misc 5; Mr J. Thraves for the papers of J.W. Thraves (7776); Mr N. van der Bijl for the papers of N. van der Bijl (3893); Mrs P. Clegg for the papers of Major T.H. Westmacott (1290).

Every effort has been made to trace copyright holders, and the Publisher and the Imperial War Museums would be grateful for any information which might help to trace those whose identities or addresses are not currently known. Should the copyright holders of the following collections come forward, the author will happily acknowledge them in future editions.

The papers of Trooper J. Bassam (2841); the papers of Major General T.H. Birkbeck CBE DSO (4224); the papers of Captain P. Caddick-Adams; the papers of H. Calvert (3509); the papers of M. Carey (1919); the papers of Flight Lieutenant E. Chadwick (3667); the papers of Corporal C. Charters (3103); the papers of Captain R.G. Clover (2639); the papers of Corporal R.W. Connolly (13168); the papers of Captain C.T. Cross (771); the papers of Lance Corporal Danzig (151); the papers of Sergeant R. Fayers (1045); the papers of W.C. and D.H. Fenton (1288); the papers of Lieutenant B.L. Francis (8240); the papers of Captain S. Gordon (774); the papers of Second Lieutenant R.P. Hamilton (1334); the papers of Lieutenant P.R.

Hampton (9165); the papers of Colonel P.R. Hill OBE (3741); the papers of Captain J.T. Keeping (745); the papers of Reverent Cannon C. Lomax (1289); the papers of W.J. Lynas (278); the papers of I.J. McKay MC (317); the papers of Lance Corporal I. McMenemy (13000); the papers of Sergeant Major J. Milne (1635); the papers in the collection of Misc 4; the papers in the collection of Misc 93; the papers of Captain E.S. Probst (14346); the papers of Colour Sergeant T. Proudfoot (5991); the papers of F. Ranken (1521); the papers of Lieutenant G.M. Renny (1374); the papers of Major G. Ritchie (11549); the papers of Private N. Robertshaw (1151); the papers of Lieutenant W. Leefe Robinson (200); the papers of D.L. Rowlands (2329); the papers of Major H.G. Scott (1386); the papers of Pilot Officer M.A. Scott (431); the papers of Captain D.L. Sheldon (126); the papers of Flying Officer G.A. Stillingsfleet (846); the papers of C. Tames (3475); the papers of Major General T.S. Taylor (6022); the papers of N. Thomas (2616); the papers of Captain E.T. Townsend (3389); the papers of H.E. Upton (2777); Captain R. Whitticase (2026); Flight Lieutenant R.H. Williams (2287); the papers of Lieutenant N.L. Woodroffe (3260); the papers in the collection of Lance Corporal J.A. Wyatt.

INDEX

Aden 231, 250
Afghanistan (2001–) 12, 13, 16, 235, 273–300
Al Qaeda 235, 276
Alacrity, HMS 259
Alexandria, Egypt 64–65, 144–145
Algeria 177
ANA (Afghan National Army) 287, 292, 295, 298
ANSF (Afghan National Security Forces) 300
Anderton, Harold 42–44
Antelope, HMS 252
Anzio, battle for (1944) 179
Argentina 232, 253
armistice, World War I 13, 26, 42, 109–110
Arras, battle of (1917) 25
Arrow, HMS 257
ARRSE (British Army Rumour Service) 16
Atatürk, Kemal 24
Attlee, Clement 229
Auchinleck, General Claude 119

Baghdad, Iraq 234, 267, 269
Bain, D.M. 34
Baker, Lance Corporal Fred 165–167
Basra, Iraq 234, 268, 270–271
Bassam, Trooper John 173–174
Battle of Britain (1940) 116–117, 140, 254
Baylis, Lionel 131–134
Beaverbrook, Lord 116
Beer, Jack 96–97
BEF (British Expeditionary Force) 17, 22, 43, 75, 98, 105, 109, 115, 130–131
Belfast, HMS 12
Belgium
    World War I 22–23, 78, 99, 111
    World War II 115, 125–126, 131, 133, 135, 206, 208–209, 211, 214–215
Benghazi, Libya 146
Benn, Tony 269
Benton, Maurice 273, 275, 277

Bergen-Belsen concentration camp 222
BFPO (British Forces Post Office) 72, 249, 252, 254–257, 263
bin Laden, Osama 235, 286
Birkbeck, Major General Theodore Henry 246–248
Blitz, the 114-117, 125, 140, 217, 263
Bonaventure, HMS 144
Bosnian conflict (1992–95) 233
Boyle, Captain 75
Bradley, Major Simon 279–282
Bremmer, Paul 271
Brighten, Colonel George Stanley 109–110
Brind, Lieutenant Colonel F.H.W. 248
Britland, Bernard 72–75
Brown, Ronald 102–103
Bulge, battle of the (1944) 121
Burma 118, 122, 181, 183, 200–201, 204

Caddick-Adams, Captain Peter 262–264
Calvert, Brigadier Mike 204
Calvert, Harry 135–137
Canberra, SS 261
Canham, Glen 257–259
Carey, Michael 222–225
Casablanca Conference (1943) 119
censorship 14–15, 18, 116, 253
Chadwick, Flight Lieutenant 174–177
Chamberlain, Neville 114
Charters, Corporal Cyril 206–210
Chater, Corporal Alfred Dougan 32–35
Chichester, A. 164–165
Chilton, Sergeant Major Gary 12
China 150, 228–229
Christmas Day truce (1914) 14, 33–35
Churchill, Winston 18, 114–115, 117–119, 137, 152
Clark, Lieutenant General Mark 119
Clover, Captain Gordon 147–149, 179
concentration camps 222–223
Connolly, Corporal Bob 185–188
Conqueror, HMS 232

Conscientious Objectors 14, 54-55, 129
Courageous, HMS 114
Coventry, HMS 256
Crested Eagle (British steamer) 127
Crete 117, 145–146, 256
Crooks, Teddy 135
Cross, Captain Chris T. 194–200
Cyprus 230–231, 248

D-Day landings (1944) 120, 185, 189,
    192, 195–196, 255
Dambusters raid (1943) 161
Danzig, Private George 30–31
Denmark 114, 209
Dietrich, SS-Oberstgruppenfuhrer 120
Dimoline, Major General William Alfred
    247–248
Dodecanese campaign (1943) 167
doodlebugs 216
Douie, Charles 17
Dove, Ben 163
Dowding, Air Chief Marshal 116
Downes, Tony 12
Drew, Private John E. 170–173
Duff, Lieutenant Patrick 63–69
Dunkirk, evacuation of (1940) 115,
    125–126, 131, 133, 135, 137, 185
Durant, Captain Norman 203–205
Dutch East Indies 118
Duxford airfield 12

Egypt 96, 117, 119, 156, 168, 230
Eisenhower, Lieutenant Colonel Dwight D.
    119–121, 177
El Alamein, battle of (1942) 13, 119, 170,
    174, 177
ENSA (Entertainments National Service
    Association) 196
Entente Cordiale 22
Ethniki Organosis Kyprion Agoniston
    (National Organisation of Cypriot
    Fighters – EOKA) 231, 248

Falklands War (1982) 232, 251,
    253–254, 260
Fayers, Sergeant Reg 161–165
Fearless, HMS 251–256

Fenton, Acting Sergeant David 91–94
Fenton, Major William 91
Ferdinand, Archduke Franz,
    assassination of 22
Ferguson, Professor Niall 15
Finland 114
France
    World War I 22–25, 27, 30-32,
        35–37, 41–43, 48, 61, 77, 96,
        98–99
    World War II 115–116, 121, 123,
        128, 132–133, 135, 167, 182, 188,
        192–193, 195, 197, 206, 210–212,
        219, 233, 293
Francis, Lieutenant Brin 213–214
Fraser, Captain Duncan 298–300
Friedeburg, Admiral Hans-Georg von 121
FSA (Federation of South Arabia) 231

Gallipoli (1915) 18, 24, 35, 62–64, 67,
    96, 111
Galtieri, General Leopoldo 232
Gautier, Albert 91
Gautier, Sergeant Francis Herbert
    11, 90–91
Gautier, Wilfred 91
Gazala Line, the 146, 156, 167
General Belgrano (Argentine cruiser) 232
German surrender, World War II
    199, 209–210
Germany 13, 22–26, 59–60, 77, 99,
    108–111, 114–118, 121, 130, 145,
    158, 161, 180, 198, 207–209, 216,
    219, 222, 264
Gibbs, Lieutenant Anthony 275–277
Gill, Lieutenant Robert 237–240
Glamorgan, HMS 258
Goebbels, Joseph 121
Goody-Orris, Joanne 273, 275, 277
Gordon, Captain S. 188–192
Gort, Lord 115
Graf Spee (German battleship) 114
Graziani, Marshal 117
Greece 117, 146, 231, 248
Guderian, General Heinz 115
Gulf War (1991) 233, 267
Gurung, Captain Kulbahadur 277–278

Gustav Line, Italy 179
Haig, Alexander 252–253
Haig, General Sir Douglas 18, 86, 252
Hamilton, Second Lieutenant Robert
   Peyton 55-58
Hampton, Lieutenant P.R. 107–108
Heligoland Bight, battle of (1914) 94
Helmand 12, 235, 276, 278, 298
Hermes, HMS 158, 232
Hill, Major Peter 128–130
Hindenburg, General Paul von 23
Hiroshima (1945) 122
Hitler, Adolf 114–118, 121, 125, 140,
   145, 158, 212
Holland 115, 131, 209
Hong Kong 118, 181, 237
Houghton-Brown, Peter J. 248–250
Hungary 117
Hussein, Saddam 233–234, 264
Hymers, Lance Corporal William 219–220

Idzi, Lance Corporal Ryan 12
IED (improvised explosive device) 234–235,
   275, 282, 284–285, 293
IFOR (International Stabilisation Force) 263
Imjin River, battle of the (1951) 229, 240
Imphal, battle of (1944) 185, 200
India 23, 115, 181, 183, 185, 200–201
Innes-Ker, William 220–221
Intrepid, HMS 262
Invincible, HMS 232
Iraq War (2003–2009) 234
ISAF (International Security Assistance
   Force) 235, 275
Italy 65, 98, 105, 119, 121, 141, 179–180
Iwo Jima, battle of (1945) 122

Jacob, General 111
Jarmain, John 167–170
Jeffries, Major 204–205
Jellicoe, Admiral Sir John 25
Jenkins, Sergeant J. 204–205
Jodl, General Alfred 121

Karzai, Hamid 235
Keeping, Captain J.T. 52
Kemal, Mustafa 24

Kembs Barrage raid (1944) 161
Kemp, Marine Mark 278–279
Kenya 230, 246–247
Kiel Canal, Germany 146
Kimathi, Didan 230
Korean War (1950–53) 237
Kuala Lumpur 118
Kuwait 233, 264, 266, 268, 270
Kyte, Captain Kit 273–275

Lancaster, Captain 75
Landrecies, battle of (1914) 27
Lathbury, General 247
Le Maitre, Lieutenant 126
Le Verguier, France 101
Leach, Admiral Sir Henry 232
Leather, Lance Corporal J.H. 59–61
Lee, Captain 92
Lewis-Stempel, John 18
Libya 117, 145, 147, 177
Lille, France 26
Lloyd George, David 18
Lock, Major Nick 271–273
Lomax, Reverend Canon Cyril 61–62
Loos, battle of (1915) 24, 85
Lucas, Brigadier 154
Ludendorff, General 26
Lusitania (British liner) 24, 65
Lynas, William 40–42

MacArthur, General Douglas 122, 229
Macmillan, Harold 17
MacPherson-Smith, Sergeant Pete 267–269
Maddocks, Staff Sergeant Ritchie 12
Maissemy, France 101
Major, John 267
Malaya 150, 181, 230, 245
Malta 35, 141–145
Manchuria, occupation of (1931) 150
Mannen, John 28
Mannering, E. 60–61
Manteuffel, General Hasso von 120
Mao Zedong 228
Marchant, Lieutenant Eric 17
Marne, Second Battle of the (1918)
   13, 105-106
Marshall, General George 118

Mau Mau Uprising 230–231, 246–247
McConnell, Second Lieutenant Robert 18
McCrae, John 47
McKay, Sergeant Ian 259–260
McKerrow, Captain Charles 18, 79–90
McMenemy, Lance-Corporal Iain 270
McNab, Brigadier J.F. 248,
Meuse-Argonne, battle of the (1918) 26
Midway, battle of (1942) 122
Milne, Colour Sergeant Major James 'Jim'
    105–106
MNLA (Communist Malayan National
    Liberation Army) 229
Mons, retreat from (1914) 27
Monte Cassino, battle of (1944) 119
Montgomery, Lieutenant General Bernard
    119, 170
Monywa, battle for (1942) 122
Morocco 177
Mortimore, Lance Corporal Andrew
    260–262
Mussolini, Benito 119, 121, 145

Nagasaki (1945) 122
NATO (North Atlantic Treaty
    Organisation) 262
Neuve Chapelle, France 23
Nimitz, Admiral Paul 122
Norway 114–115

O'Kelly, J.H. 53–54
O'Loughlin, Marine John 282–297
Operation *Barbarossa* (1941) 117, 263
Operation *Dante* (1955) 247
Operation *Desert Storm* (1991) 233
Operation *Enduring Freedom* (2001) 235
Operation *Herrick* (2002–) 273, 277–279,
    282, 284
Operation *Husky* (1943) 179
Operation *Lightfoot* (1942) 170
Operation *Market Garden* (1944)
    120, 214
Operation *New Dawn* (2003) 234–235
Operation *Overlord* (1944) 119
Operation *Sealion* (1940) 116
Operation *Supercharge* (1942) 170

Operation *Telic* (2003) 271
Operation *Torch* (1942) 177
Operation *Varsity* (1945) 193
Orr, John 247
Osmond, Captain 75
Owen, John 94-96
Owen, Lieutenant Rowland H. 94–96
Owen, Wilfred 47

Pakistan 235
Palestine 96
Parkin, 'Colours' 93
Passchendaele 13, 26, 78
Payne, Private Hedley S. 102–105
Pearl Harbor, attack on (1941) 118, 150
Pétain, Marshal Philippe 115
Peterkin, Flying Officer Anne 250–251
Philippines, the 118, 122
Philips, David 177–178
poetry 47–48, 58, 79, 138, 167–168
Poland 23, 114, 123, 219, 224
Potter, Julian 240–241
Prince of Wales, HMS 118
prisoners of war (POWs)
    Argentine 255–256
    British 107–108, 156–157, 165,
        179–181, 219–222
    German 76, 84–85, 89, 215, 217
Probst, Lance Sergeant Ernest 123–126,
    140–141
Proudfoot, Colour Sergeant Tom
    201–202

RAMC (Royal Army Medical Corps)
    62, 83, 135
Ranken, Sergeant Freddie 181–183
Reagan, Ronald 253
religion 16–17, 40–42, 74, 76, 100, 150
Renny, Lieutenant Gerry M. 53–54
Repulse, HMS 118
Reynaud, Paul 115
Ritchie, Eddie 135
Ritchie, Major Gerald 192–194
Robertshaw, Private Neil 264–265
Robinson, Lieutenant William Leefe 17, 38
Rodker, John 48

Romania 117, 182
Rommel, General Erwin 117, 119, 147, 156, 167, 170
Roosevelt, Franklin D. 118–119
Rosenberg, Isaac 47
Rowlands, D.L. 'Laurie' 98–100
Rugman, Michael 245–246

Salerno landings (1943) 119, 141
Sandbostel prisoner of war camp 222
Schlieffen Plan 22–23
Scott, Major Henry Granville 49–52
Scott, Pilot Officer Michael A. 137–140
Seoul, South Korea 229, 237–241
September 11 attacks 235
Sheffield, HMS 254, 257–258
Sheldon, David 214–219
shell shock 16, 99
Sicily 119, 145, 179
Siddons, Reverend Don 156–158
Siegfried Line 214
Simeons, Captain Edward 78–79
Singapore 118, 152–153, 155, 181, 220, 228
Sir Galahad, RFA 261
Slim, General William 122
Smith, Lieutenant Garry 241–244
Soldiers, The (group) 12
Somme, First Battle of the (1916) 25, 40, 60, 80, 84
Somme, Second Battle of the (1918) 26, 102, 263
Speer, Albert 121
Stalag XXA war camp, Poland 219
Stalin, Josef 117, 228
Stillingfleet, Flying Officer Geoff 141–147
Student, General Kurt 117
Suez Canal 231, 250

Taliban, the 235–236, 274, 276, 279, 282, 284, 286–288, 296
Tame, Charles 75–78
Tannenberg, battle of (1914) 23
Taylor, Lieutenant Colonel Tim 152–155
Templer, General Sir Gerald 230
Thatcher, Margaret 232

Thomas, Norman 54–55
Tirpitz (German battleship) 161
Tito, Marshal 233
Tobruk, Libya 118–119, 147, 156, 179
Townsend, Captain Eric 70–71
Tripoli, Libya 117–118, 145, 174
Truman, Harry 229
Tufnell, Timothy 212
Tunisia 174, 177
Turkey 23

United Nations (UN) 229, 233, 235, 237, 241, 245, 262
Upton, Harold 183–185
USSR 117, 228–229

V1 flying bombs (doodlebugs) 216–217
Van der Bijl, Staff Sergeant Nick 251–257
Verdun, battle of (1916) 24–25, 115
Vermand, France 101
Villecholles, France 101
Voluntary Aid Detachment (VAD) Hospital, Essex 90

Walls, Howard 126
war poetry 47–48, 58, 79, 138, 167–168
Watson-Gandy, Lieutenant Colonel C.V. 248
Wavell, General 117
Webster, Captain Michael G.T. 210–213
Westmacott, Major Thomas Horatio 101–102
White Brigade, Belgium 209
Whitticase, Lieutenant Richard 266
Wilhelm II, Kaiser 26
Williams, Flying Officer Ron 158–161
Williams, Jack 213
Wingate, Major General Orde 200
Woodroffe, Second Lieutenant Neville Leslie 19, 27
Wyatt, Lance Corporal John 150

Yarmouth, HMS 258
Ypres 24, 26, 29, 49, 50, 52, 72, 75, 77–78, 89, 91, 99, 133, 263
Yugoslavia 117, 233, 262

About the Author

Andrew Roberts is the author of *Masters and Commanders: How Four Titans Won the War in the West* (which won the International Churchill Society Book Award) and *A History of the English-Speaking Peoples since 1900* (which won the Intercollegiate Studies Institute Book Award). His other books include *Napoleon and Wellington*, *Eminent Churchillians* and *Salisbury*, which won the Wolfson History Prize. His latest book, *The Storm of War*, won the British Army Military Book of the Year for 2010. A Fellow of the Royal Society of Literature, he holds a PhD in History from Cambridge University and lives in New York City.

About the Imperial War Museums (IWM)

IWM tells the stories of people who have lived, fought and died in conflicts involving Britain and the Commonwealth since the First World War. Our unique collections, made up of the everyday and the exceptional, help to tell the stories of people's spirit, resilience, creativity and innovation in the face of adversity.

IWM's five branches are IWM London, IWM's flagship branch which is being transformed for the First World War Centenary in 2014; IWM North, housed in an iconic award-winning building designed by Daniel Libeskind; IWM Duxford, a world-renowned aviation museum and Britain's best-preserved wartime airfield; Churchill War Rooms, housed in Churchill's secret headquarters below Whitehall; and the Second World War cruiser HMS *Belfast*.

iwm.org.uk